JOKER:
KILLER SMILE

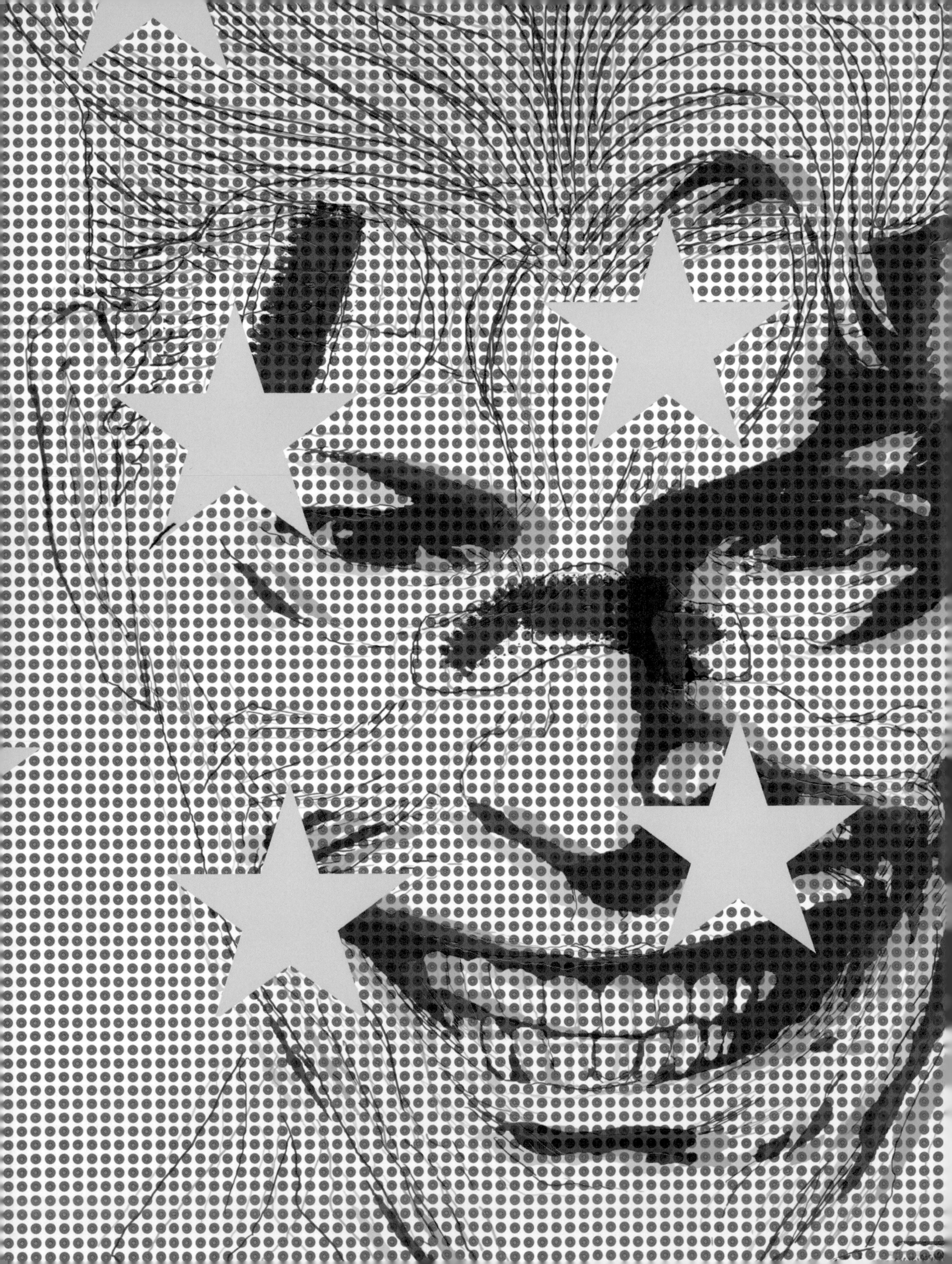

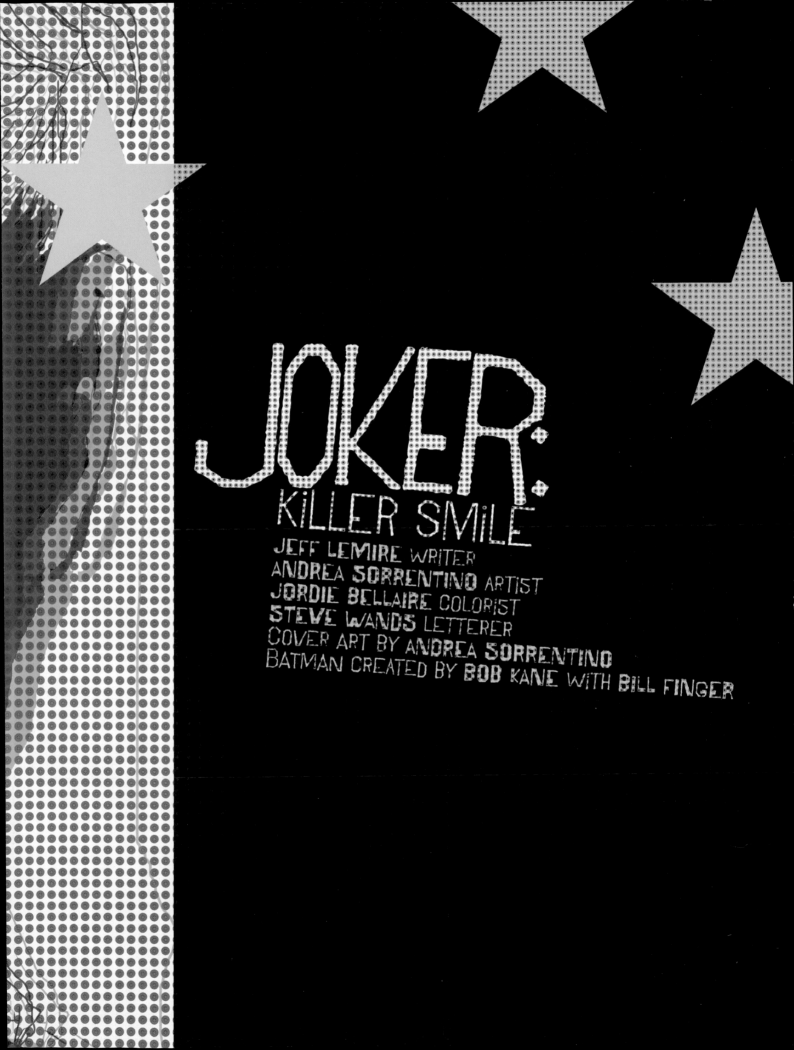

JOKER: KILLER SMILE

JEFF LEMIRE WRITER
ANDREA SORRENTINO ARTIST
JORDIE BELLAIRE COLORIST
STEVE WANDS LETTERER
COVER ART BY ANDREA SORRENTINO
BATMAN CREATED BY BOB KANE WITH BILL FINGER

JOKER: KILLER SMILE

PUBLISHED BY DC COMICS. COMPILATION AND
ALL NEW MATERIAL COPYRIGHT © 2020 DC COMICS.
ALL RIGHTS RESERVED. ORIGINALLY PUBLISHED IN
SINGLE MAGAZINE FORM IN *JOKER: KILLER SMILE* 1-3,
BATMAN: THE SMILE KILLER 1. COPYRIGHT © 2019,
2020 DC COMICS. ALL RIGHTS RESERVED. ALL
CHARACTERS, THEIR DISTINCTIVE LIKENESSES, AND
RELATED ELEMENTS FEATURED IN THIS PUBLICATION
ARE TRADEMARKS OF DC COMICS. THE STORIES,
CHARACTERS, AND INCIDENTS FEATURED IN THIS
PUBLICATION ARE ENTIRELY FICTIONAL. DC COMICS
DOES NOT READ OR ACCEPT UNSOLICITED
SUBMISSIONS OF IDEAS, STORIES, OR ARTWORK.
DC – A WARNERMEDIA COMPANY.

DC COMICS, 2900 WEST ALAMEDA AVE.,
BURBANK, CA 91505
PRINTED BY TRANSCONTINENTAL INTERGLOBE,
BEAUCEVILLE, QC, CANADA. 8/7/20. FIRST PRINTING.
ISBN: 978-1-77950-269-8

LIBRARY OF CONGRESS CATALOGING-IN-PUBLICATION
DATA IS AVAILABLE.

CHRIS CONROY EDITOR – ORIGINAL SERIES
MAGGIE HOWELL ASSOCIATE EDITOR – ORIGINAL SERIES
JEB WOODARD GROUP EDITOR – COLLECTED EDITIONS
SCOTT NYBAKKEN EDITOR – COLLECTED EDITION
STEVE COOK DESIGN DIRECTOR – BOOKS
LOUIS PRANDI PUBLICATION DESIGN
SUZANNAH ROWNTREE PUBLICATION PRODUCTION

BOB HARRAS SENIOR VP – EDITOR-IN-CHIEF, DC COMICS
MARK DOYLE EXECUTIVE EDITOR, DC BLACK LABEL

DAN DiDIO PUBLISHER
JIM LEE PUBLISHER & CHIEF CREATIVE OFFICER
BOBBIE CHASE VP – NEW PUBLISHING INITIATIVES
DON FALLETTI VP – MANUFACTURING OPERATIONS & WORKFLOW MANAGEMENT
LAWRENCE GANEM VP – TALENT SERVICES
ALISON GILL SENIOR VP – MANUFACTURING & OPERATIONS
HANK KANALZ SENIOR VP – PUBLISHING STRATEGY & SUPPORT SERVICES
DAN MIRON VP – PUBLISHING OPERATIONS
NICK J. NAPOLITANO VP – MANUFACTURING ADMINISTRATION & DESIGN
NANCY SPEARS VP – SALES
JONAH WEILAND VP – MARKETING & CREATIVE SERVICES
MICHELE R. WELLS VP & EXECUTIVE EDITOR, YOUNG READER

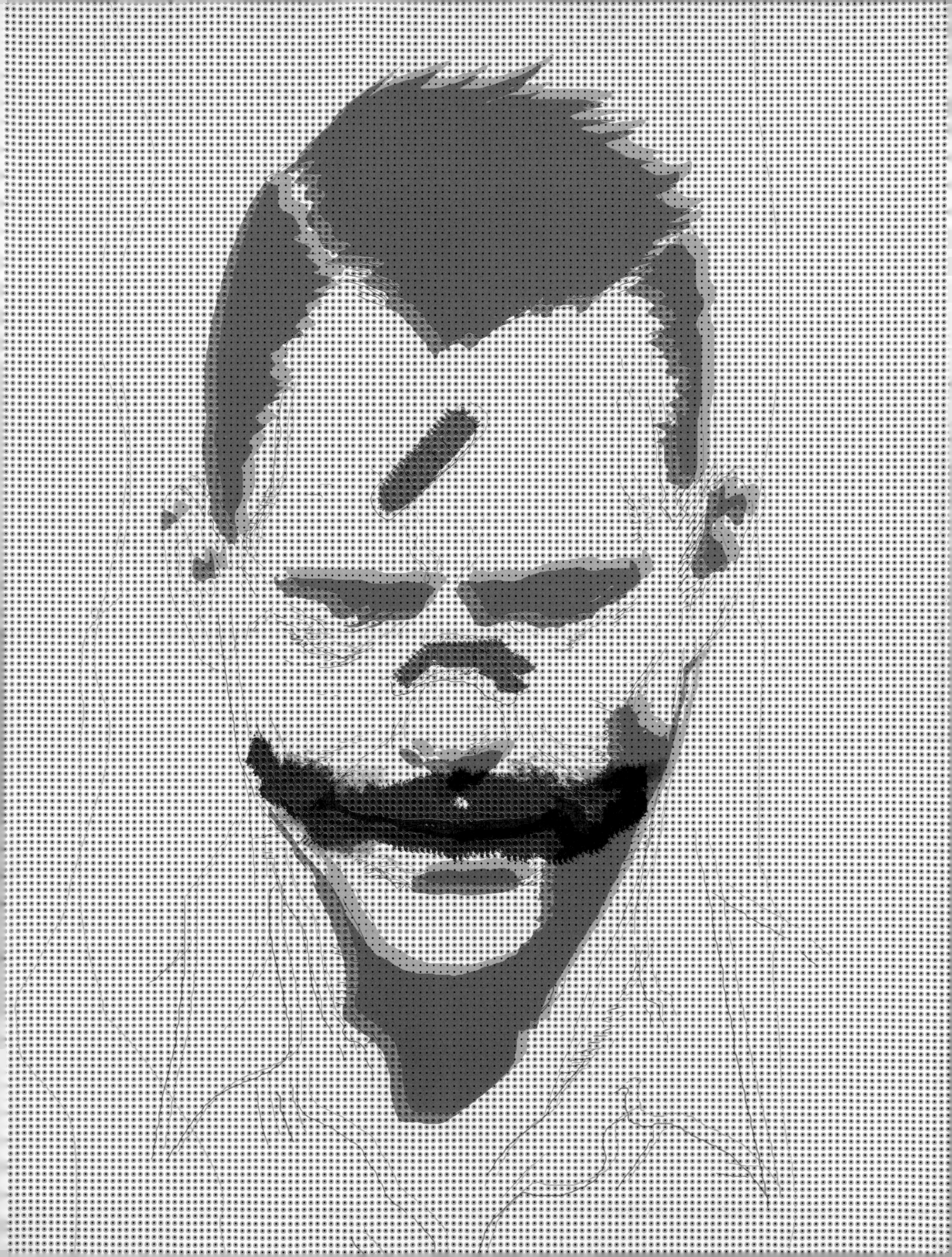

BOOK ONE

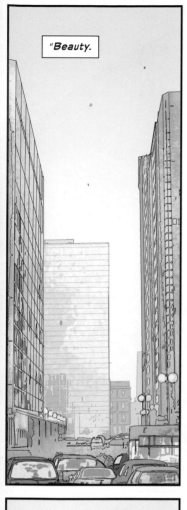

"Beauty.

"That is all I have *ever* wanted.

"You want to understand me? You *really* want to understand? Then understand *that...*

"All I have ever wanted is to create things that are *beautiful.*"

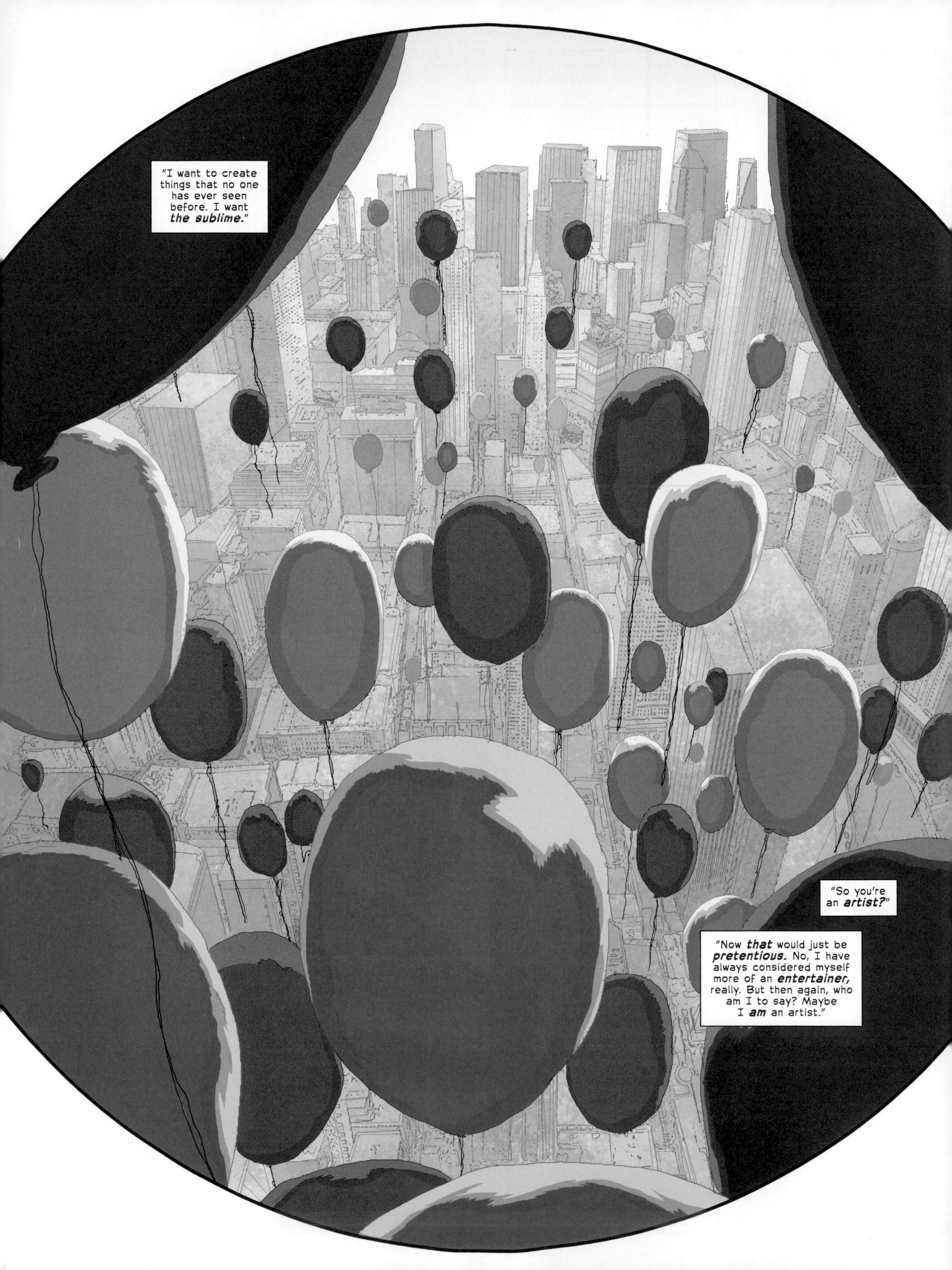
"I want to create things that no one has ever seen before. I want **the sublime.**"
"So you're an **artist?**"
"Now **that** would just be **pretentious.** No, I have always considered myself more of an **entertainer,** really. But then again, who am I to say? Maybe I **am** an artist."

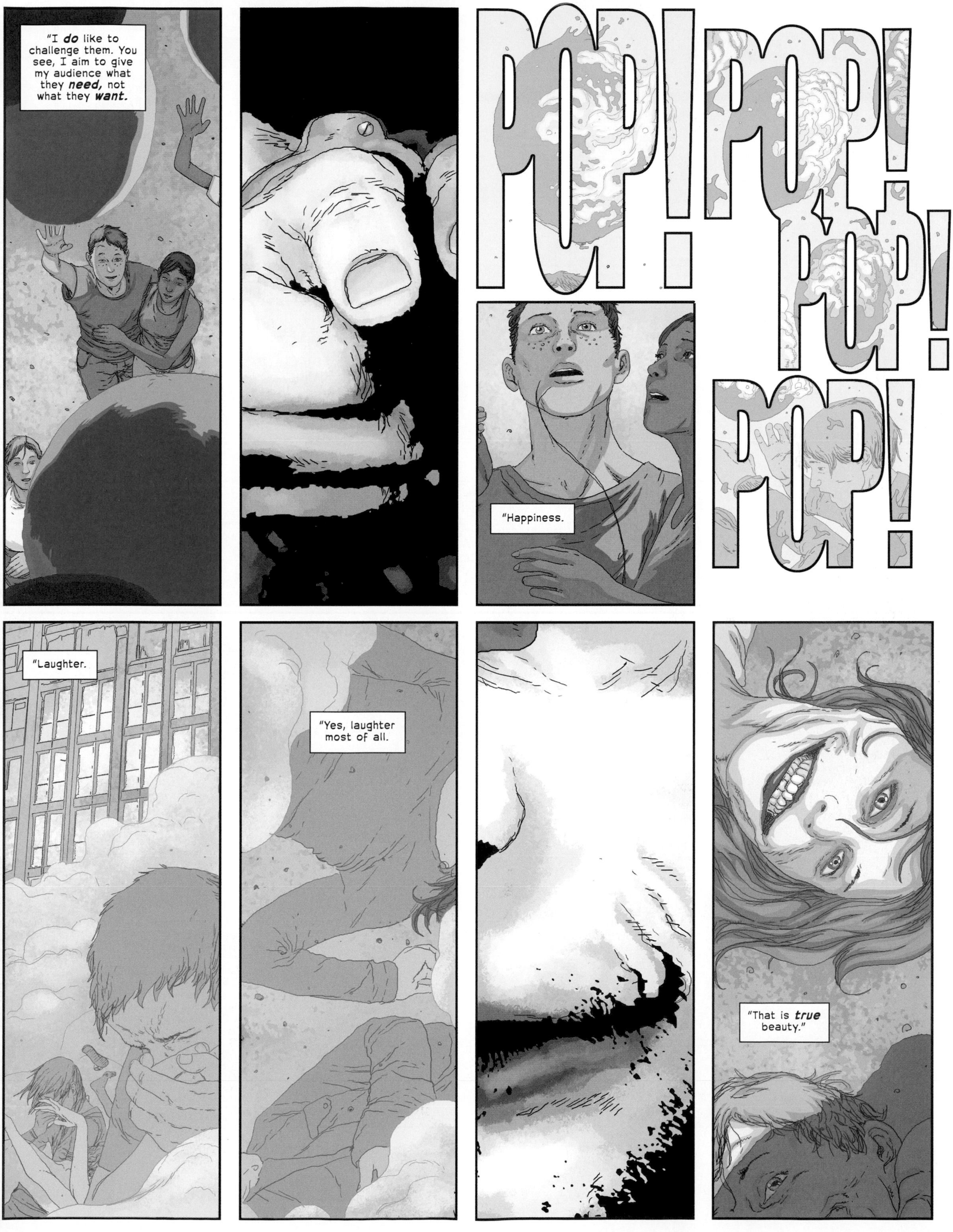
"I *do* like to challenge them. You see, I aim to give my audience what they ***need,*** not what they ***want.***
POP!
POP!
POP!
POP!
"Happiness.
"Laughter.
"Yes, laughter most of all.
"That is ***true*** beauty."

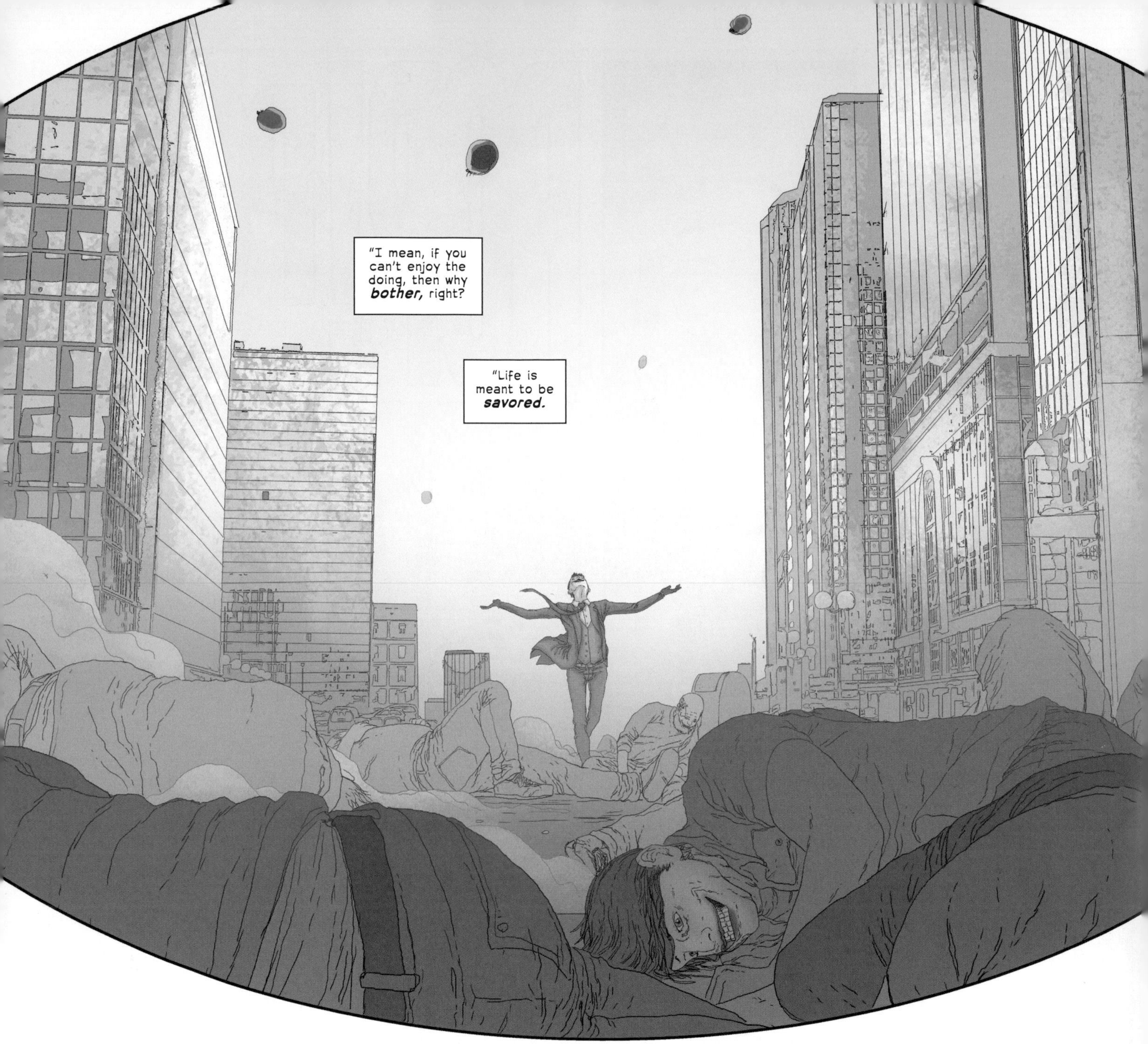
"I mean, if you can't enjoy the doing, then why *bother,* right?
"Life is meant to be *savored.*

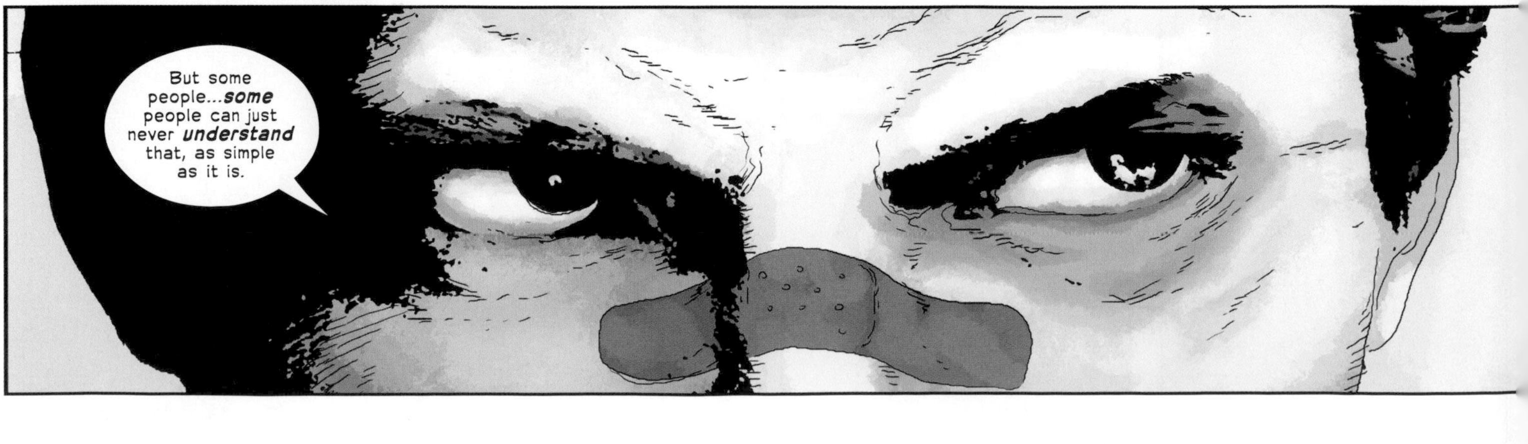
But some people...*some* people can just never *understand* that, as simple as it is.

PUNCH!

Some *people* will always want to *ruin* what is beautiful.

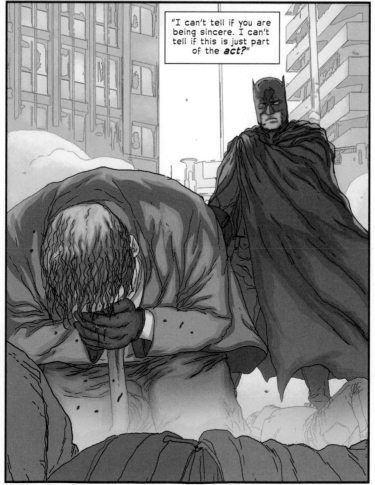

"I can't tell if you are being sincere. I can't tell if this is just part of the *act?*"

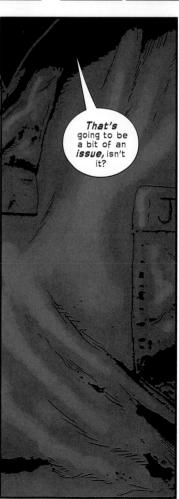

That's going to be a bit of an *issue,* isn't it?

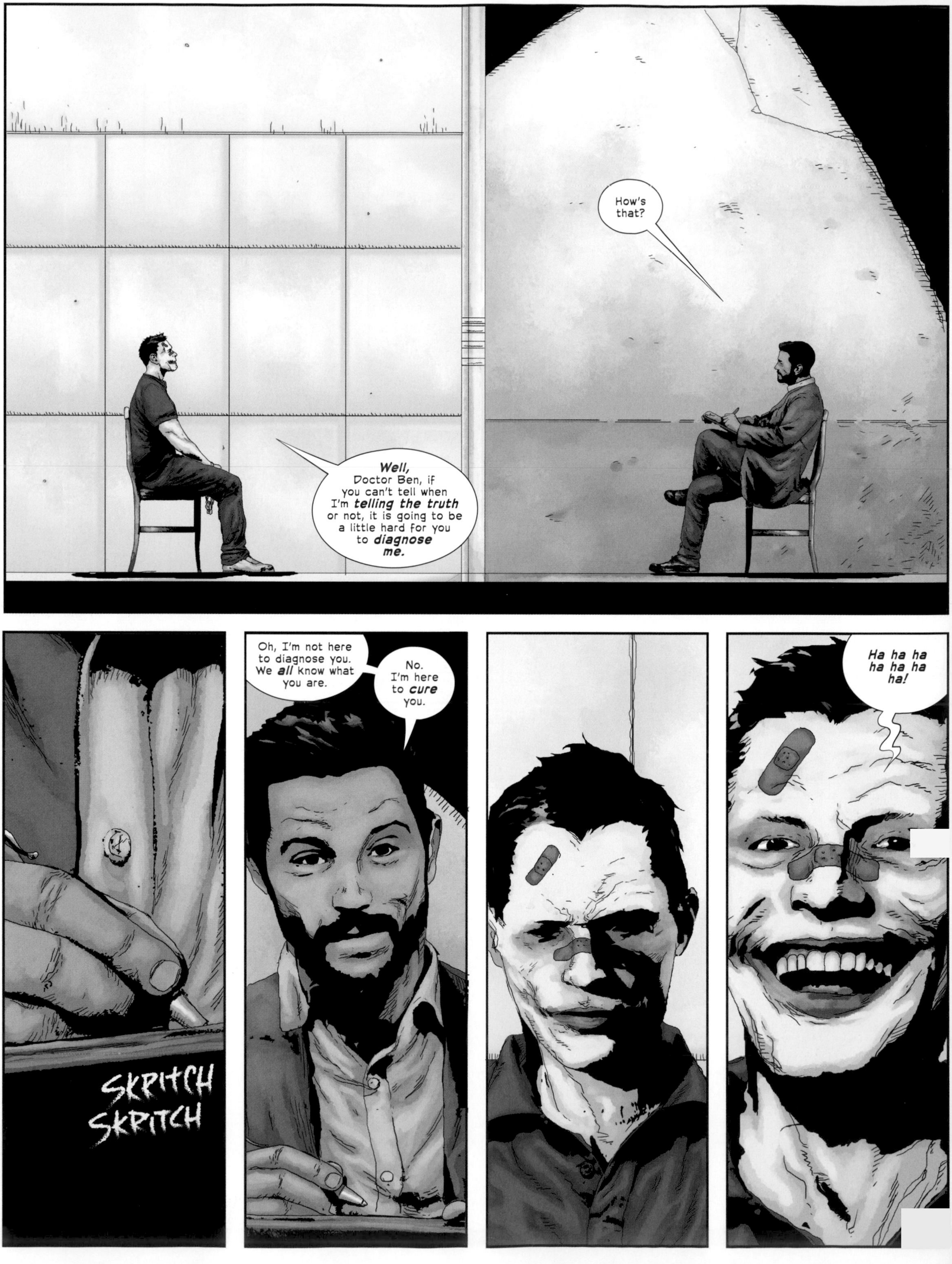

How's that?
Well, Doctor Ben, if you can't tell when I'm telling the truth or not, it is going to be a little hard for you to diagnose me.
SKRITCH SKRITCH
Oh, I'm not here to diagnose you. We all know what you are.
No. I'm here to cure you.
Ha ha ha ha ha ha ha!

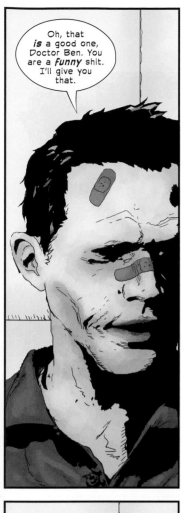

Oh, that *is* a good one, Doctor Ben. You are a *funny* shit. I'll give you that.

You don't think that's possible? You don't *want* that?

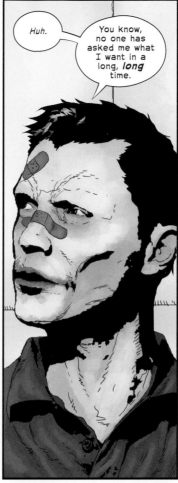

Huh.

You know, no one has asked me what I want in a long, *long* time.

But let me ask you, Doc...say you *could* do it. Say you could "cure" me. What would that do for the *hundreds of people* that I've killed?

Would creating a sane, healthy man bring them back?

But this isn't about *me* at all, is it? This isn't about my *victims* either.

It's about *you*...

...isn't it, Benji?

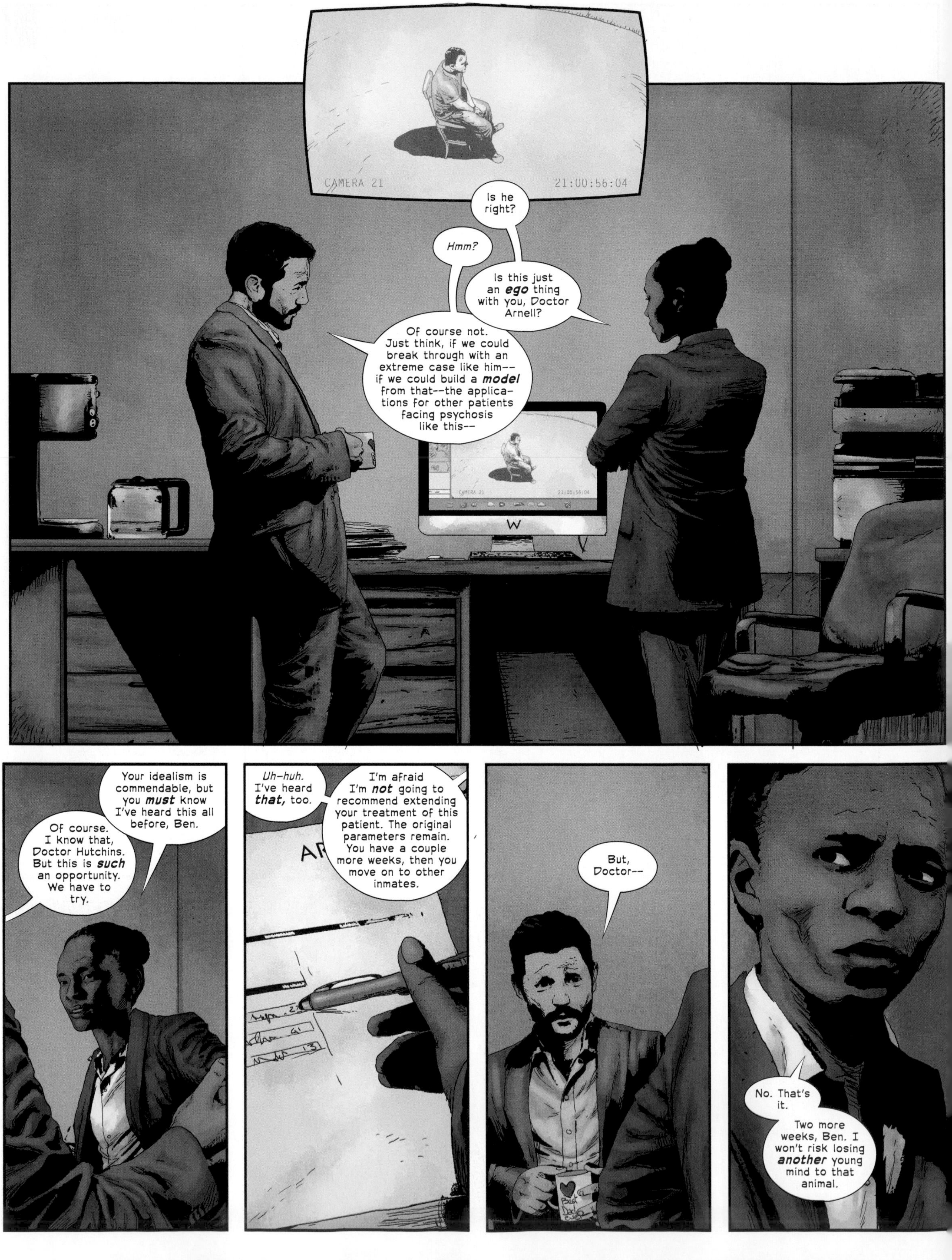
CAMERA 21
21:00:56:04
Is he right?
Hmm?
Is this just an ***ego*** thing with you, Doctor Arnell?
Of course not. Just think, if we could break through with an extreme case like him--if we could build a ***model*** from that--the applications for other patients facing psychosis like this--
CAMERA 21
21:00:56:04
Your idealism is commendable, but you ***must*** know I've heard this all before, Ben.
Of course. I know that, Doctor Hutchins. But this is ***such*** an opportunity. We have to try.
Uh-huh. I've heard ***that,*** too.
I'm afraid I'm ***not*** going to recommend extending your treatment of this patient. The original parameters remain. You have a couple more weeks, then you move on to other inmates.
But, Doctor--
No. That's it.
Two more weeks, Ben. I won't risk losing ***another*** young mind to that animal.

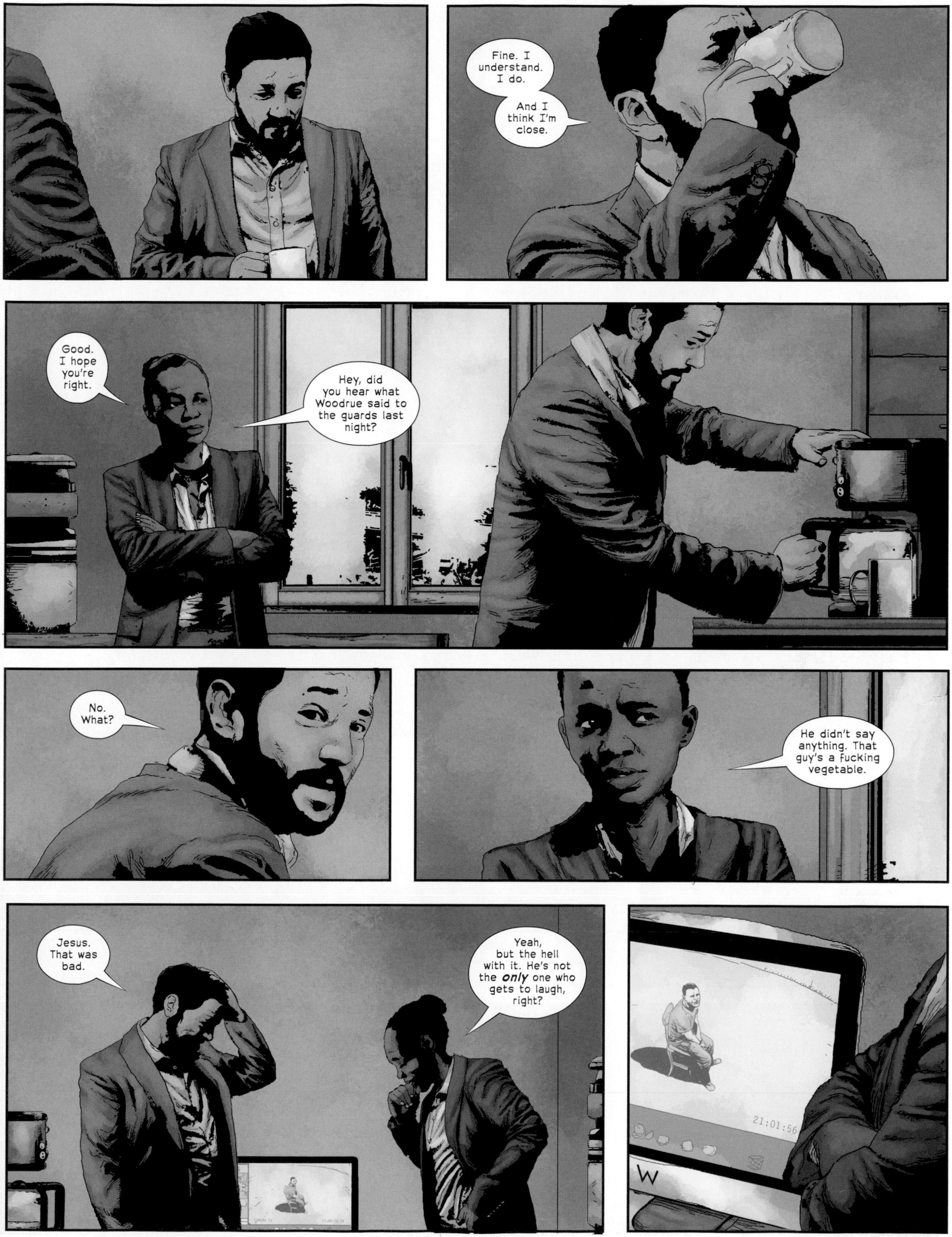
Fine. I understand. I do.
And I think I'm close.
Good. I hope you're right.
Hey, did you hear what Woodrue said to the guards last night?
No. What?
He didn't say anything. That guy's a fucking vegetable.
Jesus. That was bad.
Yeah, but the hell with it. He's not the *only* one who gets to laugh, right?
21:01:56
W

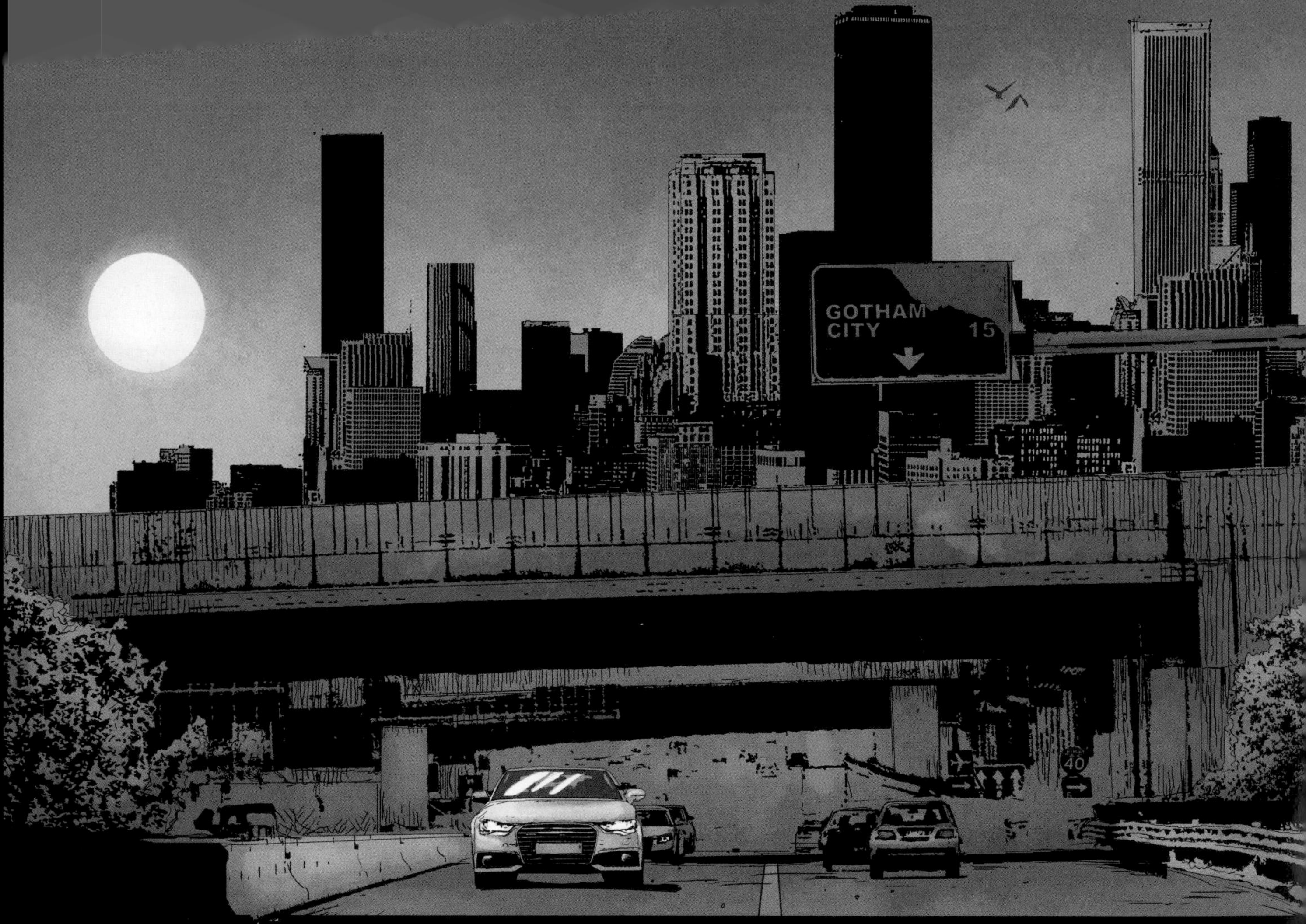
GOTHAM CITY 15
40

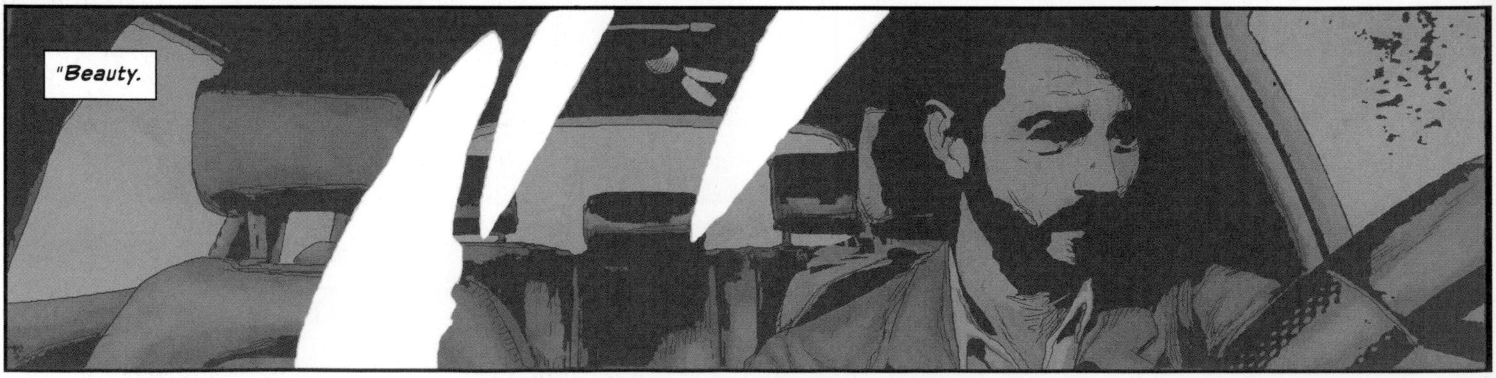
"Beauty.

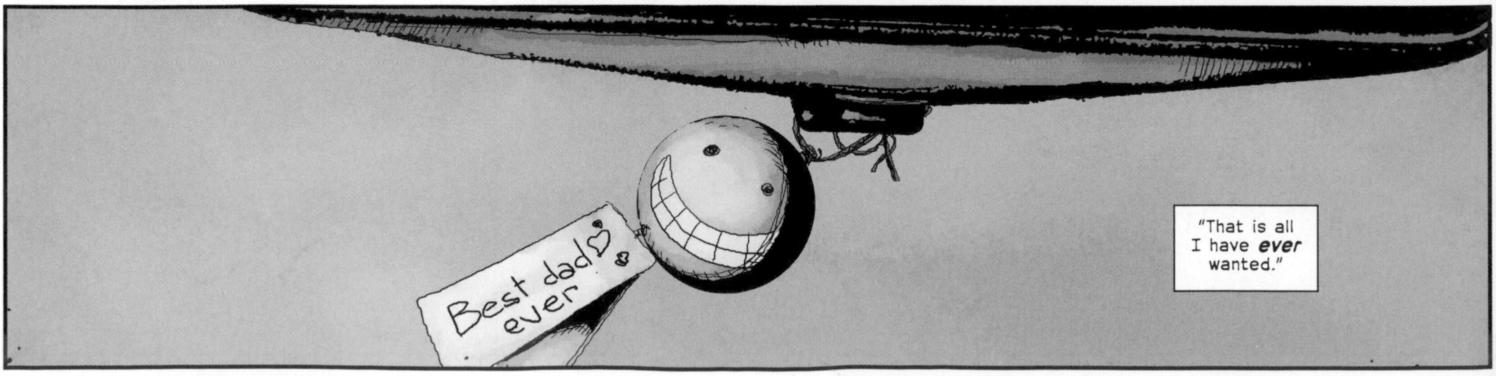
Best dad ever
"That is all I have *ever* wanted."

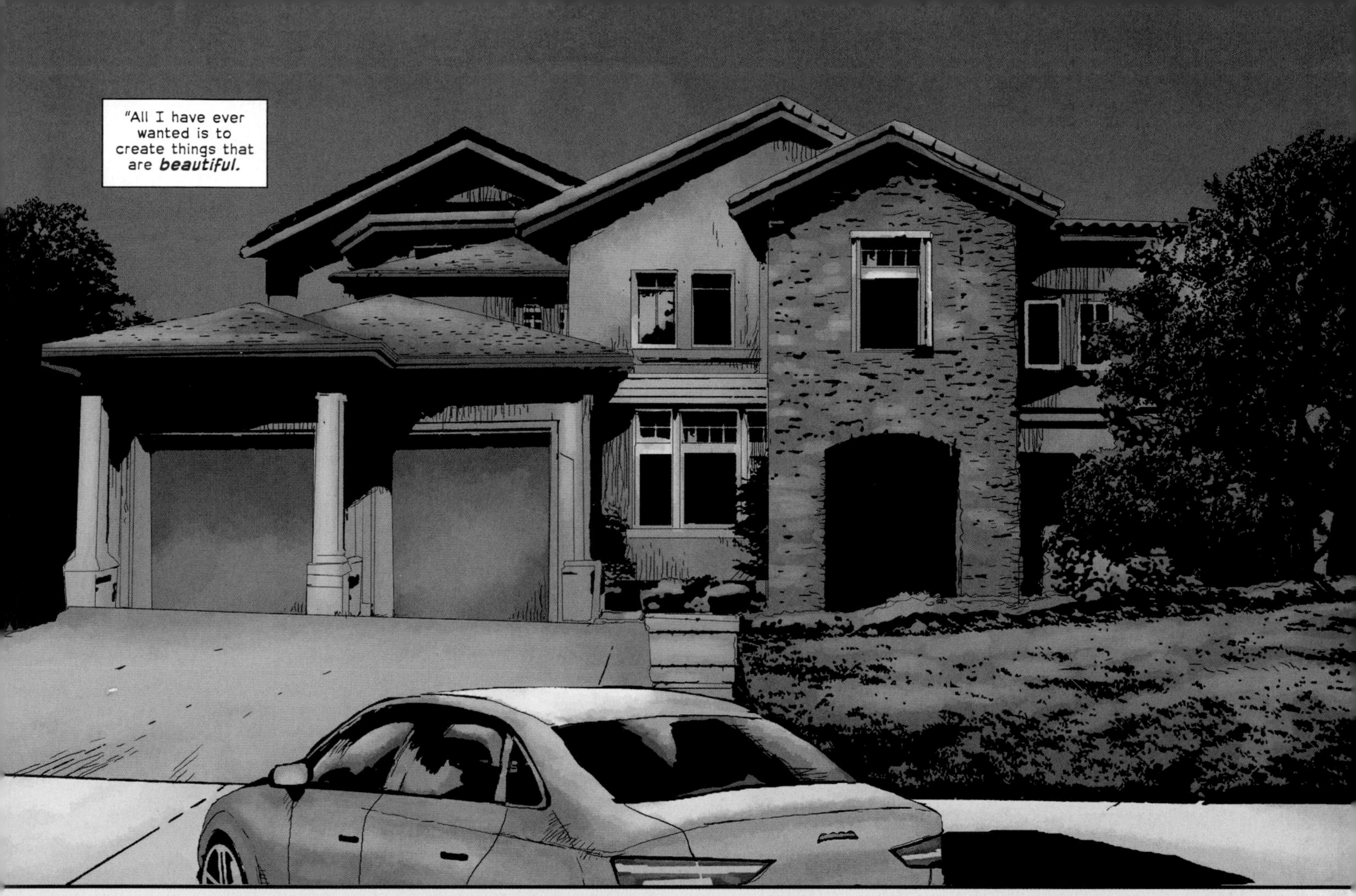
"All I have ever wanted is to create things that are *beautiful.*

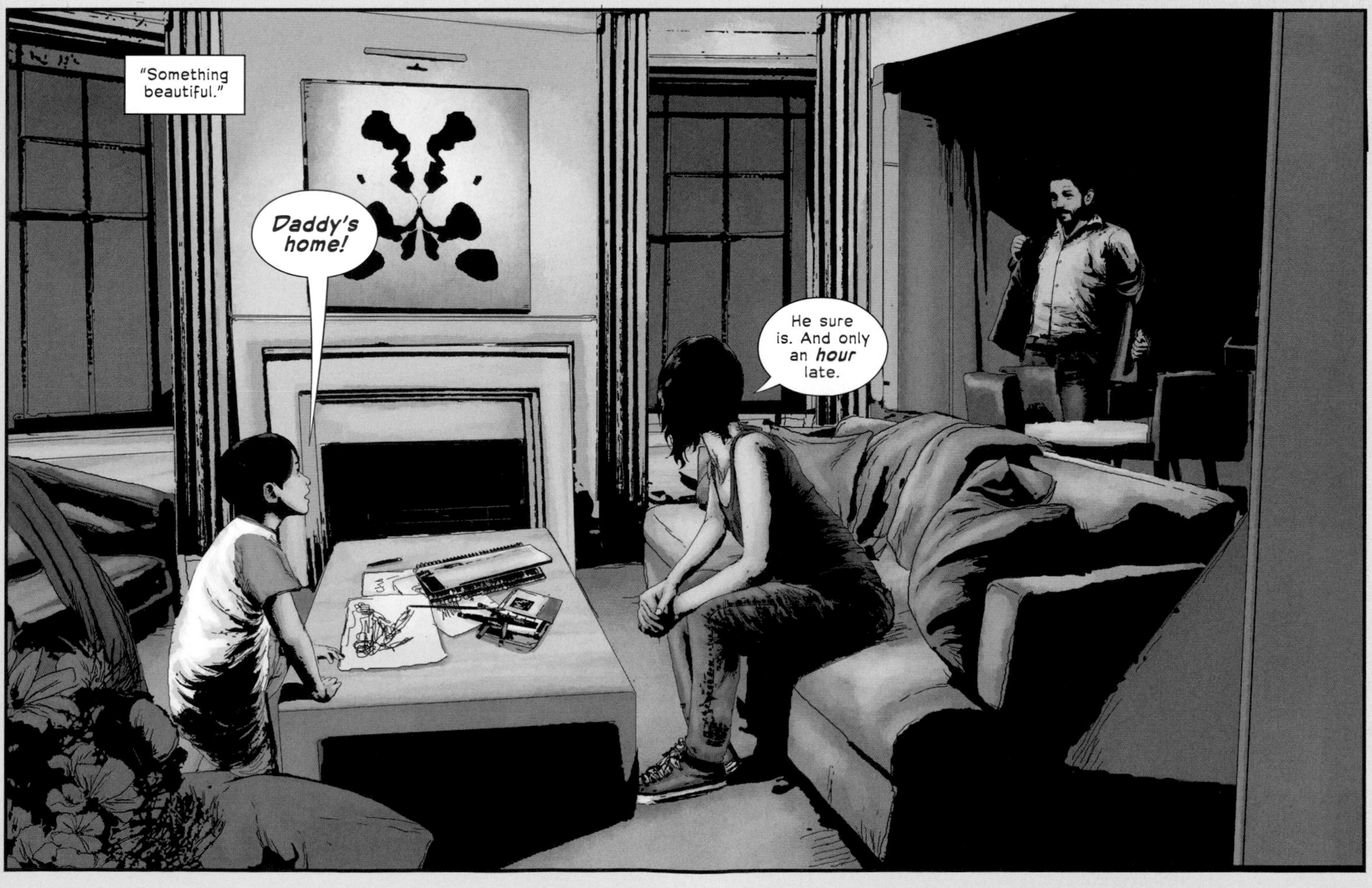
"Something beautiful."
Daddy's home!
He sure is. And only an *hour* late.

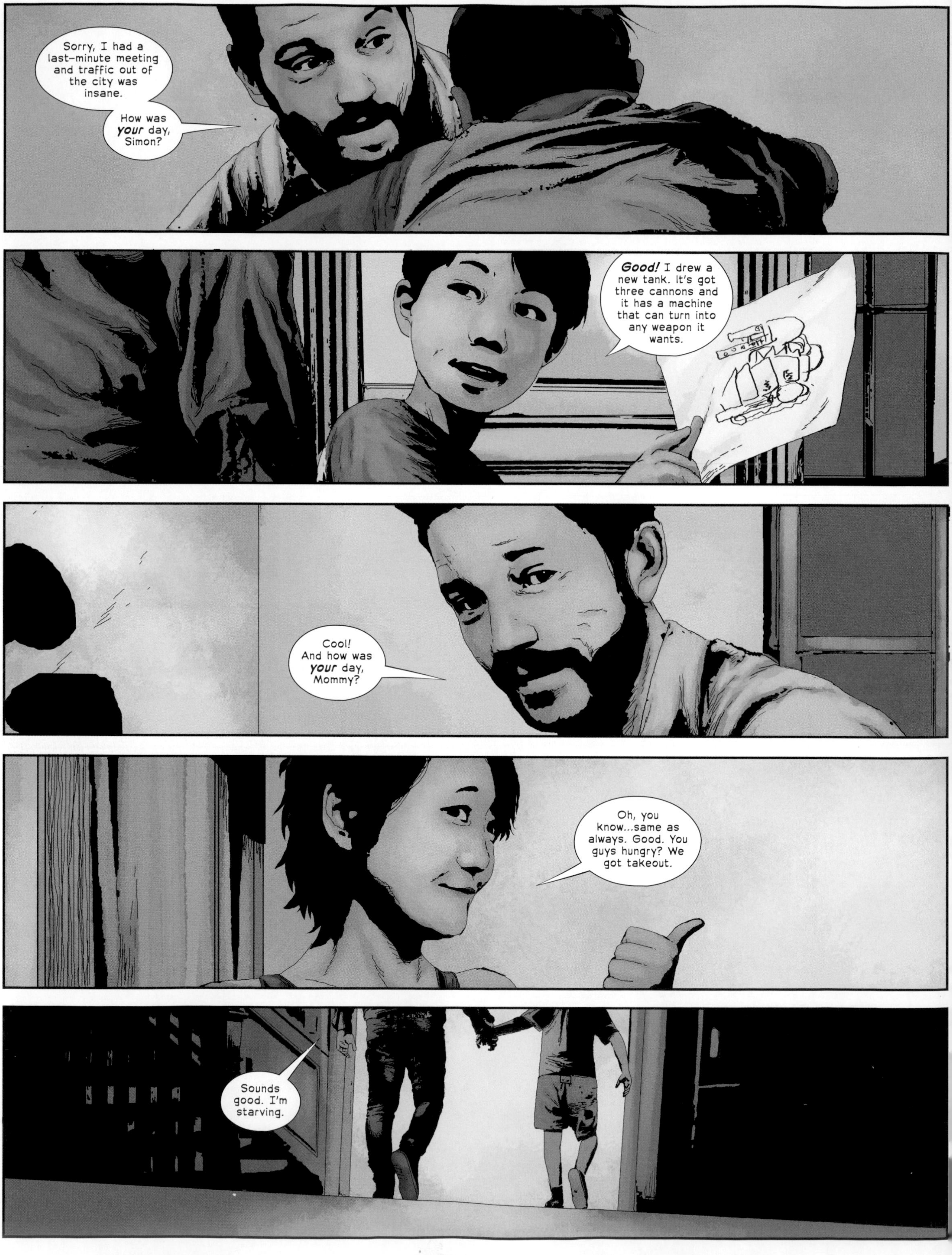
Sorry, I had a last-minute meeting and traffic out of the city was insane.
How was *your* day, Simon?
Good! I drew a new tank. It's got three cannons and it has a machine that can turn into any weapon it wants.
Cool! And how was *your* day, Mommy?
Oh, you know...same as always. Good. You guys hungry? We got takeout.
Sounds good. I'm starving.

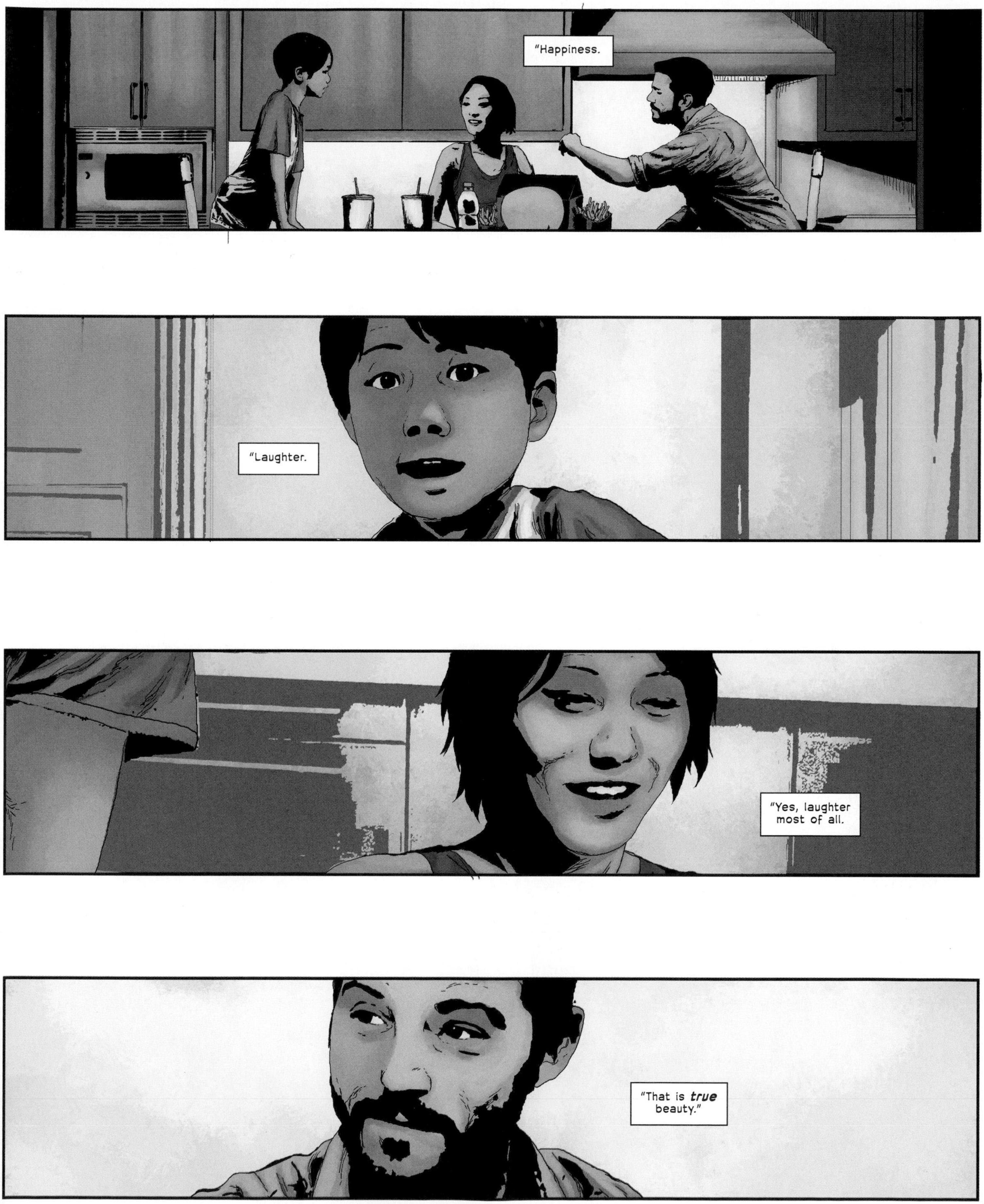
"Happiness.
"Laughter.
"Yes, laughter most of all.
"That is *true* beauty."

Once upon a very long time ago, there was a happy happy place in a happy happy forest. And wouldn't you just know it, this place was even called Happyville!

Oh, and Happyville was the happiest place there ever ever was! And everyone in Happyville knew each other, and they were all the very best of friends.

But all of that was about to change...

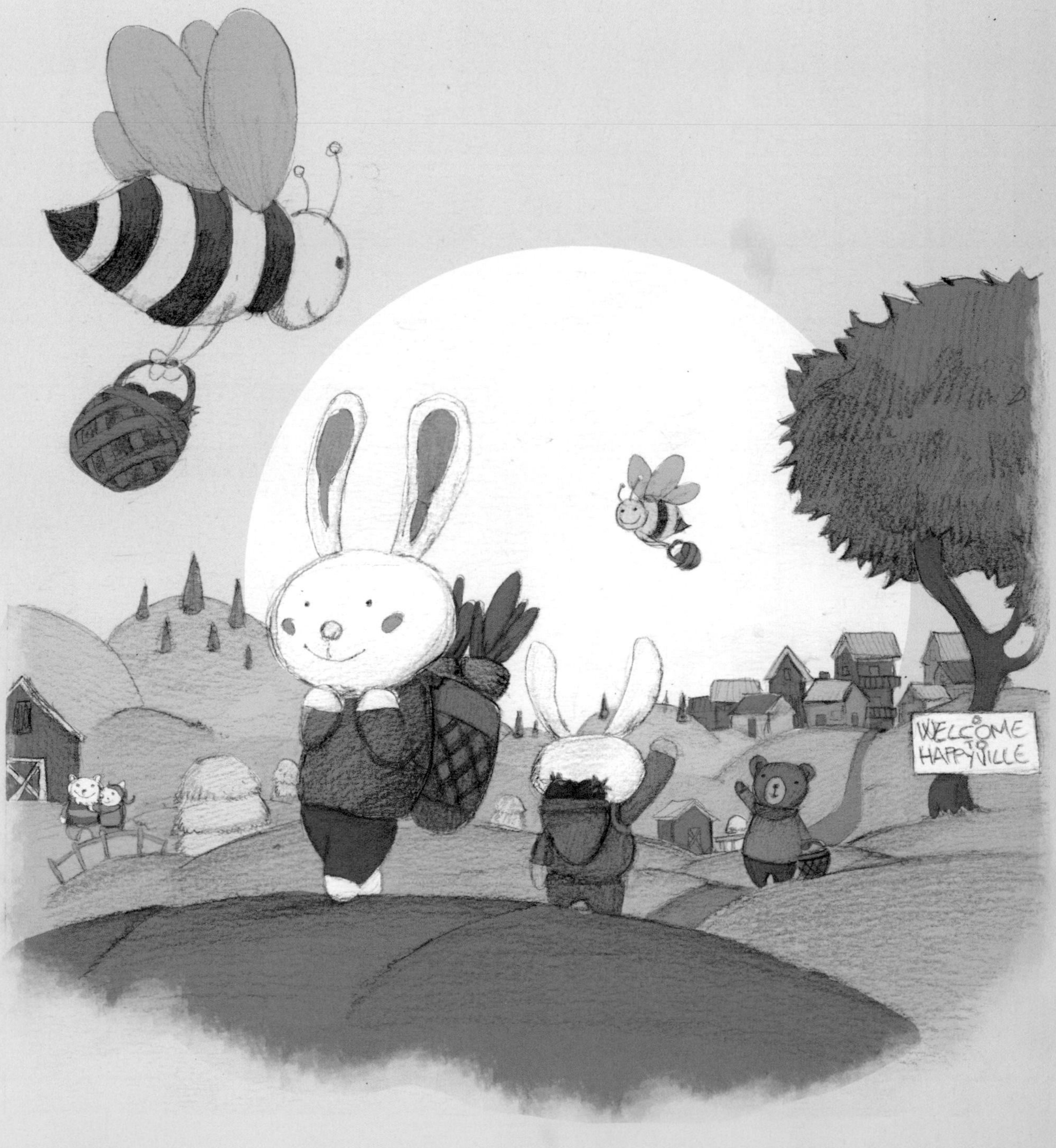
WELCOME TO HAPPYVILLE

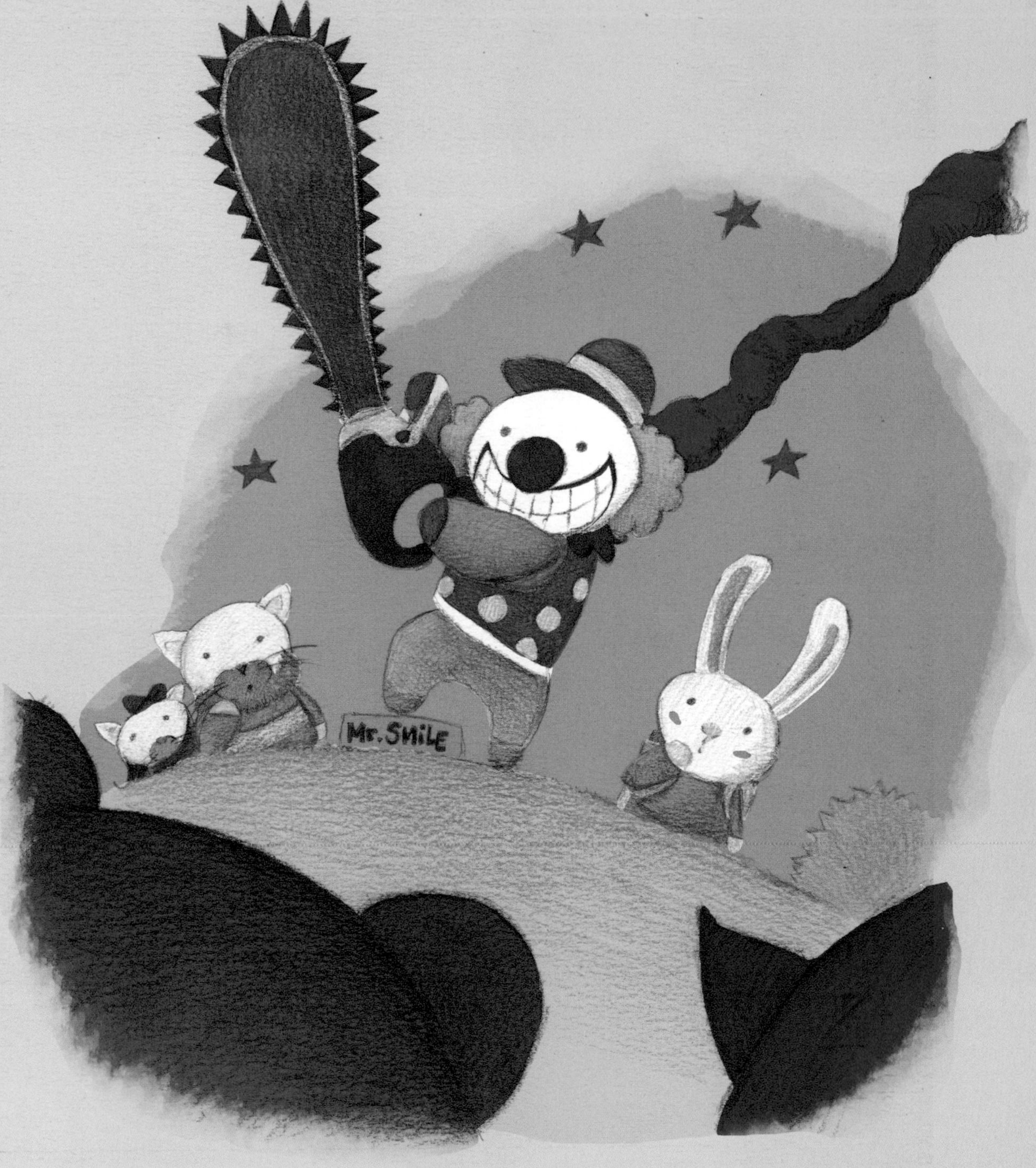
Mr. SMILE

You see, on the last Saturday of the very last week in Happyville, a new friend came to town. He called himself Mr. Smiles, and boy oh boy, was he a character!

Mr. Smiles carried a strange thing in his hand, and all the curious critters of Happyville gathered around to see what it was.

Mr. Smiles was more than happy to give a demonstration of his amazing contraption. "Step right up! Step right up!" he declared, as he pulled the starting cord, and the rumble of the device's small engine, the smell of diesel fumes, filled the spring air...

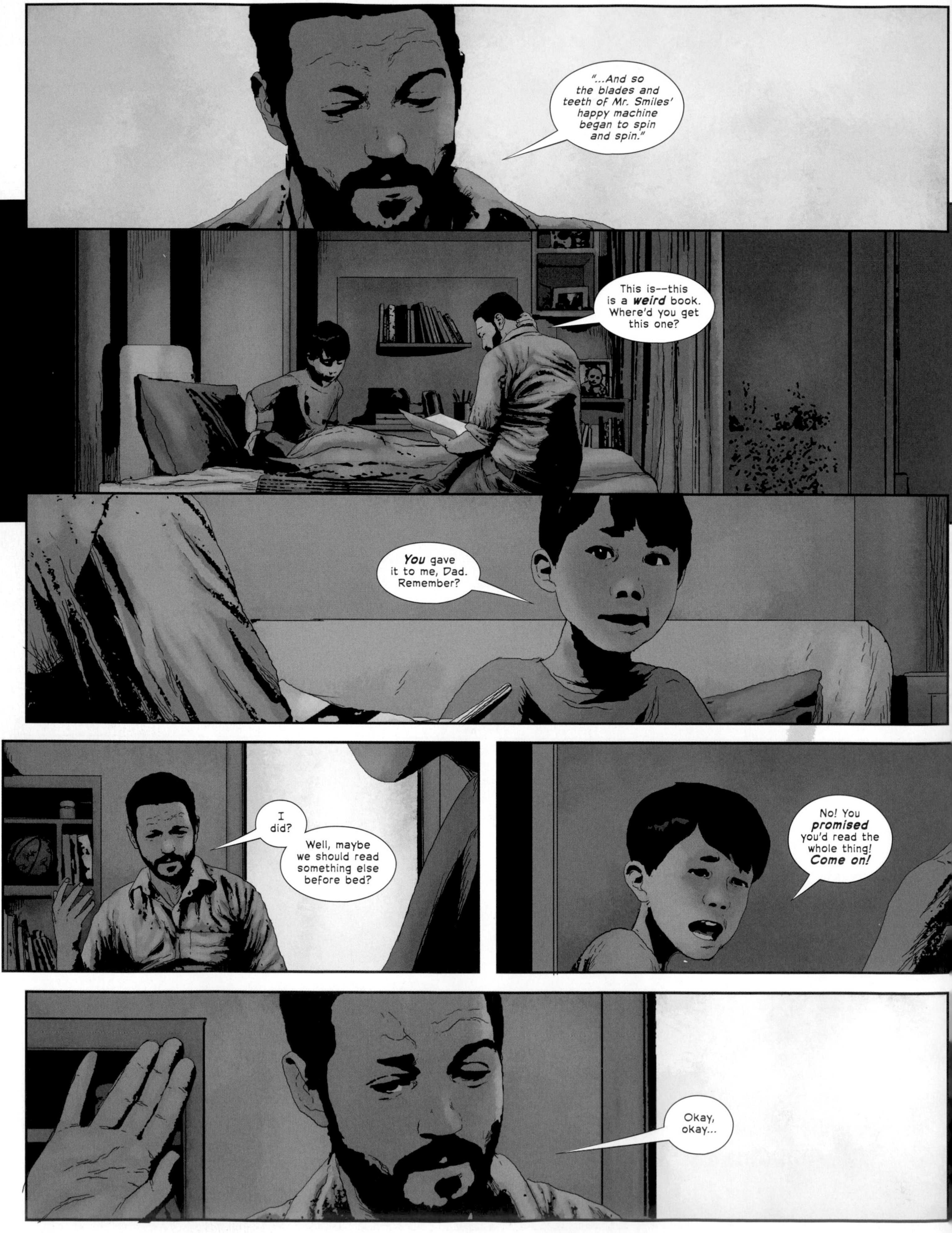
"...And so the blades and teeth of Mr. Smiles' happy machine began to spin and spin."
This is--this is a *weird* book. Where'd you get this one?
You gave it to me, Dad. Remember?
I did?
Well, maybe we should read something else before bed?
No! You *promised* you'd read the whole thing! *Come on!*
Okay, okay...

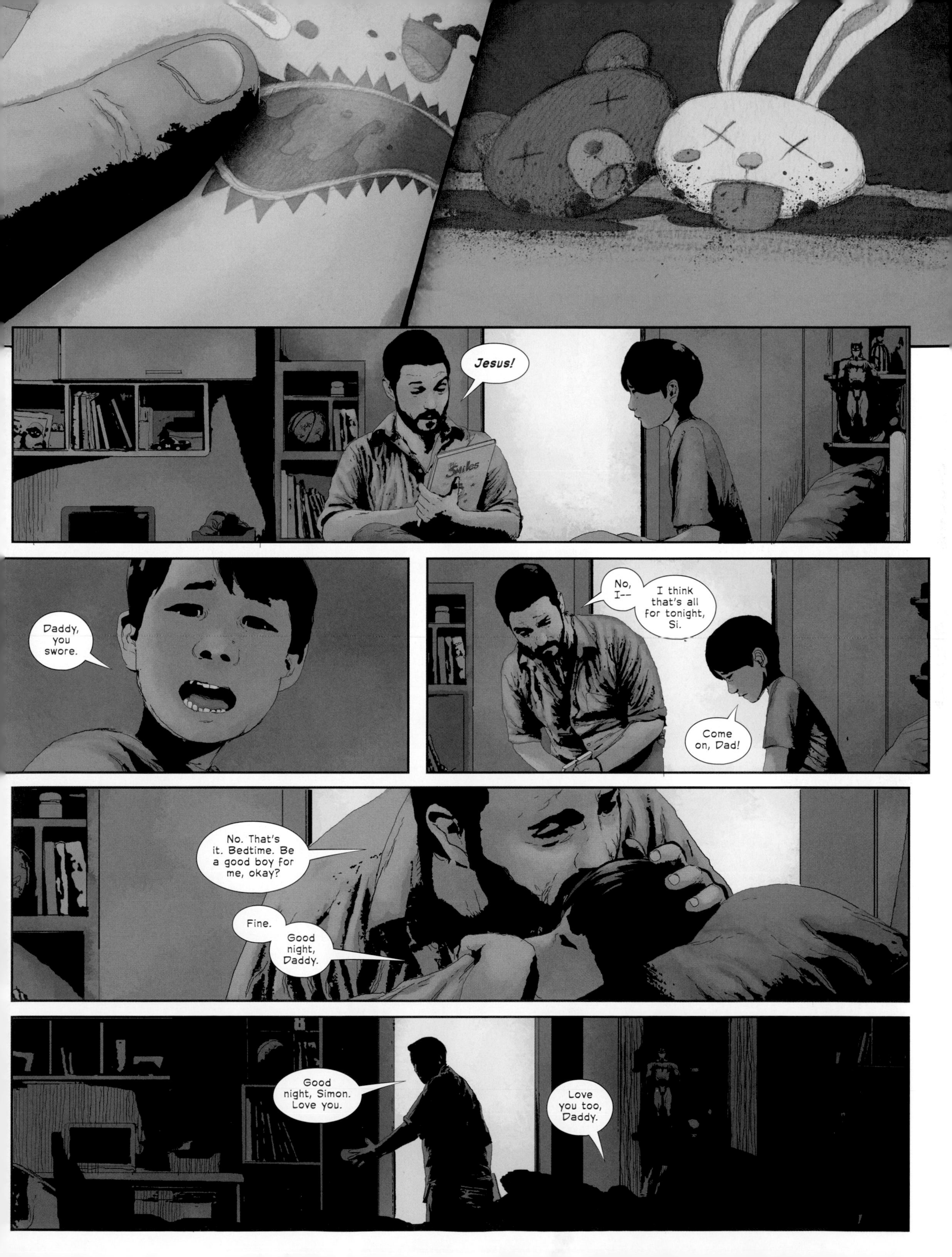
Jesus!
Daddy, you swore.
No, I--
I think that's all for tonight, Si.
Come on, Dad!
No. That's it. Bedtime. Be a good boy for me, okay?
Fine.
Good night, Daddy.
Good night, Simon. Love you.
Love you too, Daddy.

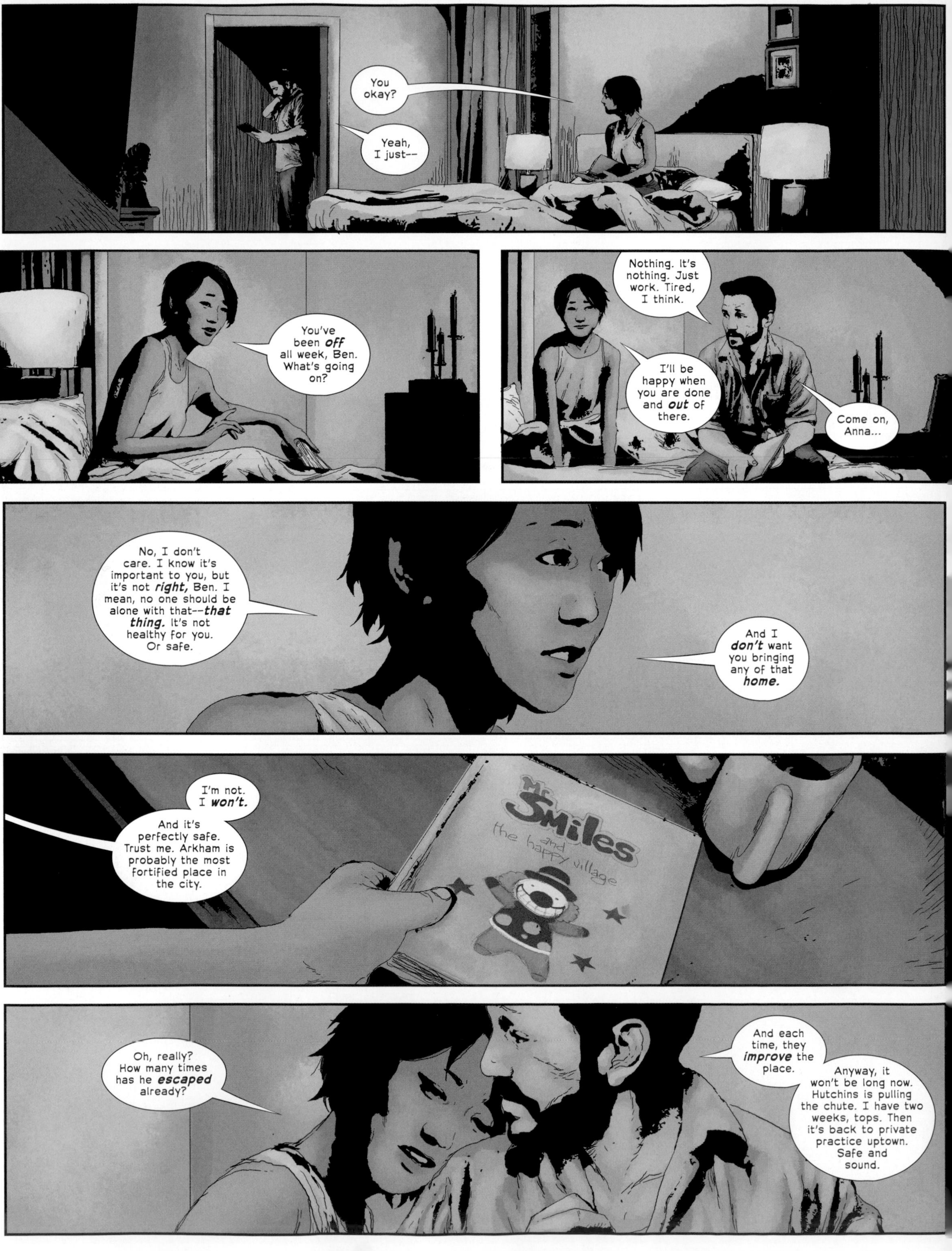
You okay?
Yeah, I just--
You've been *off* all week, Ben. What's going on?
Nothing. It's nothing. Just work. Tired, I think.
I'll be happy when you are done and *out* of there.
Come on, Anna...
No, I don't care. I know it's important to you, but it's not *right,* Ben. I mean, no one should be alone with that--*that thing.* It's not healthy for you. Or safe.
And I *don't* want you bringing any of that *home.*
I'm not. I *won't.*
And it's perfectly safe. Trust me. Arkham is probably the most fortified place in the city.
Mr. Smiles and the happy village
Oh, really? How many times has he *escaped* already?
And each time, they *improve* the place.
Anyway, it won't be long now. Hutchins is pulling the chute. I have two weeks, tops. Then it's back to private practice uptown. Safe and sound.

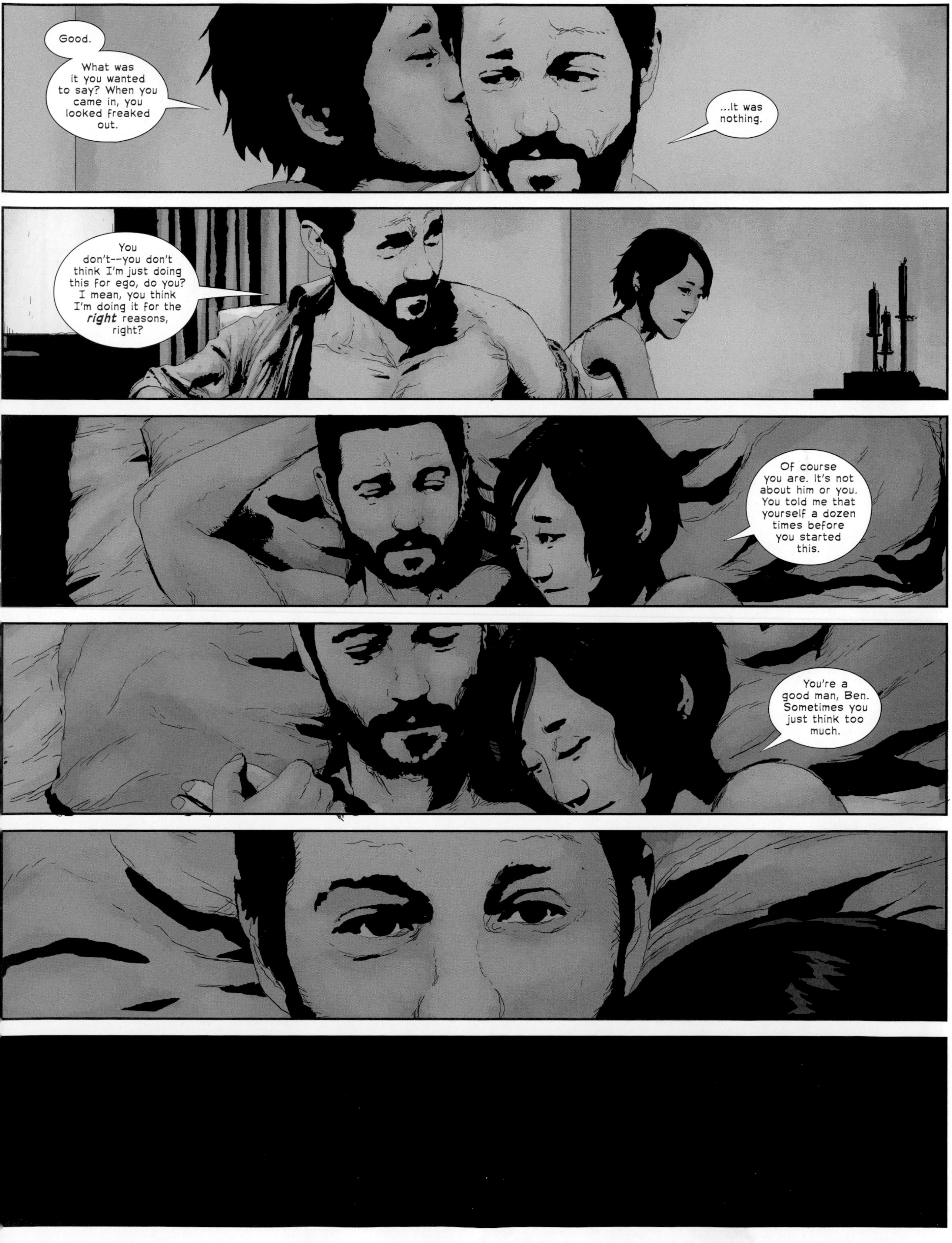
Good.
What was it you wanted to say? When you came in, you looked freaked out.
...It was nothing.
You don't--you don't think I'm just doing this for ego, do you? I mean, you think I'm doing it for the *right* reasons, right?
Of course you are. It's not about him or you. You told me that yourself a dozen times before you started this.
You're a good man, Ben. Sometimes you just think too much.

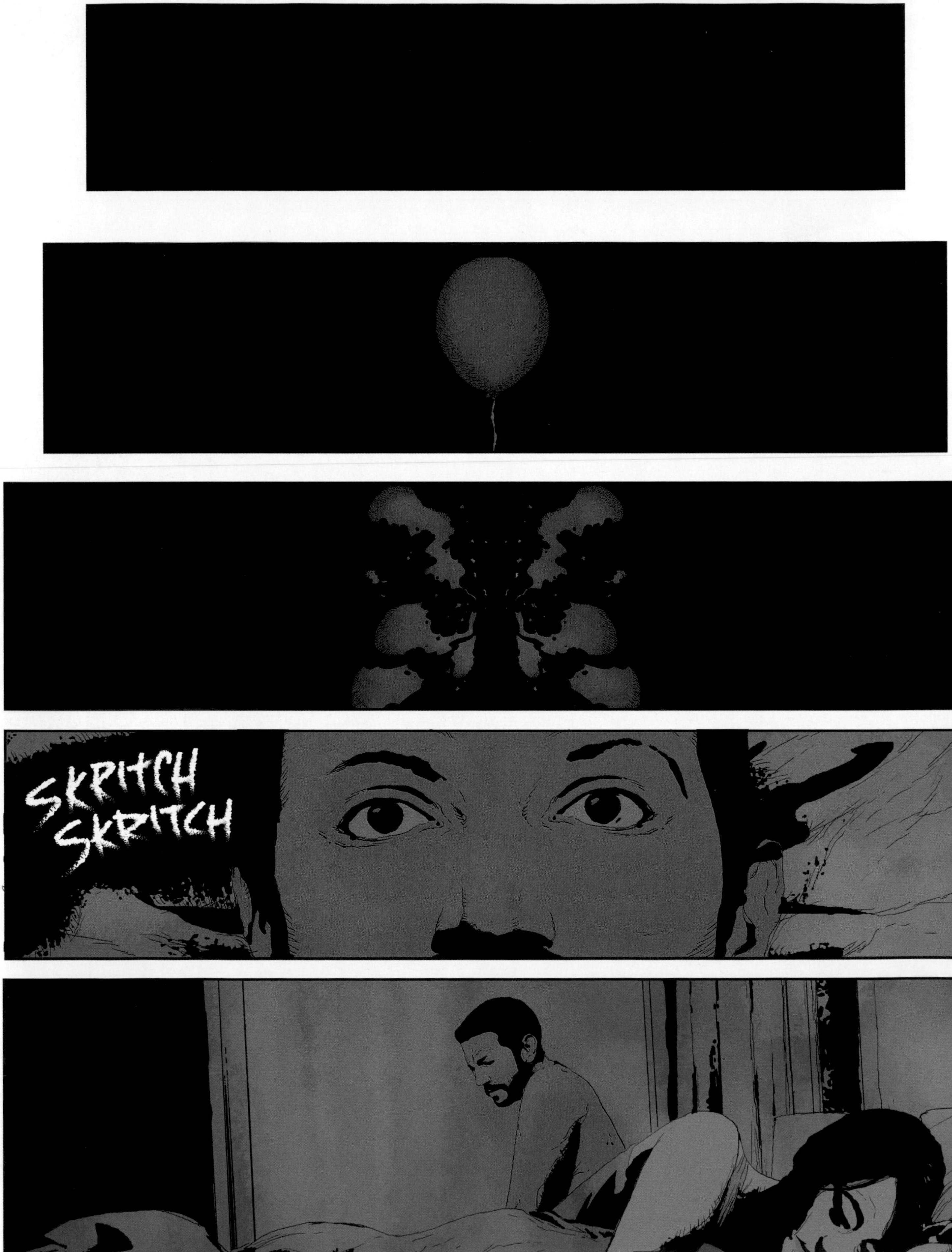
SKRITCH
SKRITCH

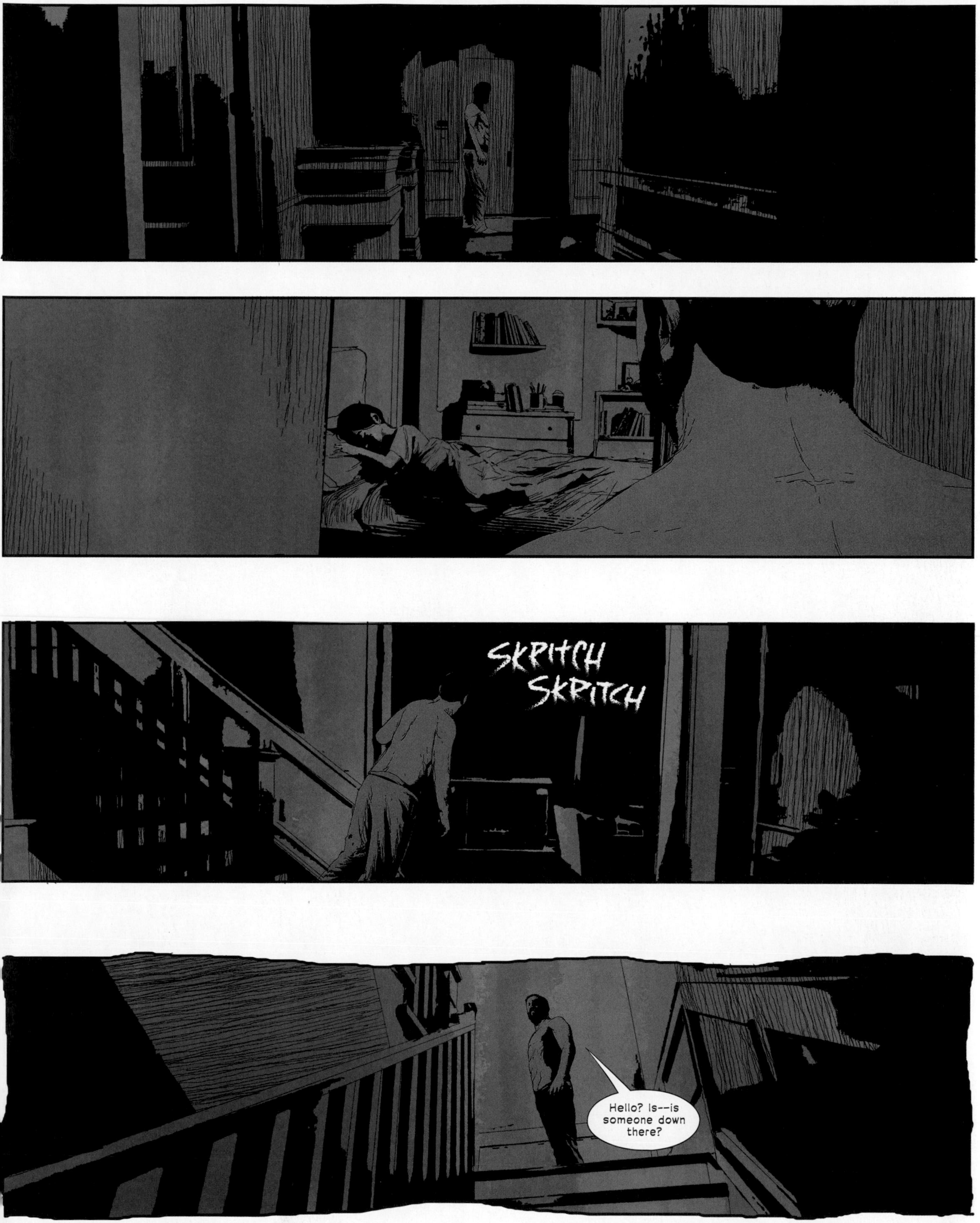
SKRITCH
SKRITCH
Hello? Is--is someone down there?

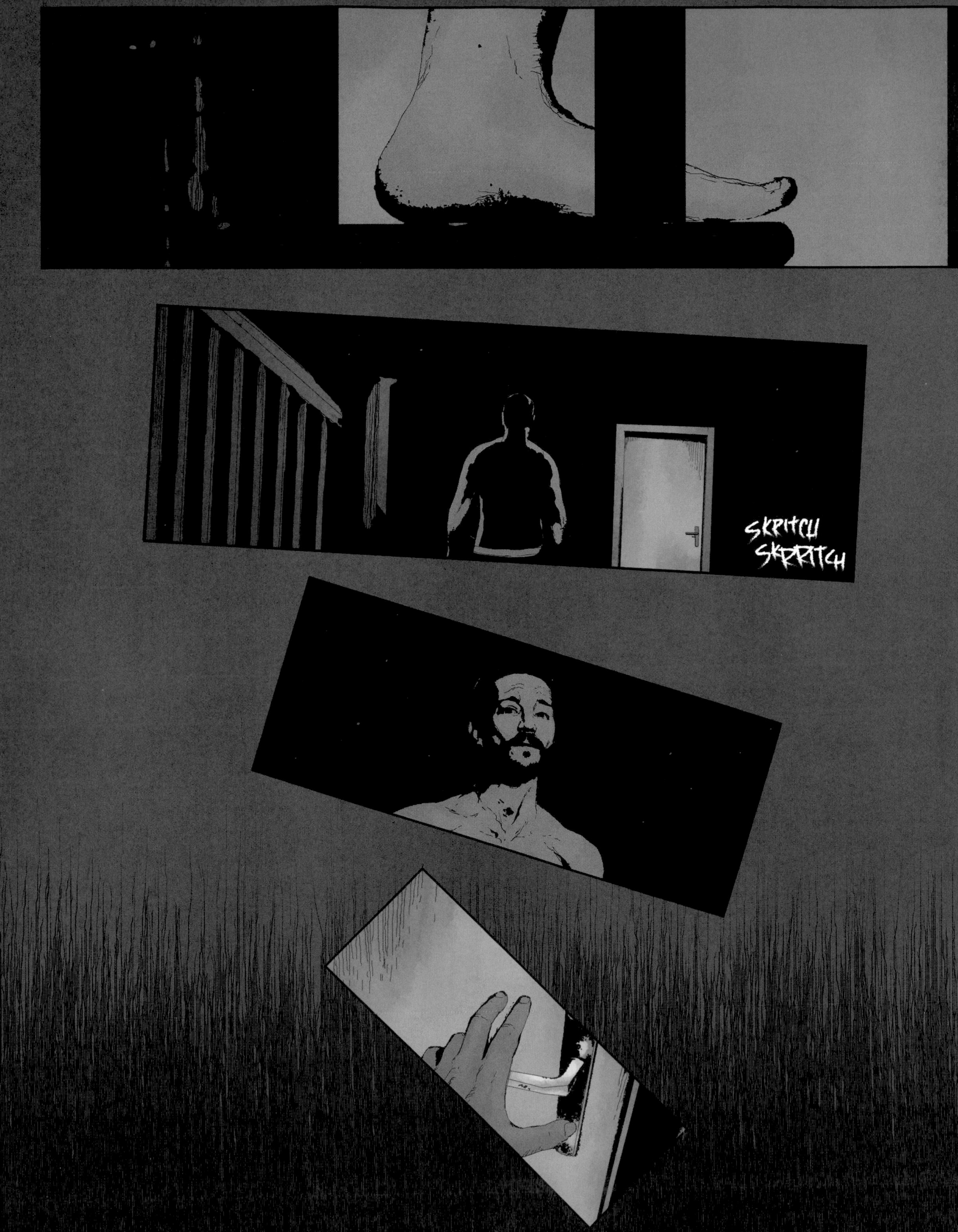
SKRITCH
SKRRITCH

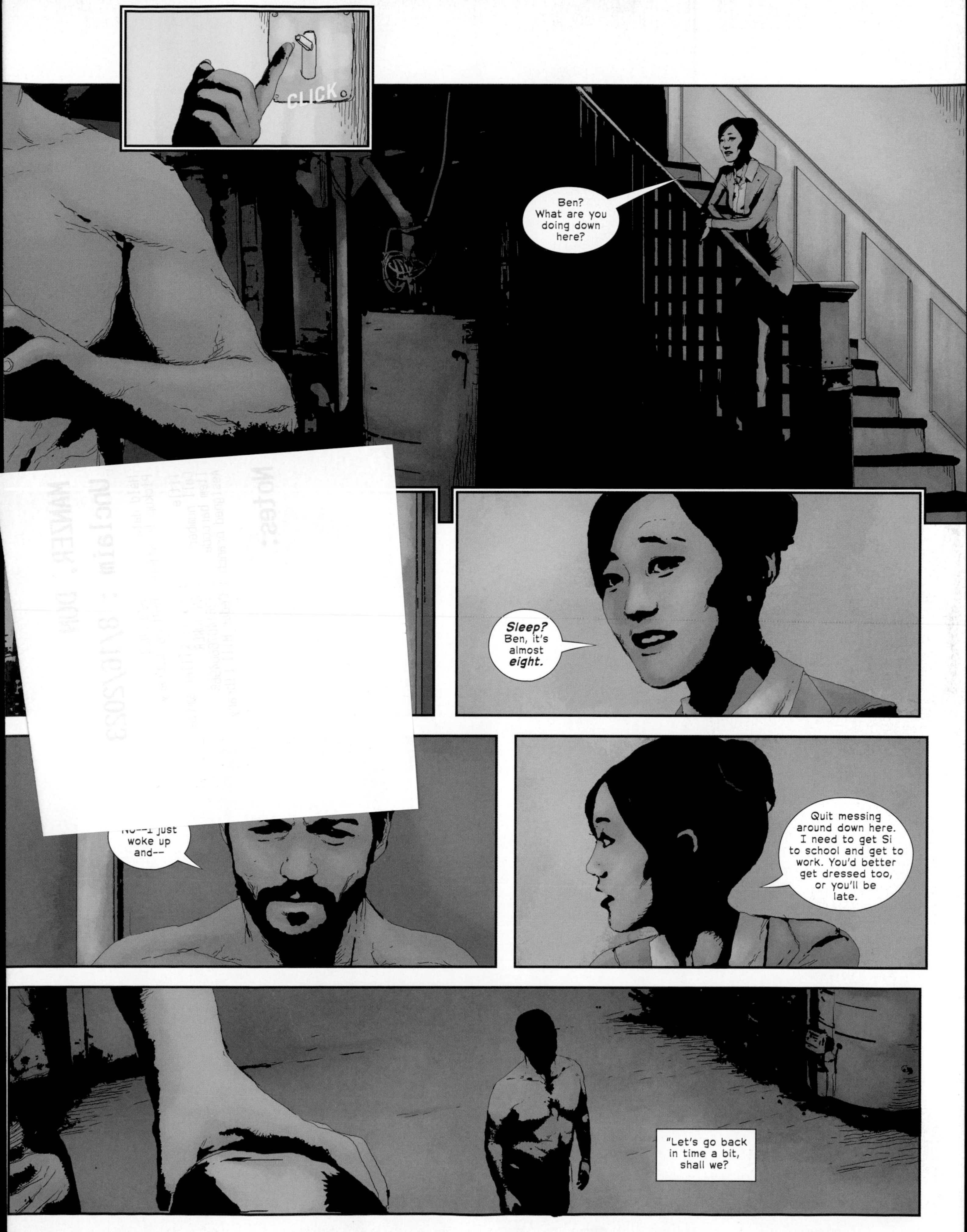
CLICK
Ben? What are you doing down here?
Sleep? Ben, it's almost eight.
No--I just woke up and--
Quit messing around down here. I need to get Si to school and get to work. You'd better get dressed too, or you'll be late.
"Let's go back in time a bit, shall we?

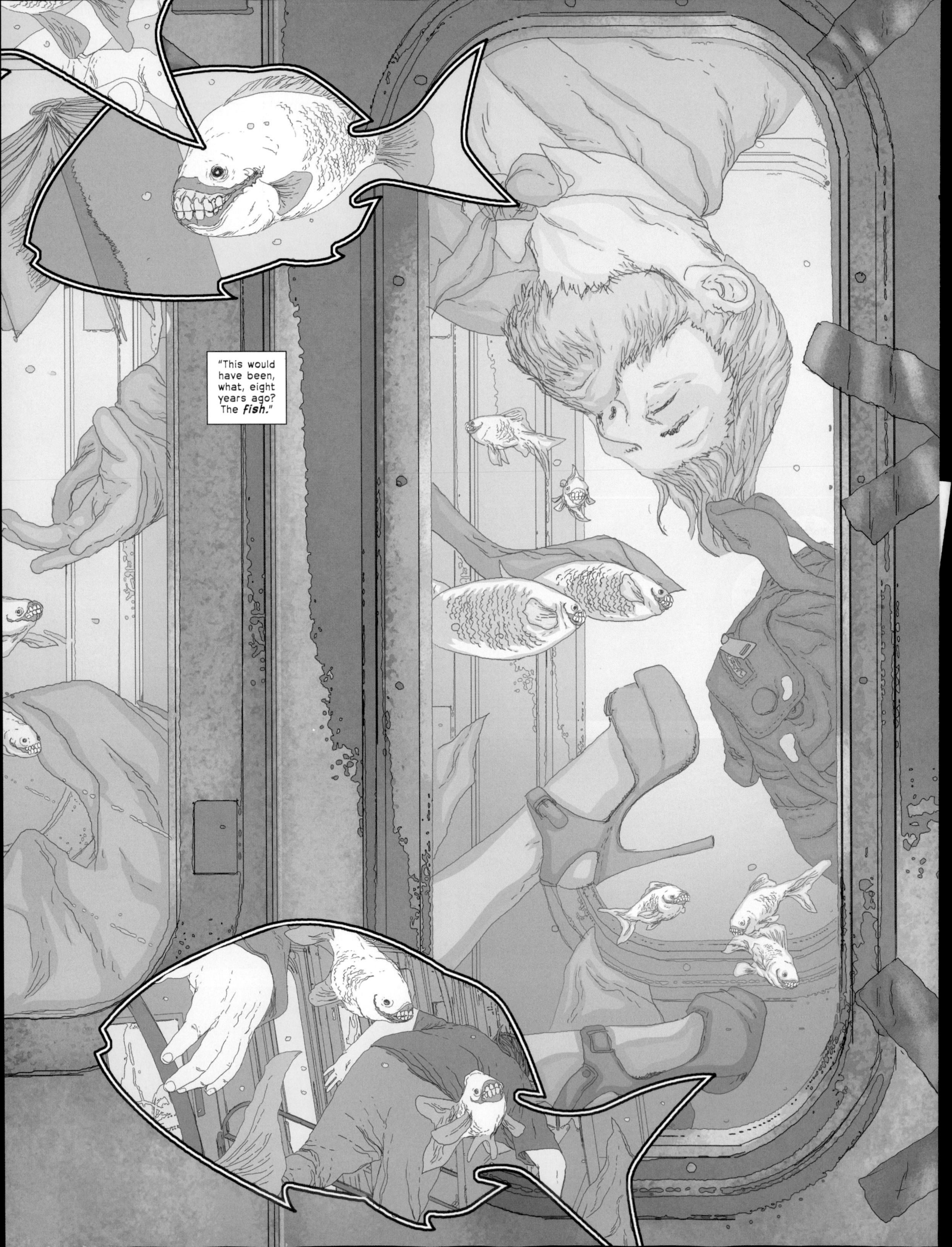
"This would have been, what, eight years ago? The *fish.*"

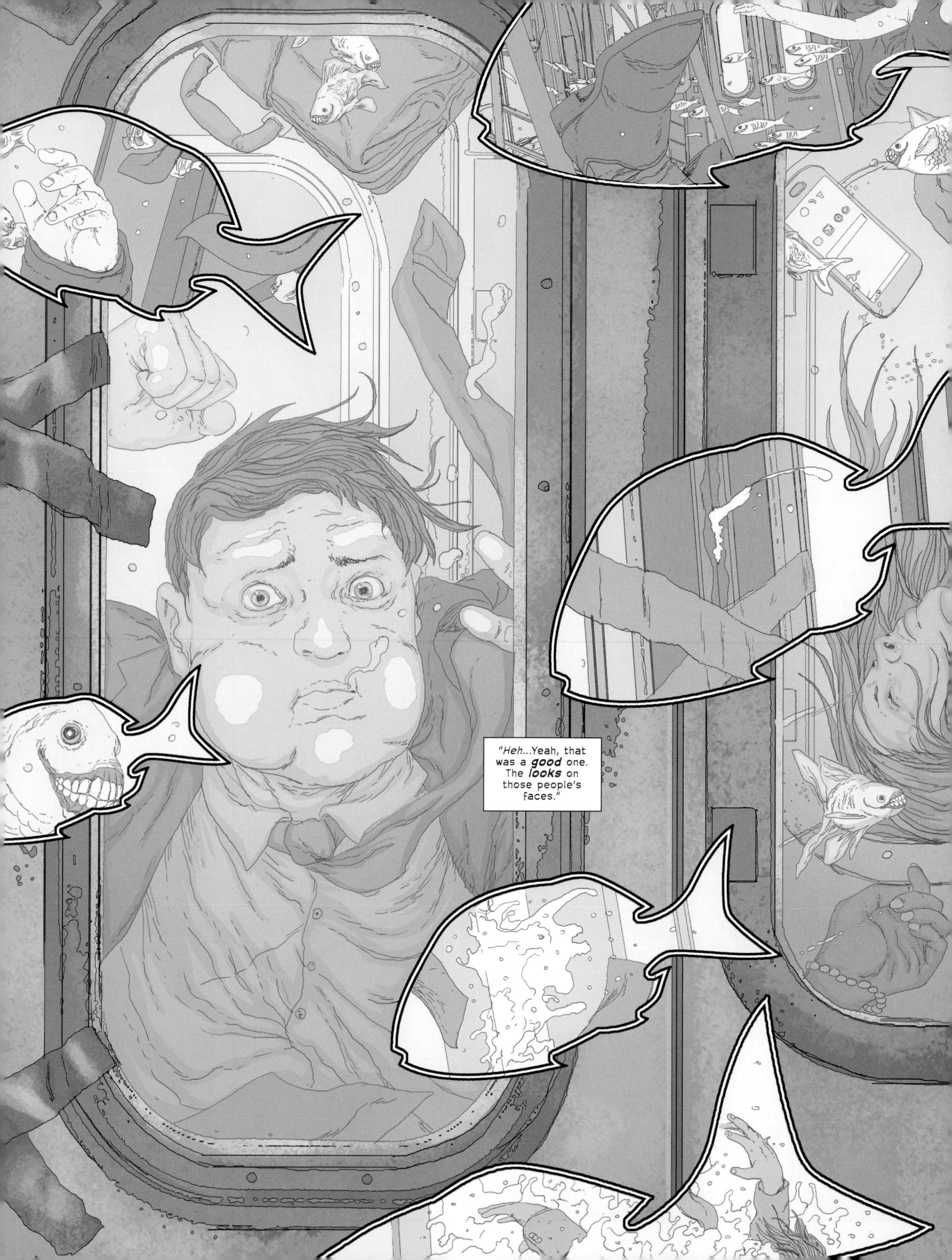
"Heh...Yeah, that was a good one. The looks on those people's faces."

"It's almost like *performance art* to you, isn't it?"

Yeah... *almost.*

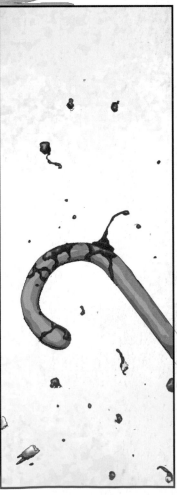

"But the fish...*how* did you do that?"

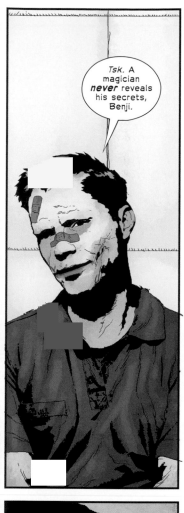

Tsk. A magician *never* reveals his secrets, Benji.

No, but seriously. You *must* have some kind of background in chemistry, right? Is that what happened to your face? A lab accident?

Oh, you wanna play the *secret origin* game? I warn you, I'm *really* good at that one. I *never* lose.

You wanna know where I *came from*, Doctor Ben?

Sure.

Once upon a very long time ago, there was a happy happy place in a happy happy forest. And wouldn't you just know it, this place was even called *Happyville!*

Oh, and Happyville was the happiest place there ever *ever* was! And everyone in Happyville knew each other, and they were all the very *best* of friends.

That is, until *Mr. Smiles* came to town.

Ha ha HAhA HA!

"After Mr. Smiles came to town, Happyville **wasn't** so happy anymore.

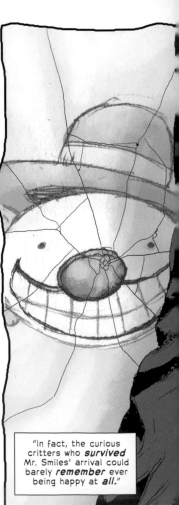

"In fact, the curious critters who **survived** Mr. Smiles' arrival could barely **remember** ever being happy at **all**."

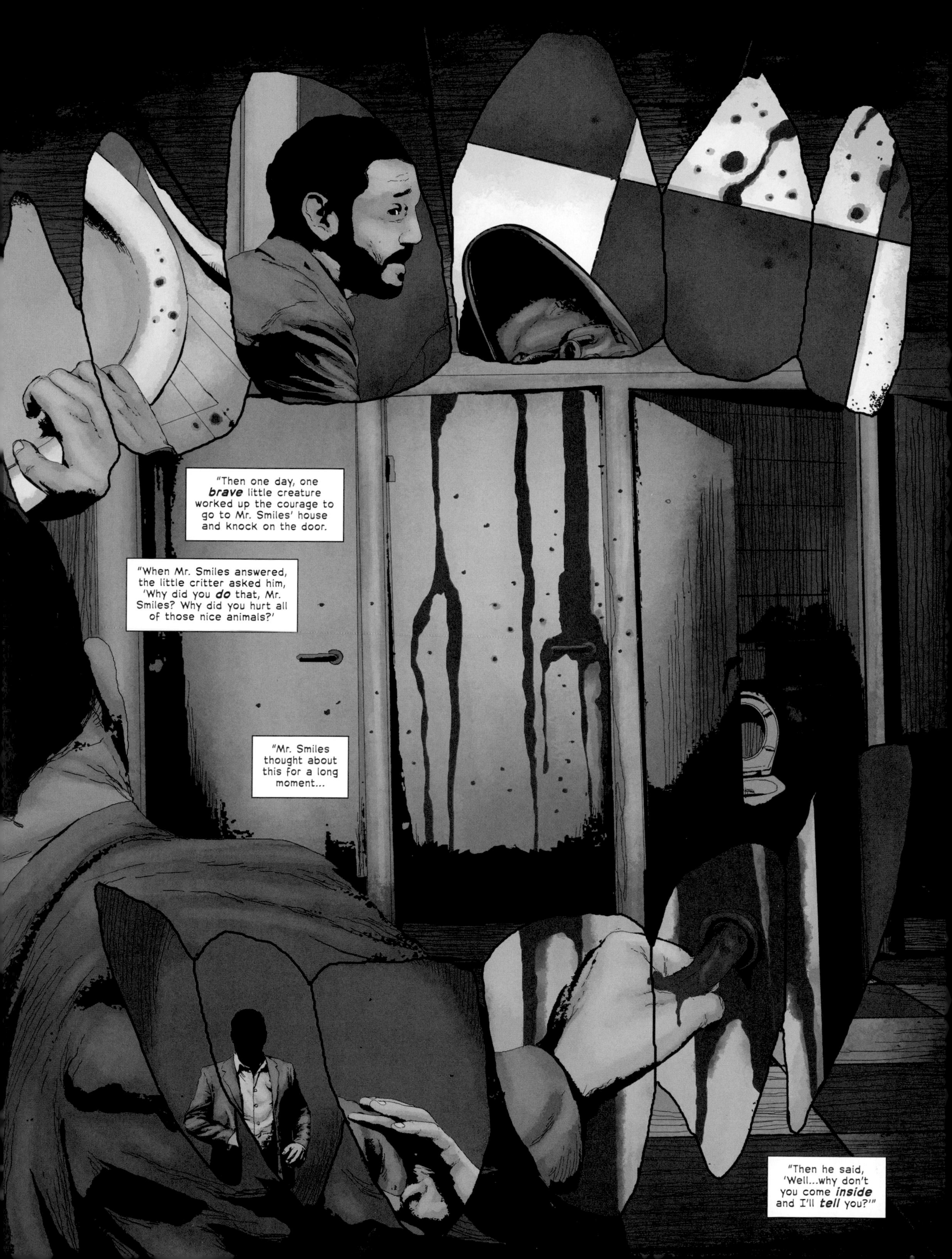
"Then one day, one *brave* little creature worked up the courage to go to Mr. Smiles' house and knock on the door.
"When Mr. Smiles answered, the little critter asked him, 'Why did you *do* that, Mr. Smiles? Why did you hurt all of those nice animals?'
"Mr. Smiles thought about this for a long moment...
"Then he said, 'Well...why don't you come *inside* and I'll *tell* you?'"

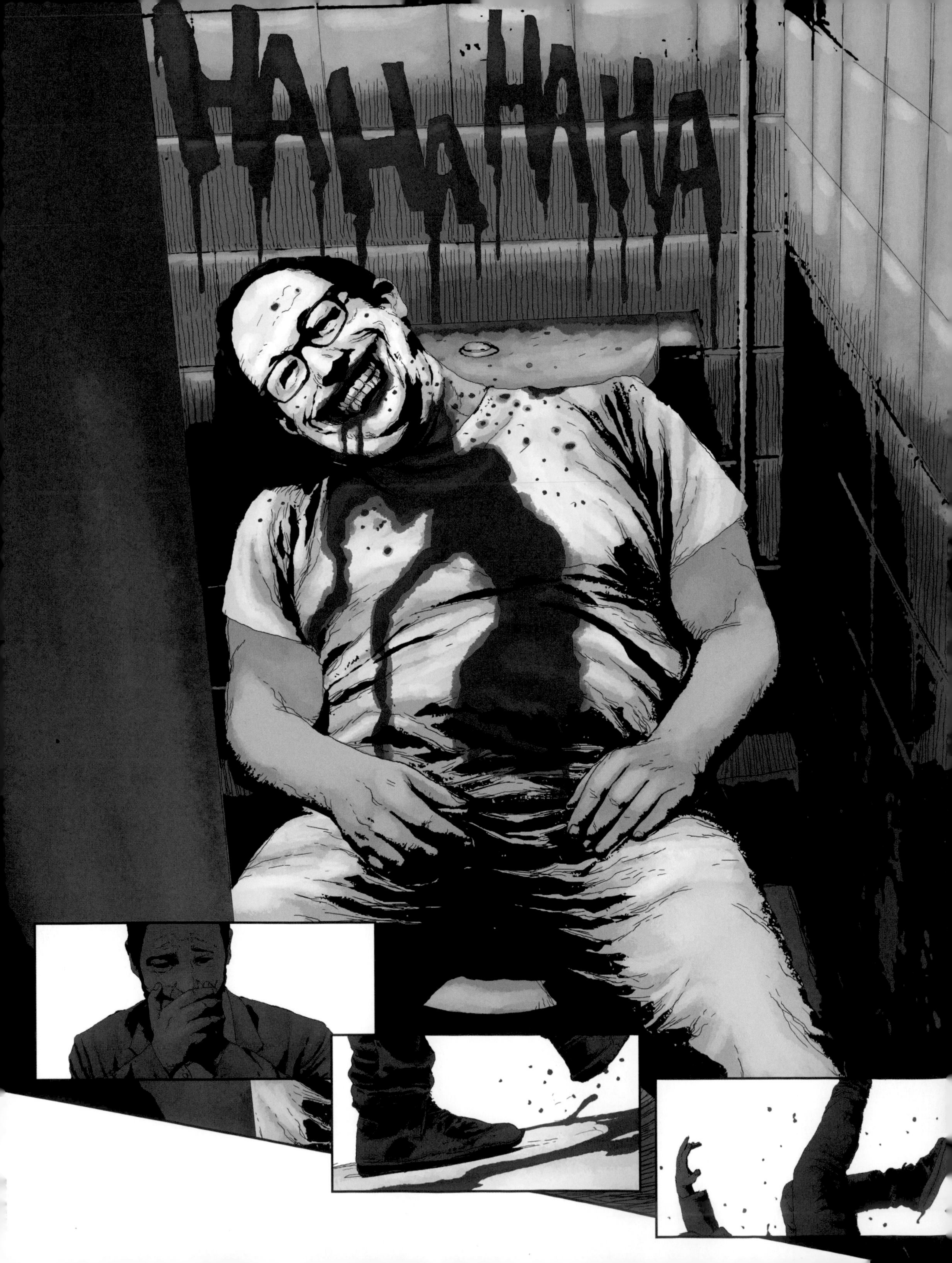
HAHAHAHAHA

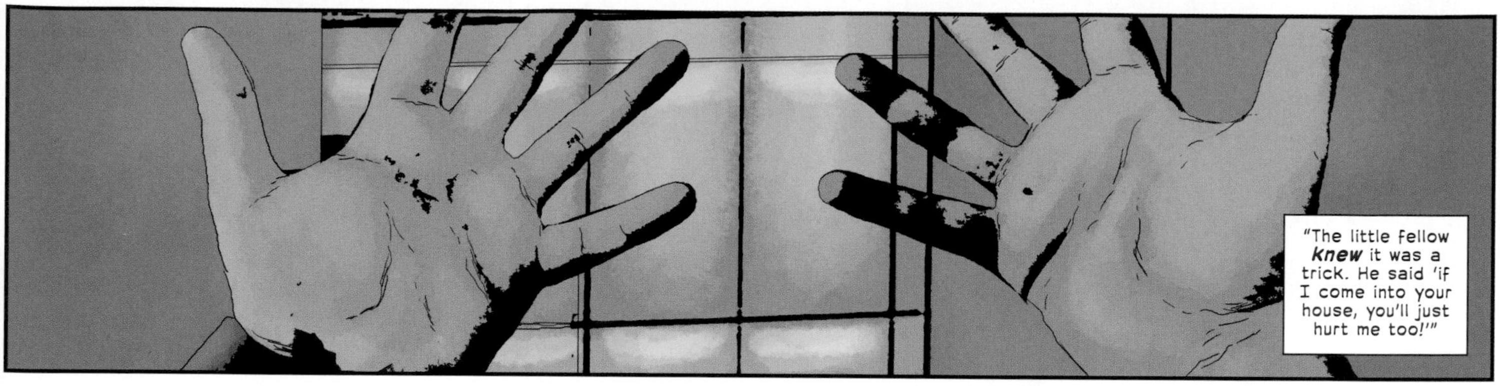
"The little fellow knew it was a trick. He said 'if I come into your house, you'll just hurt me too!'"

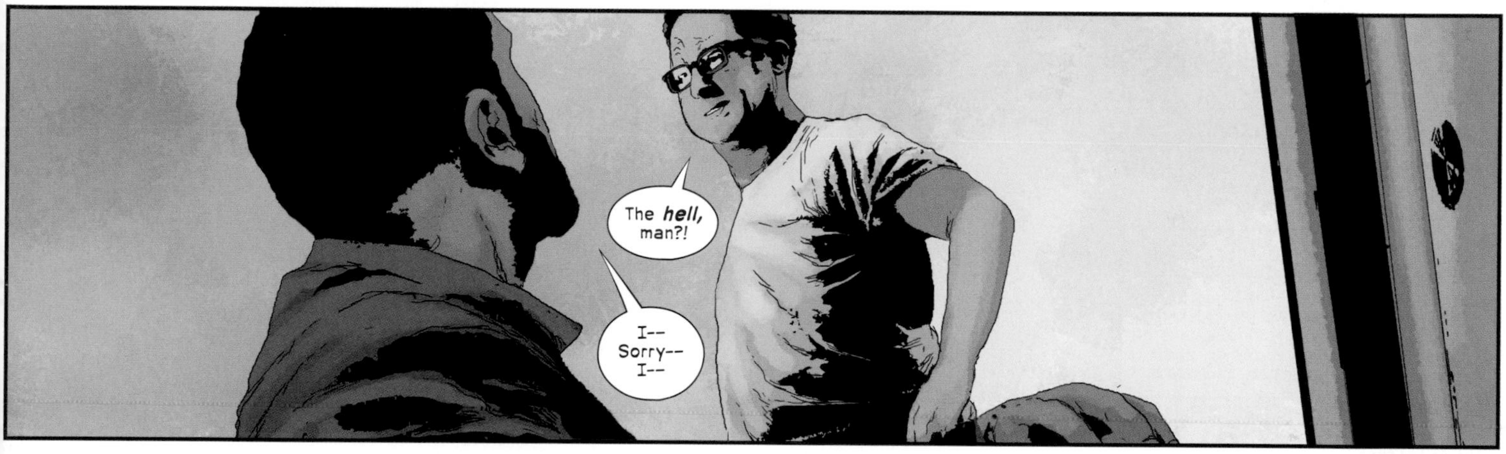
The hell, man?!
I-- Sorry-- I--

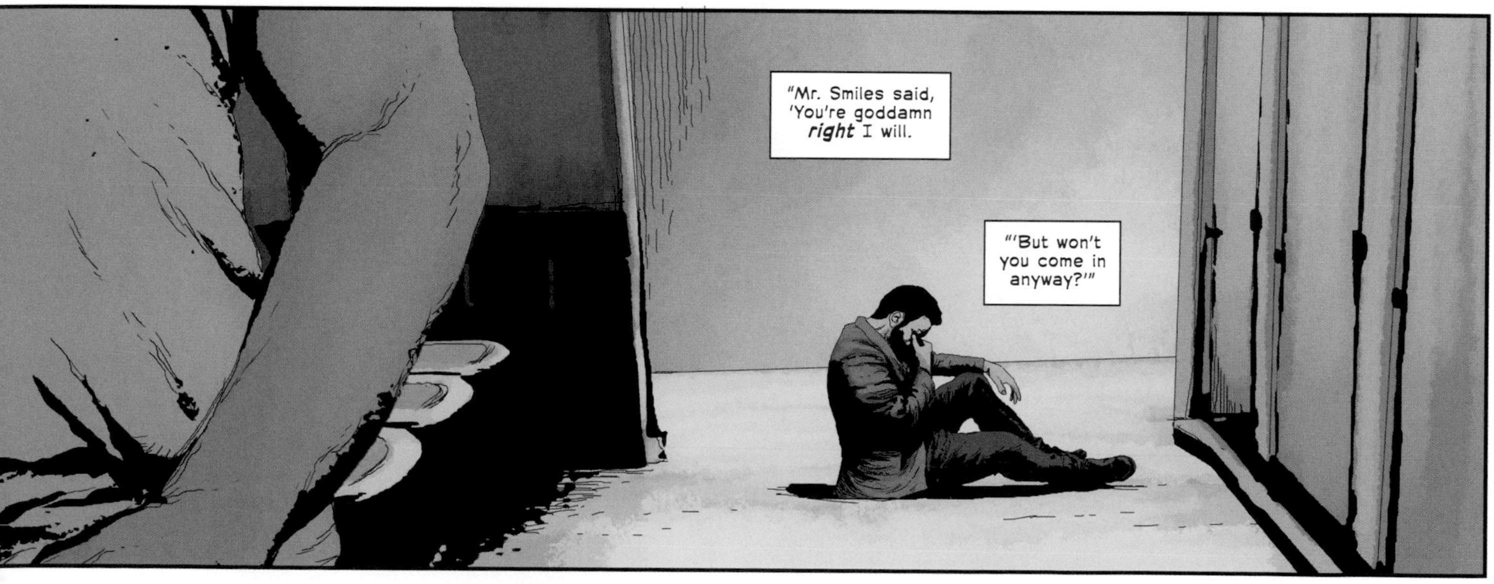
"Mr. Smiles said, 'You're goddamn right I will.
"'But won't you come in anyway?'"

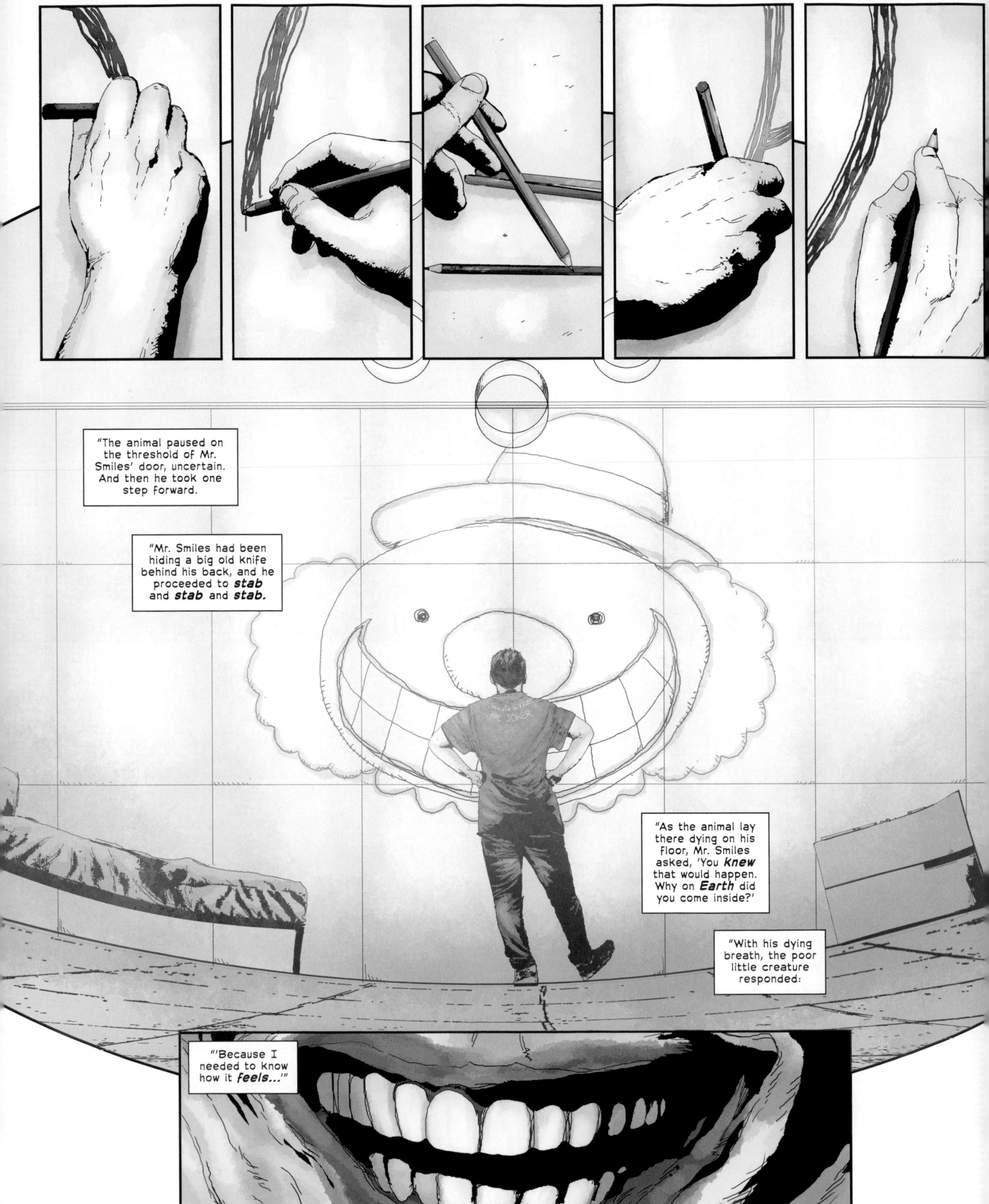
"The animal paused on the threshold of Mr. Smiles' door, uncertain. And then he took one step forward.
"Mr. Smiles had been hiding a big old knife behind his back, and he proceeded to ***stab*** and ***stab*** and ***stab.***
"As the animal lay there dying on his floor, Mr. Smiles asked, 'You ***knew*** that would happen. Why on ***Earth*** did you come inside?'
"With his dying breath, the poor little creature responded:
"'Because I needed to know how it ***feels...***'"

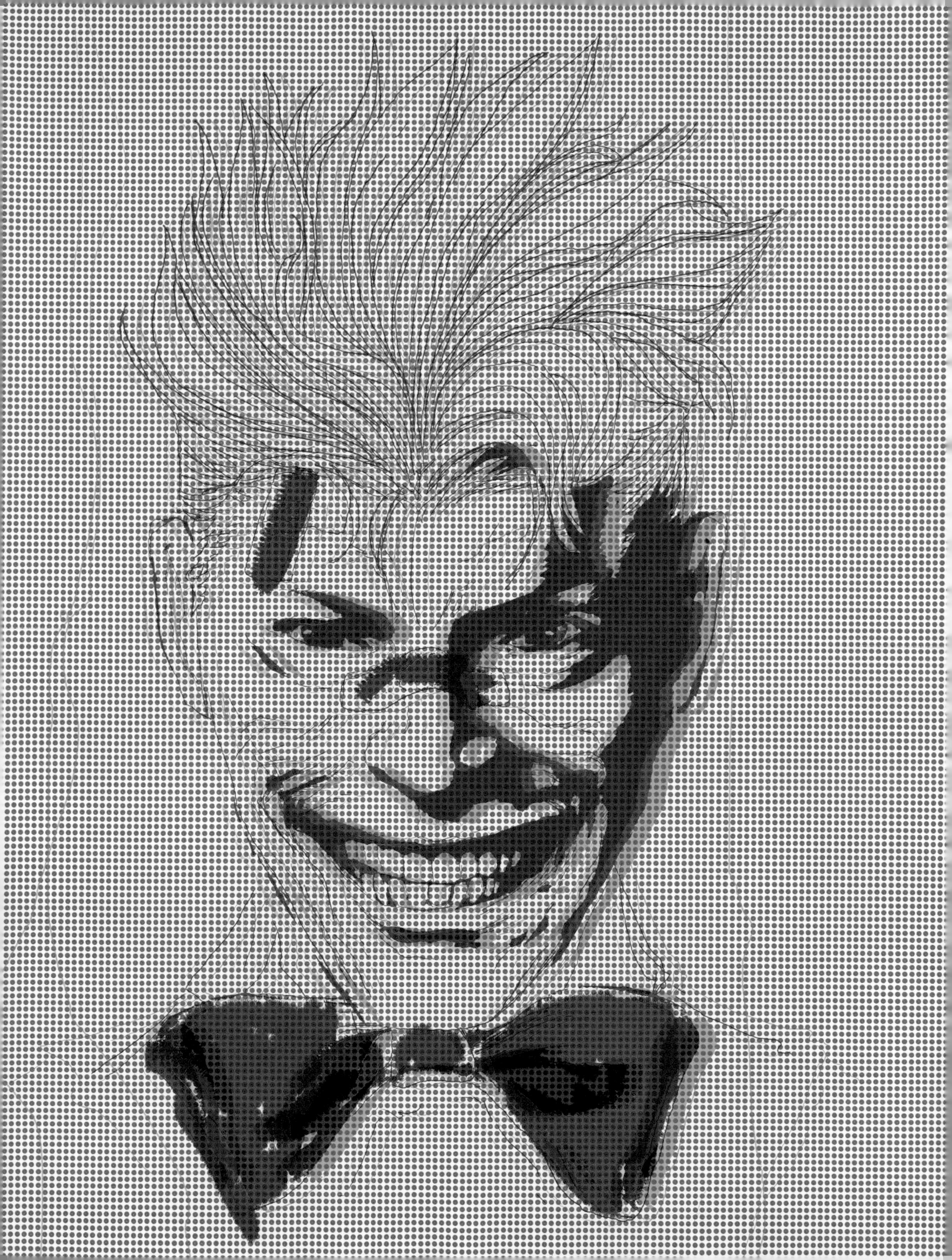

★★

BOOK TWO

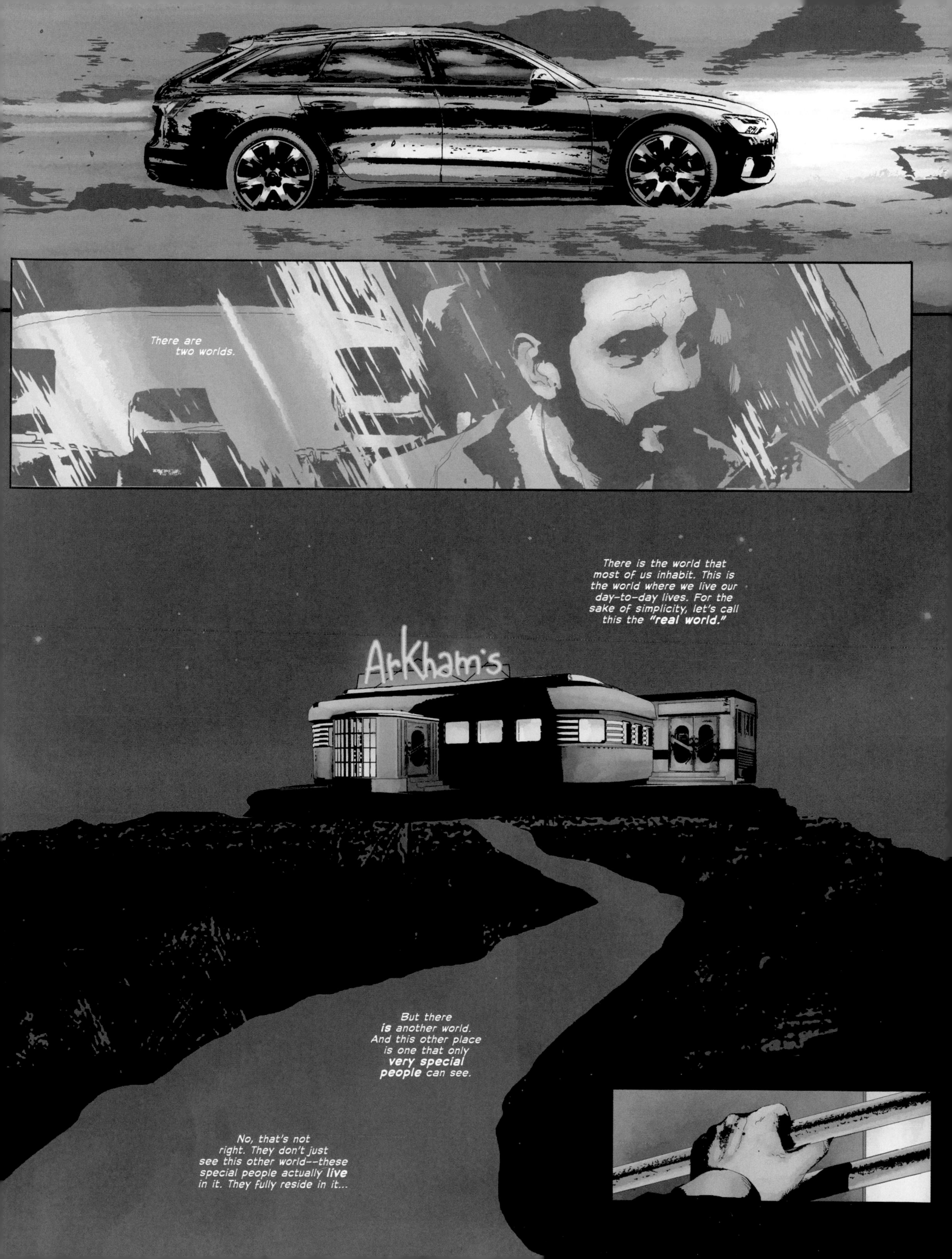

There are two worlds.
There is the world that most of us inhabit. This is the world where we live our day-to-day lives. For the sake of simplicity, let's call this the **"real world."**
ArKham's
But there **is** another world. And this other place is one that only **very special people** can see.
No, that's not right. They don't just see this other world--these special people actually **live** in it. They fully reside in it...

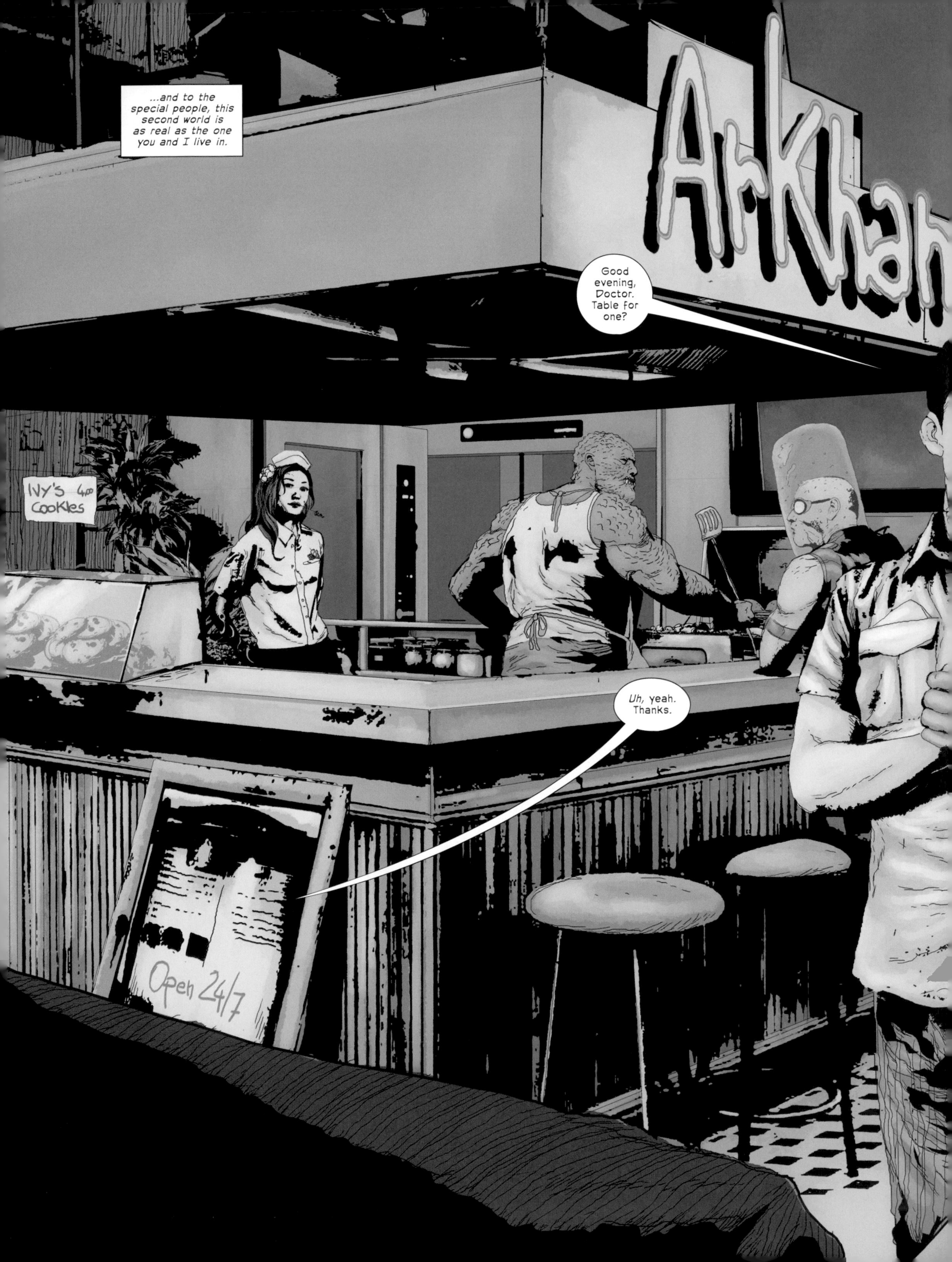
...and to the special people, this second world is as real as the one you and I live in.
Arkham
Good evening, Doctor. Table for one?
IVY'S COOKIES
Uh, yeah. Thanks.
Open 24/7

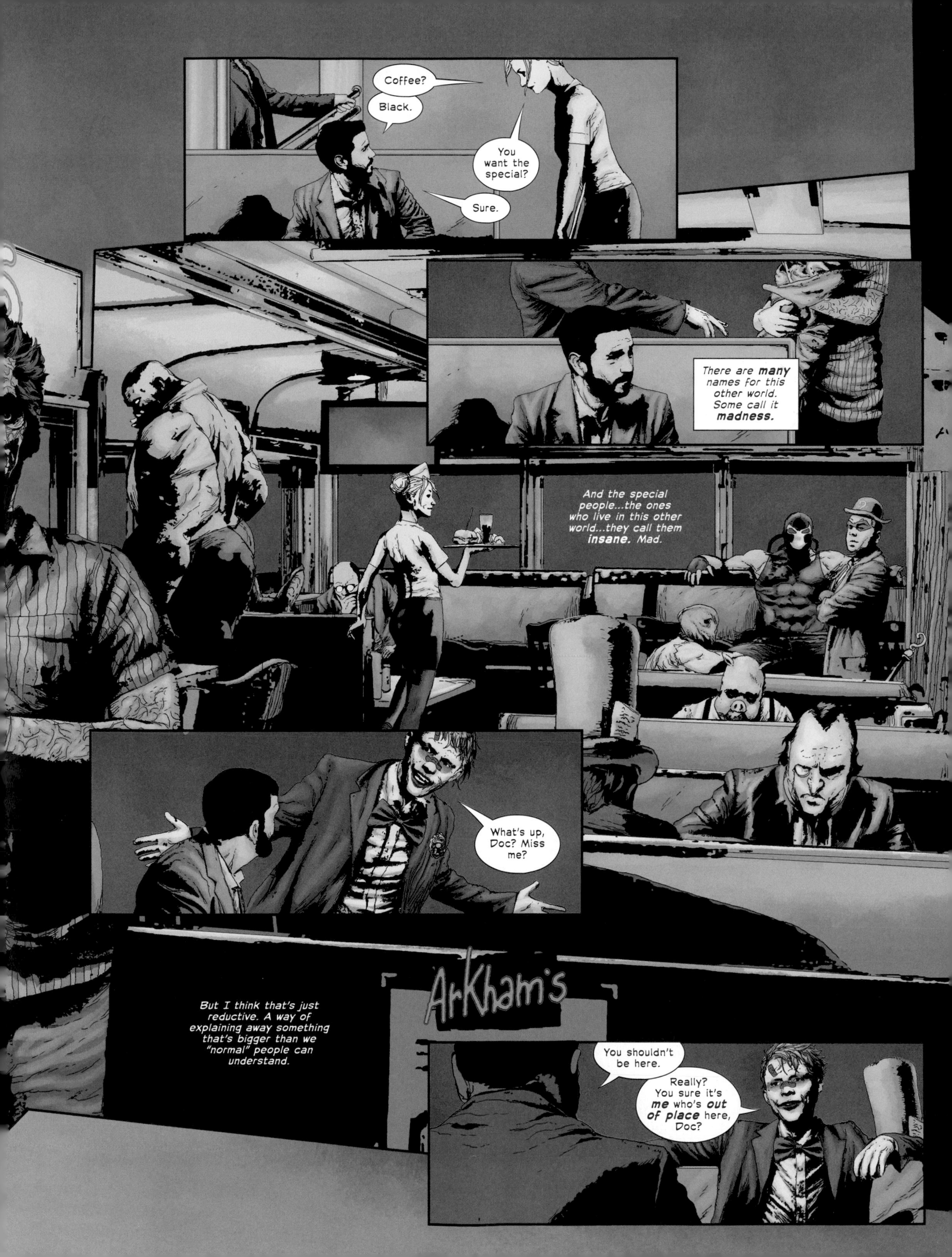
Coffee?
Black.
You want the special?
Sure.
There are **many** names for this other world. Some call it **madness.**
And the special people...the ones who live in this other world...they call them ***insane.*** *Mad.*
What's up, Doc? Miss me?
ArKham's
But I think that's just reductive. A way of explaining away something that's bigger than we "normal" people can understand.
You shouldn't be here.
Really? You sure it's ***me*** who's ***out of place*** here, Doc?

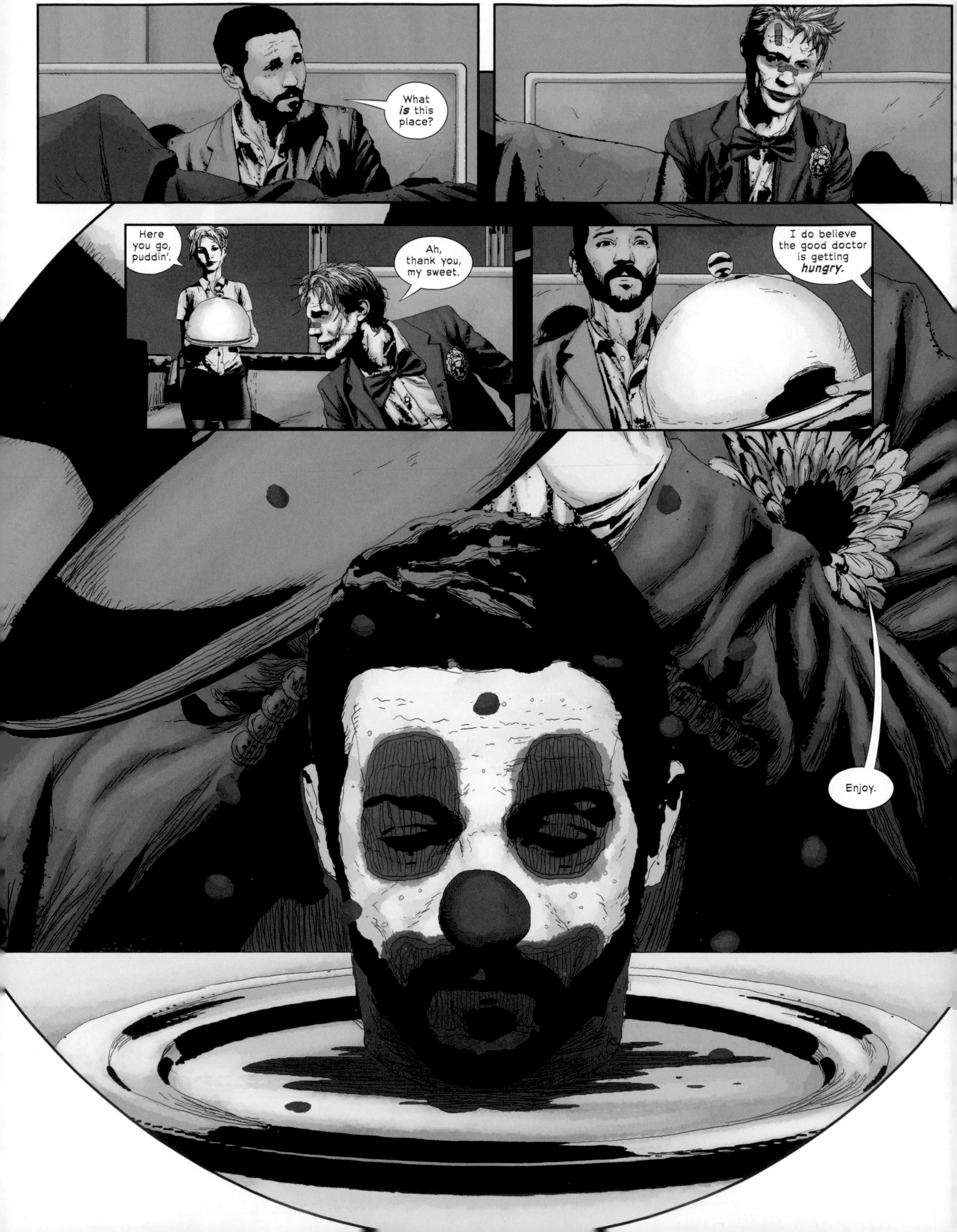

What *is* this place?
Here you go, puddin'.
Ah, thank you, my sweet.
I do believe the good doctor is getting ***hungry.***
Enjoy.

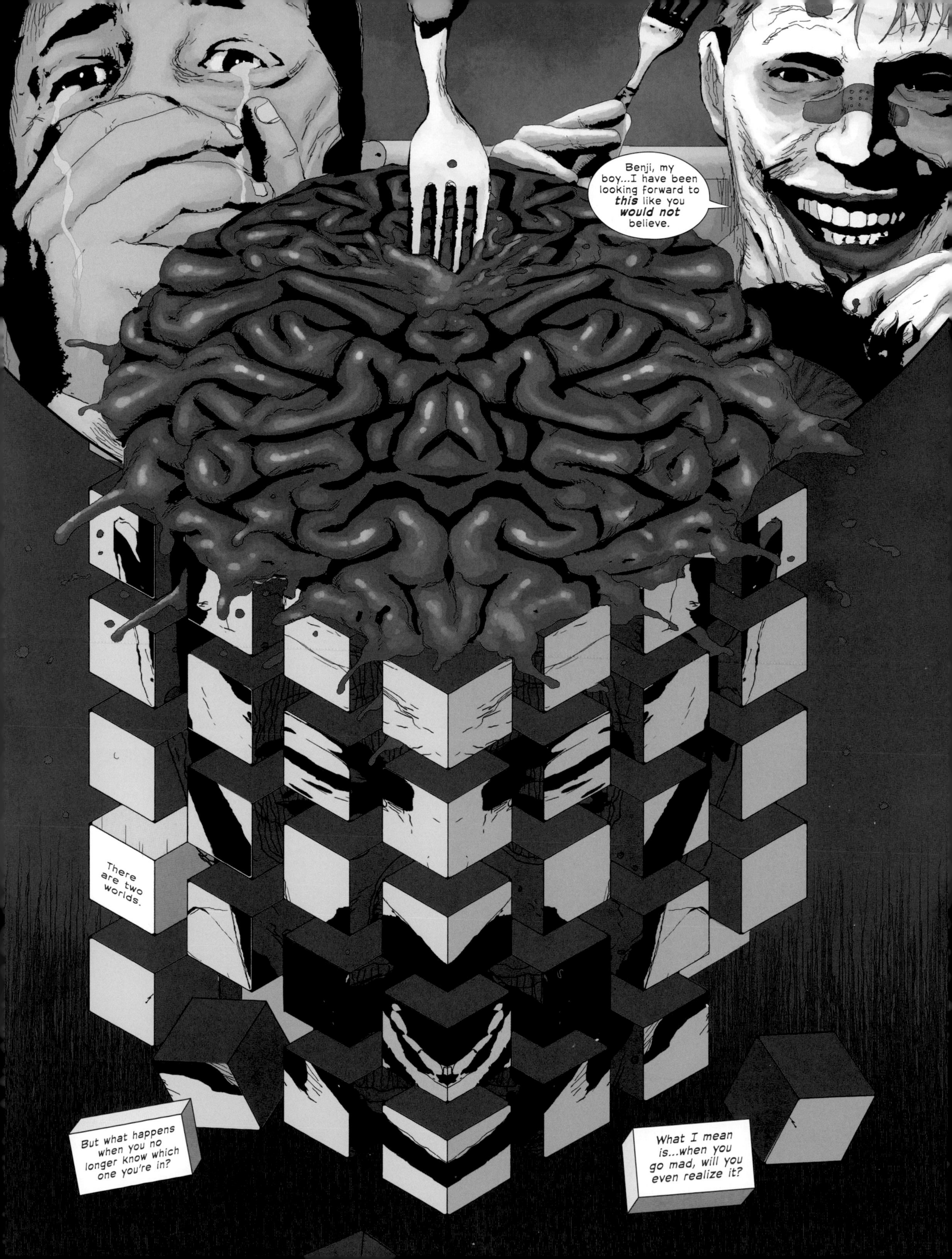
Benji, my boy...I have been looking forward to **this** like you ***would not*** believe.
There are two worlds.
But what happens when you no longer know which one you're in?
What I mean is...when you go mad, will you even realize it?

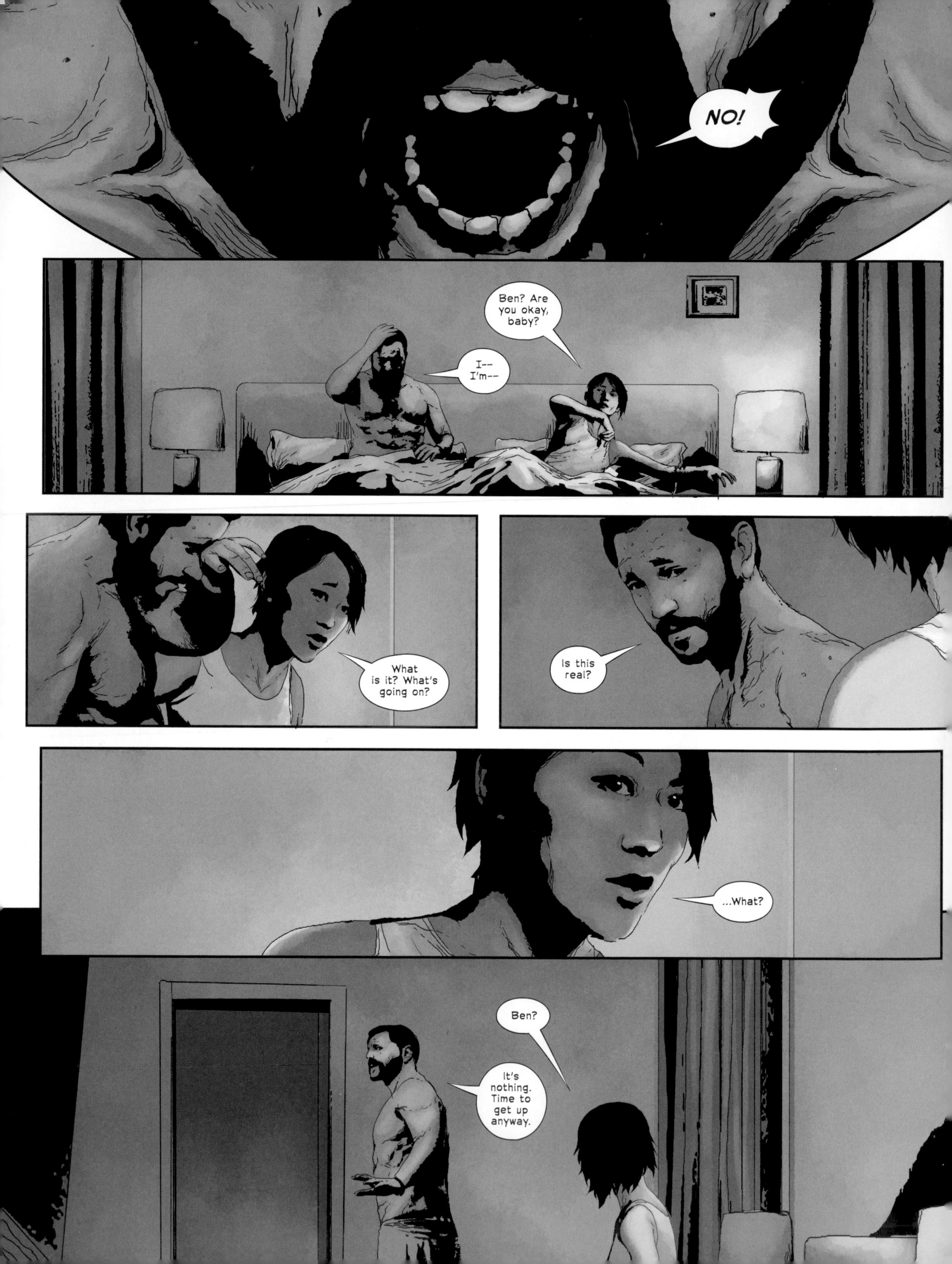
NO!
Ben? Are you okay, baby?
I-- I'm--
What is it? What's going on?
Is this real?
...What?
Ben?
It's nothing. Time to get up anyway.

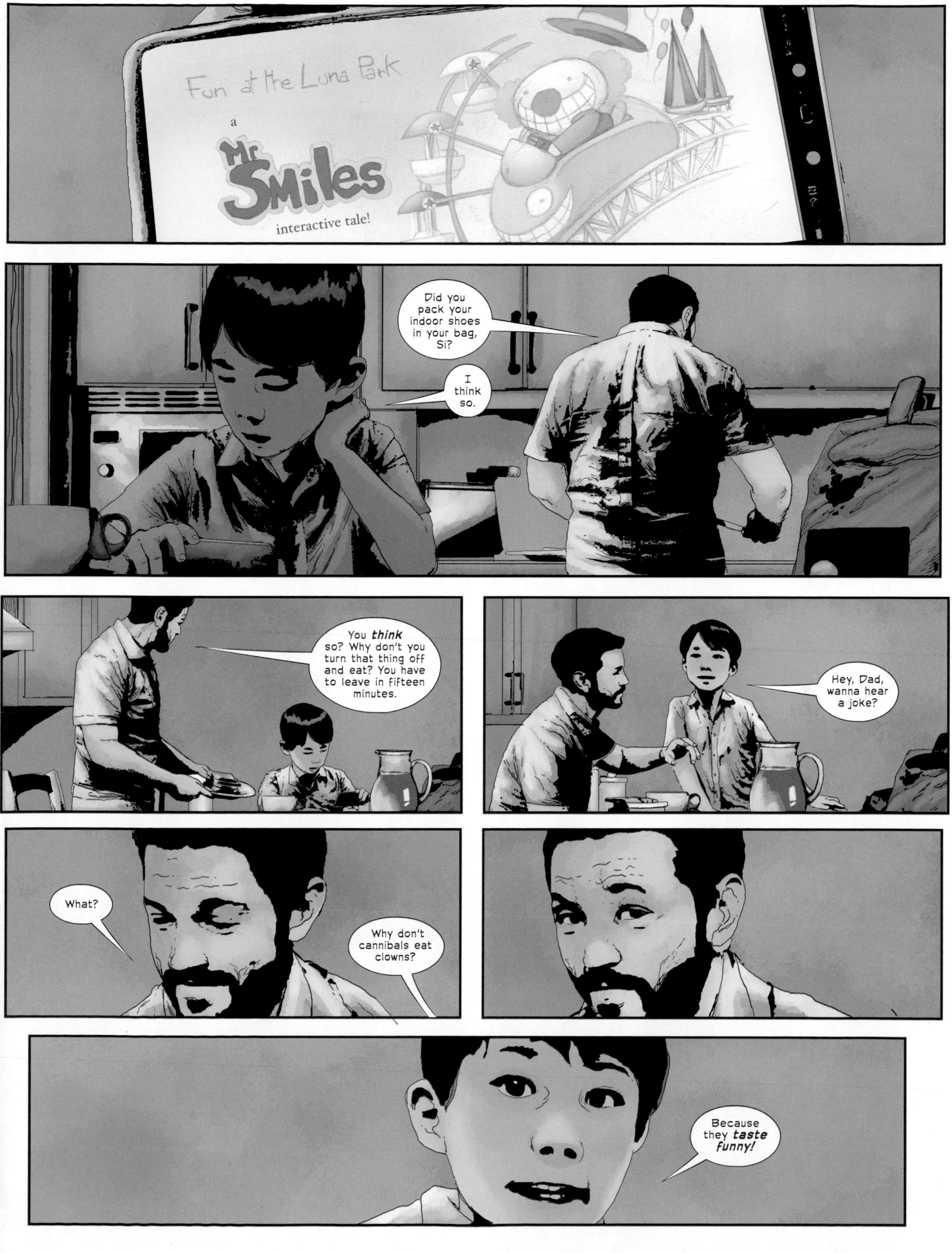

Fun at the Luna Park
a
Mr Smiles
interactive tale!
Did you pack your indoor shoes in your bag, Si?
I think so.
You *think* so? Why don't you turn that thing off and eat? You have to leave in fifteen minutes.
Hey, Dad, wanna hear a joke?
What?
Why don't cannibals eat clowns?
Because they *taste funny!*

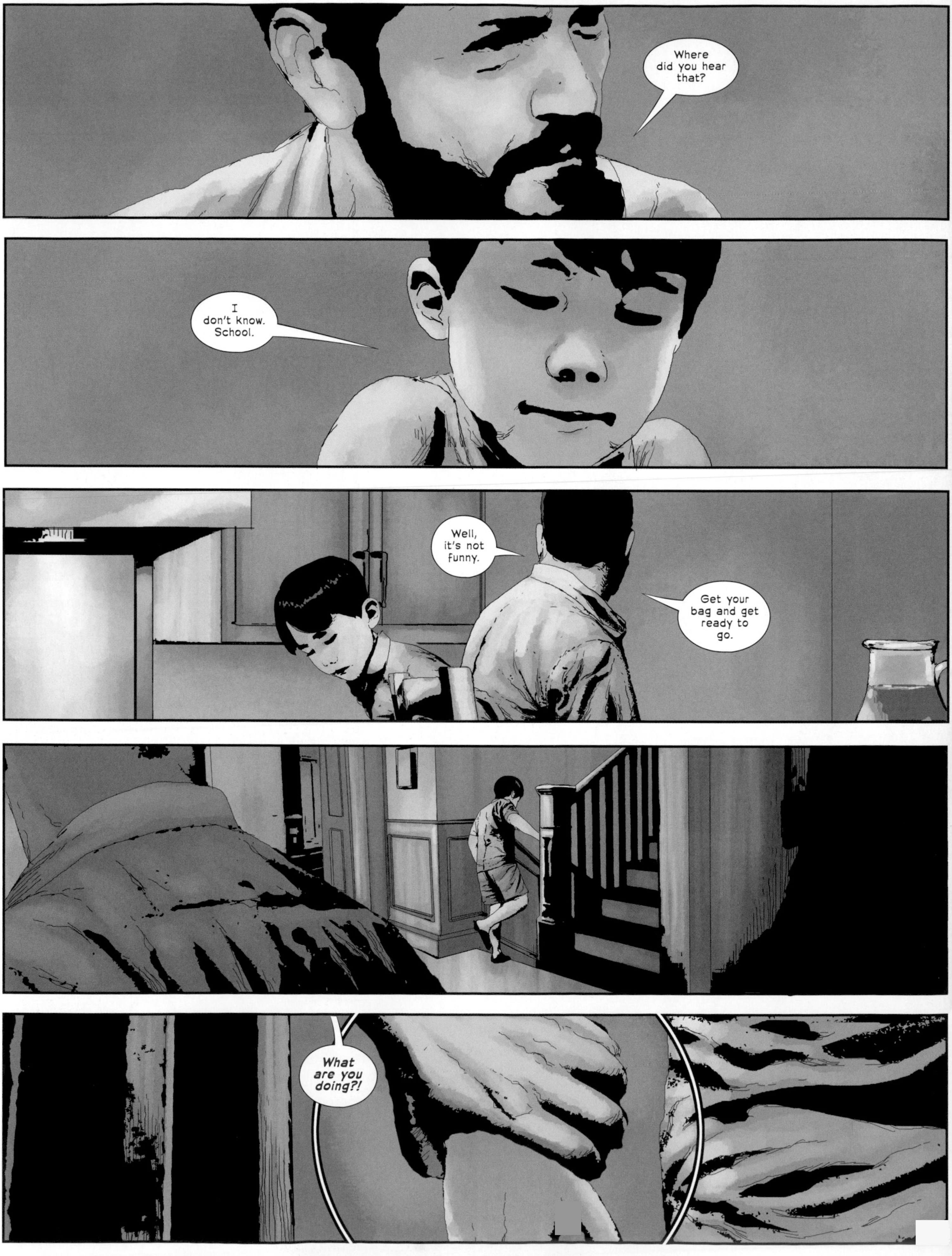

Where did you hear that?
I don't know. School.
Well, it's not funny.
Get your bag and get ready to go.
What are you doing?!

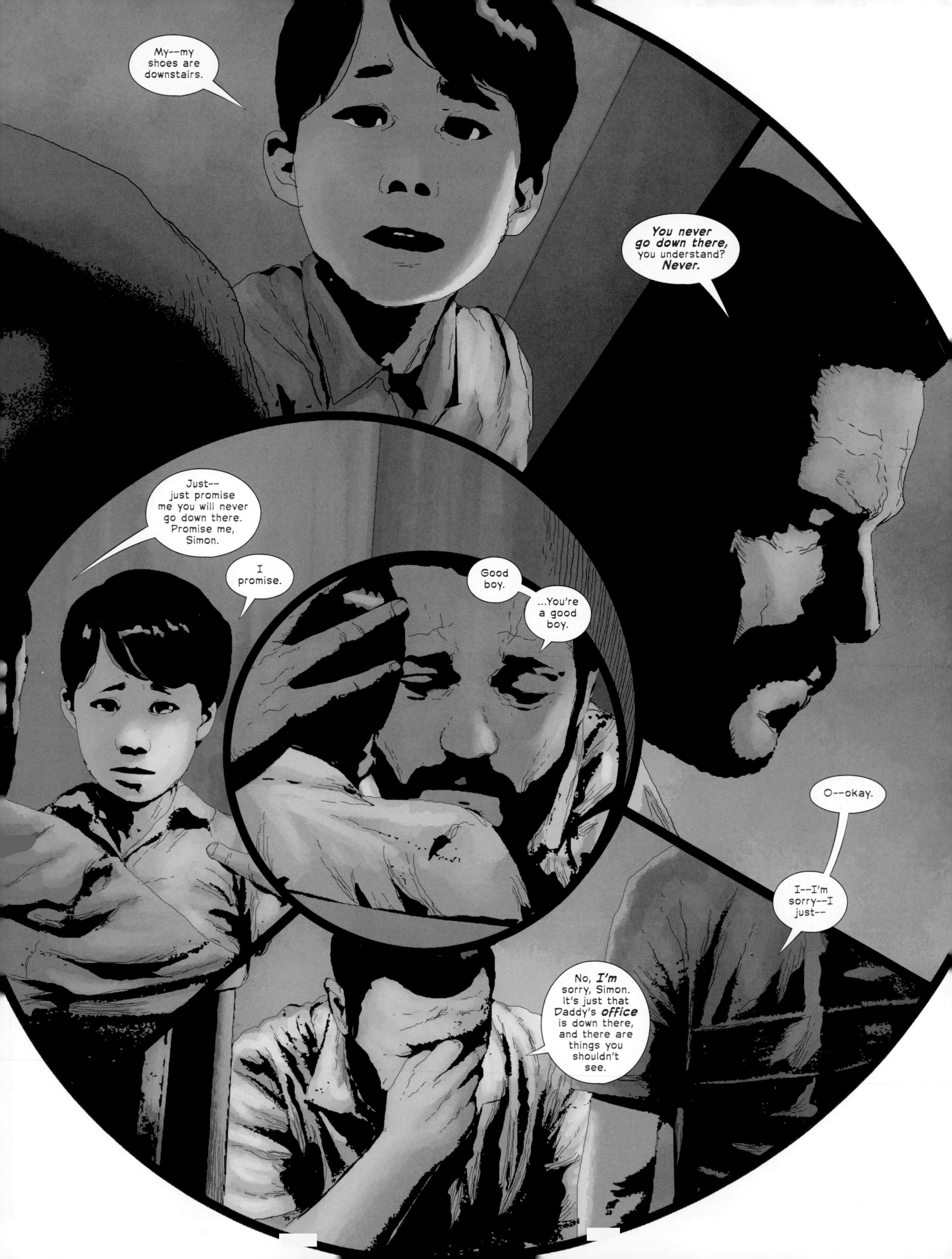
My--my shoes are downstairs.
You never go down there, you understand? Never.
Just-- just promise me you will never go down there. Promise me, Simon.
I promise.
Good boy.
...You're a good boy.
O--okay.
I--I'm sorry--I just--
No, I'm sorry, Simon. It's just that Daddy's office is down there, and there are things you shouldn't see.

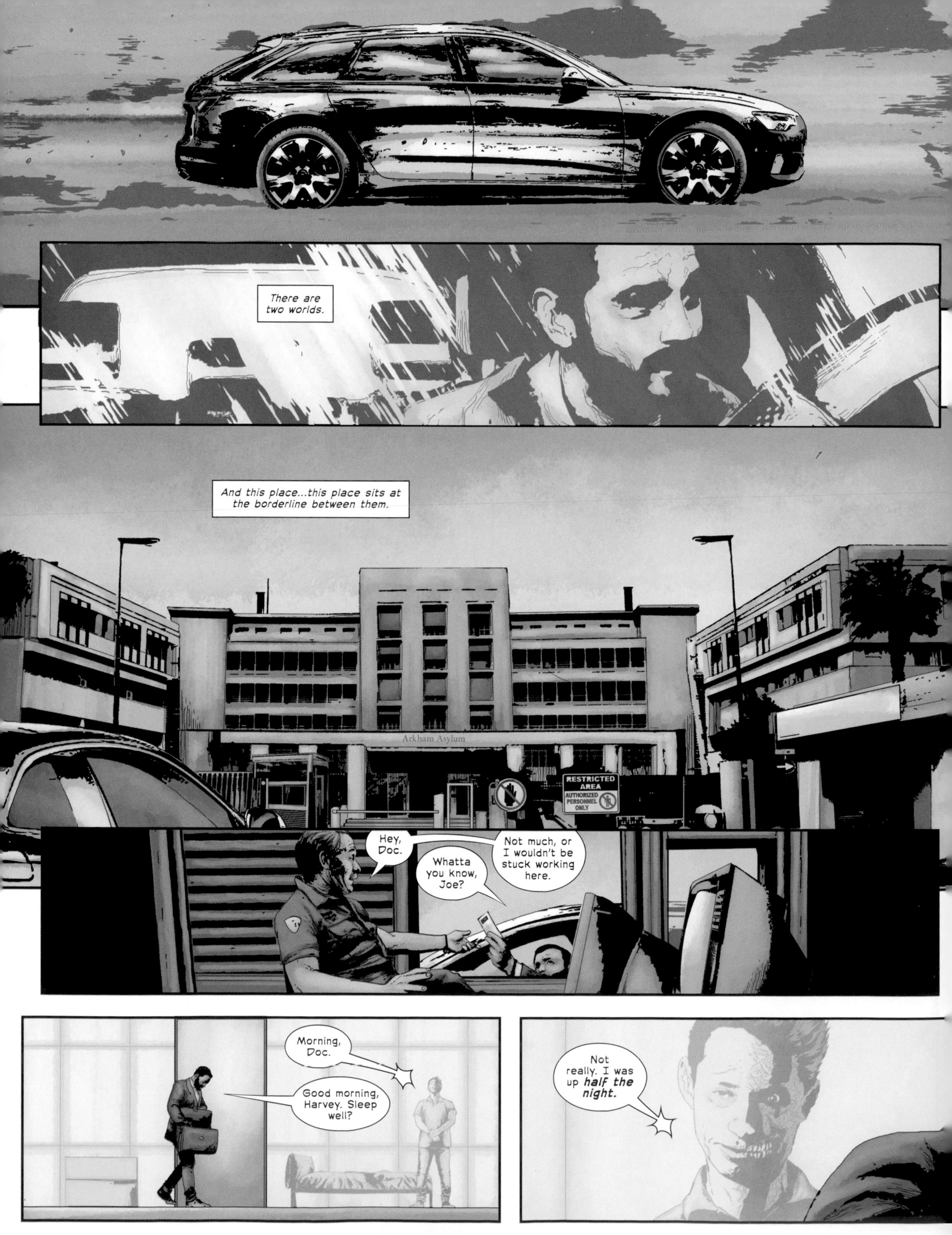

There are two worlds.
And this place...this place sits at the borderline between them.
Arkham Asylum
RESTRICTED AREA
AUTHORIZED PERSONNEL ONLY
Hey, Doc.
Whatta you know, Joe?
Not much, or I wouldn't be stuck working here.
Morning, Doc.
Good morning, Harvey. Sleep well?
Not really. I was up half the night.

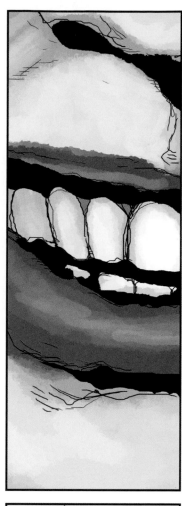

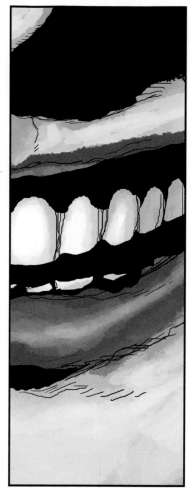

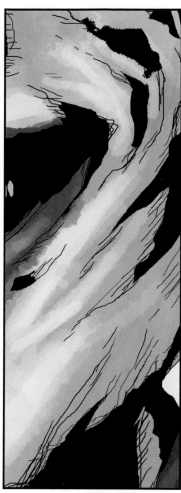

Today I would like to talk about your **beginnings.**

Which one?

Don't give me that. I know your game. Every time you talk about your origins you have another story. Each one sounds so convincing, too.

But I don't want the **stories.** I want the **truth.**

The truth?

Trust me, Benji...you **don't** want the truth. Not yet, anyway.

Stories are **so** much better. They make **sense** of things. They **comfort** us.

Do these lies comfort you? What is it that **you're** hiding from, Joker?

What scares **you?**

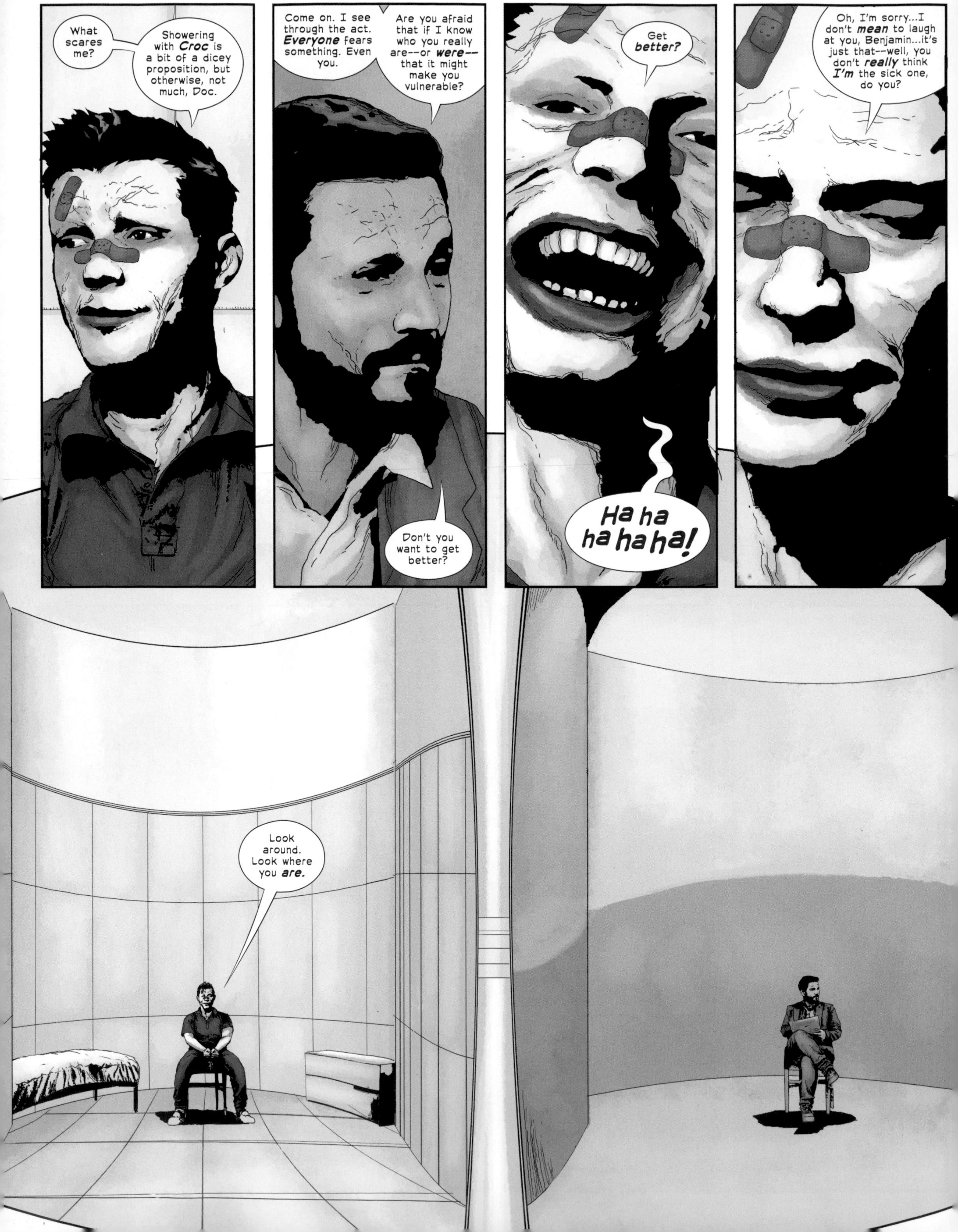

What scares me?
Showering with *Croc* is a bit of a dicey proposition, but otherwise, not much, Doc.
Come on. I see through the act. *Everyone* fears something. Even you.
Are you afraid that if I know who you really are--or *were--* that it might make you vulnerable?
Don't you want to get better?
Get *better?*
Ha ha ha ha ha!
Oh, I'm sorry...I don't *mean* to laugh at you, Benjamin...it's just that--well, you don't *really* think *I'm* the sick one, do you?
Look around. Look where you *are.*

Nice try. Let's try something else. How about the first time you met *him?*

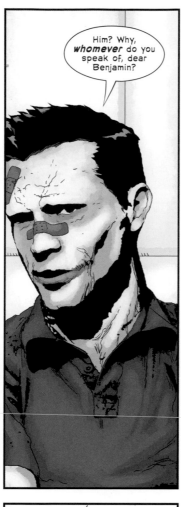

Him? Why, *whomever* do you speak of, dear Benjamin?

You *know* who.

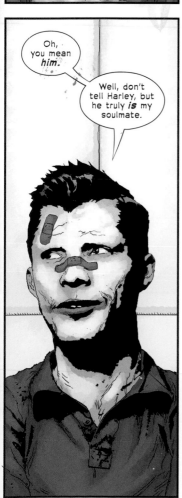

Oh, you mean *him.*

Well, don't tell Harley, but he truly *is* my soulmate.

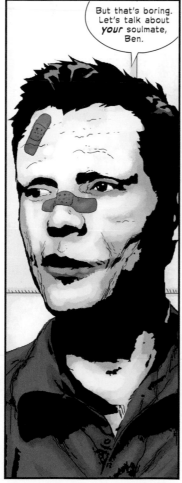

But that's boring. Let's talk about *your* soulmate, Ben.

Why don't you tell *me* something...I would love to hear about *your first time* with *Anna.*

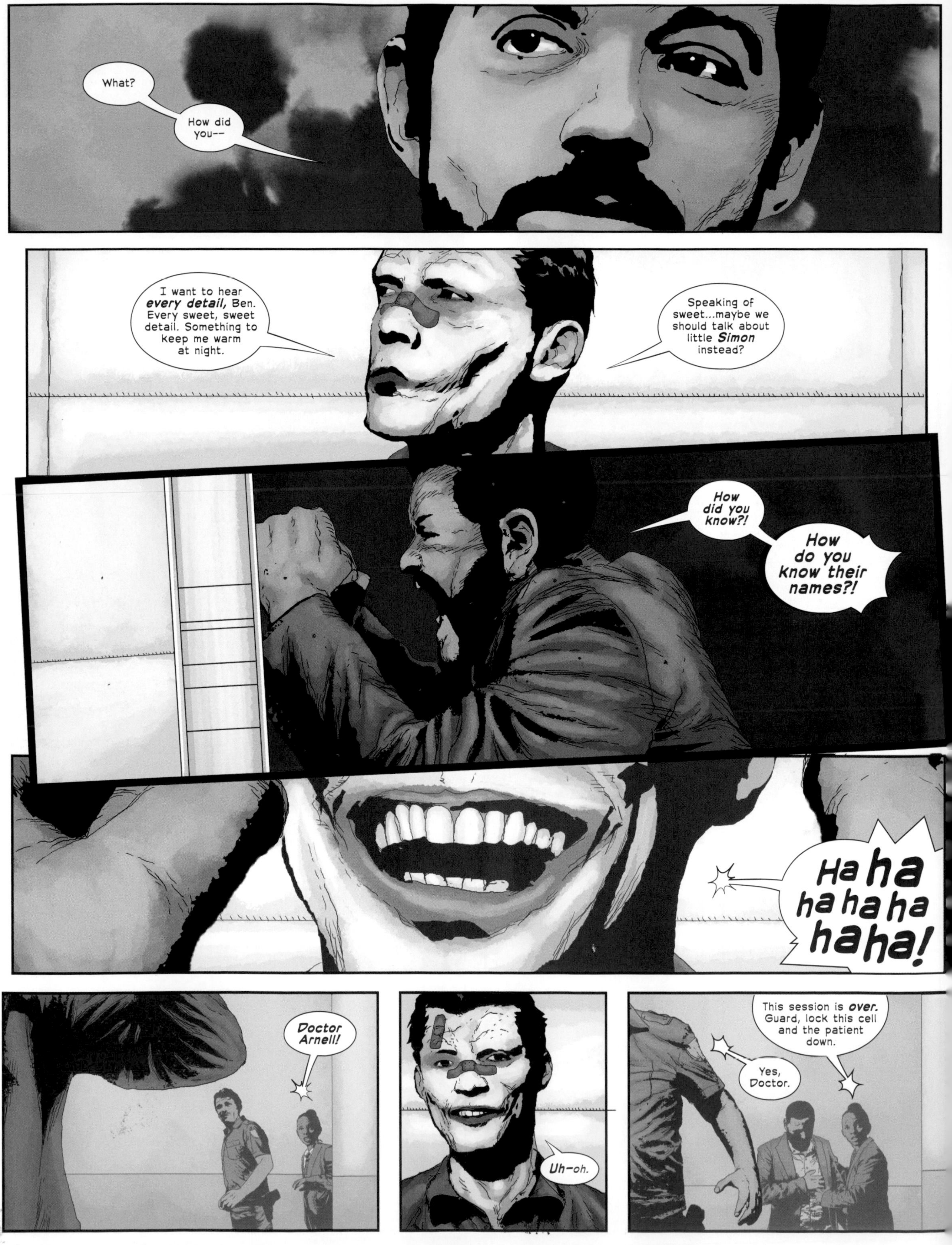

What?
How did you--
I want to hear *every detail,* Ben. Every sweet, sweet detail. Something to keep me warm at night.
Speaking of sweet...maybe we should talk about little *Simon* instead?
How did you know?!
How do you know their names?!
Ha ha ha ha ha ha haha!
Doctor Arnell!
Uh-oh.
This session is *over.* Guard, lock this cell and the patient down.
Yes, Doctor.

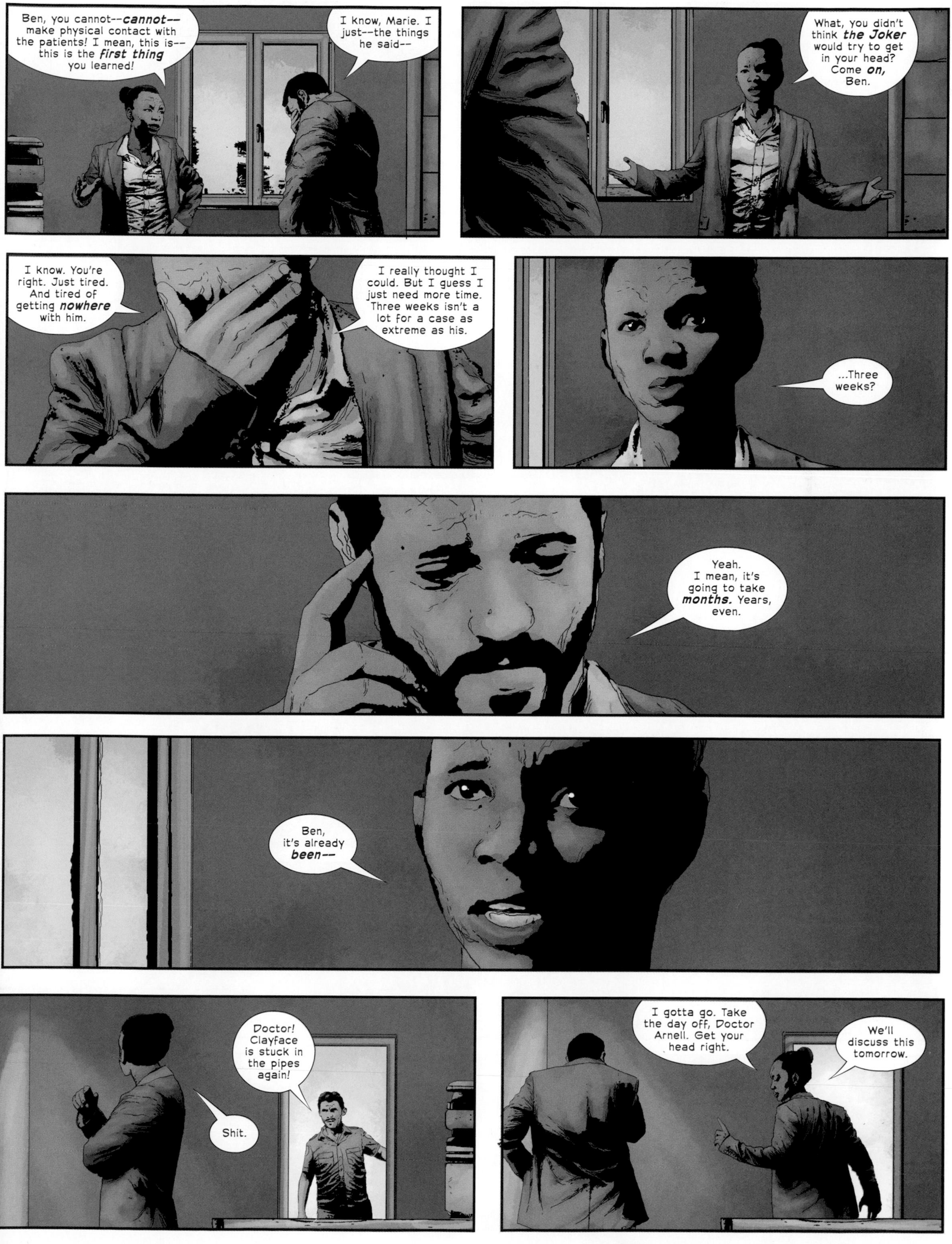

Ben, you cannot--*cannot*--make physical contact with the patients! I mean, this is--this is the *first thing* you learned!
I know, Marie. I just--the things he said--
What, you didn't think *the Joker* would try to get in your head? Come *on,* Ben.
I know. You're right. Just tired. And tired of getting *nowhere* with him.
I really thought I could. But I guess I just need more time. Three weeks isn't a lot for a case as extreme as his.
...Three weeks?
Yeah. I mean, it's going to take *months.* Years, even.
Ben, it's already *been--*
Doctor! Clayface is stuck in the pipes again!
Shit.
I gotta go. Take the day off, Doctor Arnell. Get your head right.
We'll discuss this tomorrow.

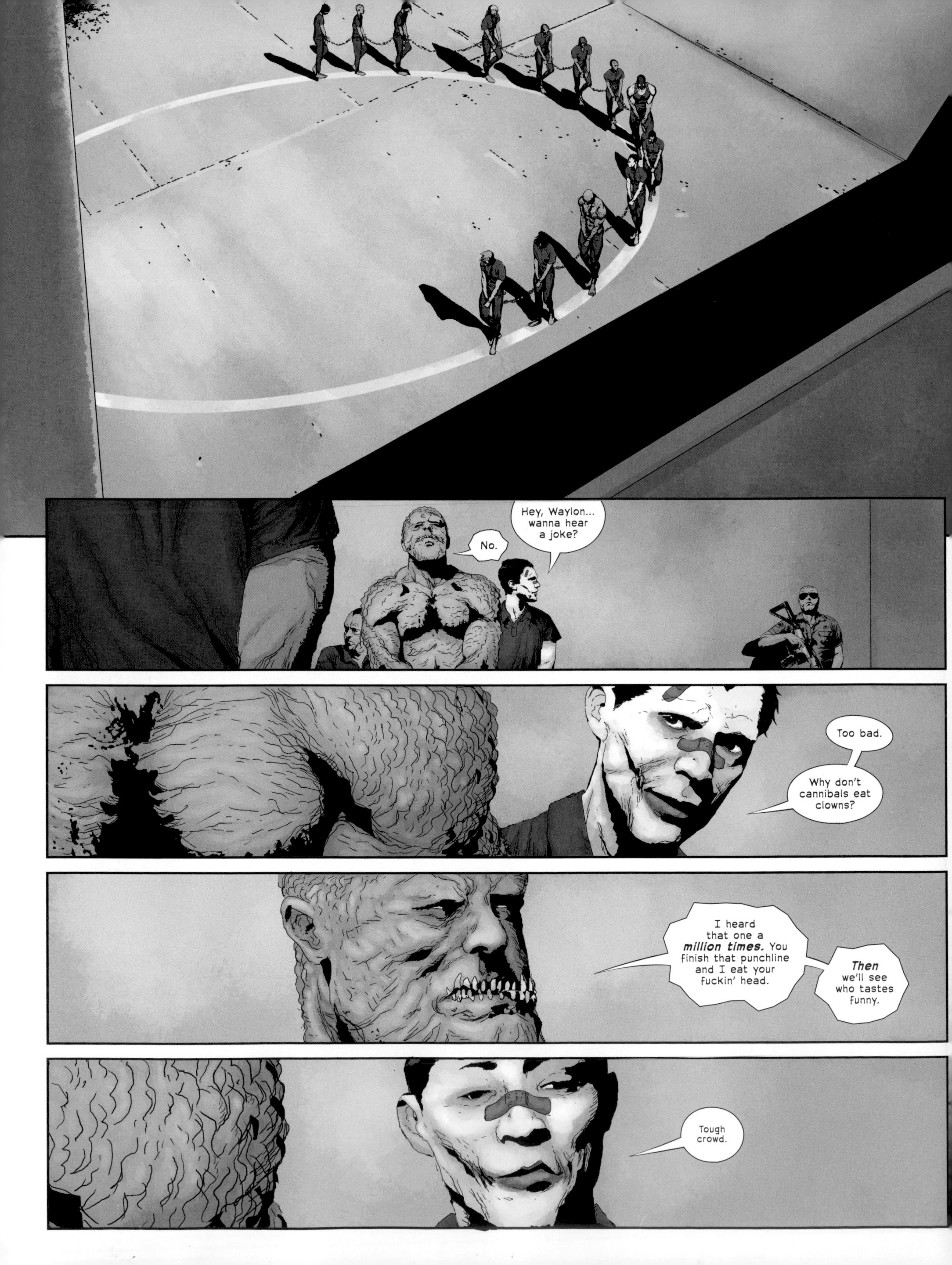
Hey, Waylon... wanna hear a joke?
No.
Too bad.
Why don't cannibals eat clowns?
I heard that one a *million times.* You finish that punchline and I eat your fuckin' head.
Then we'll see who tastes funny.
Tough crowd.

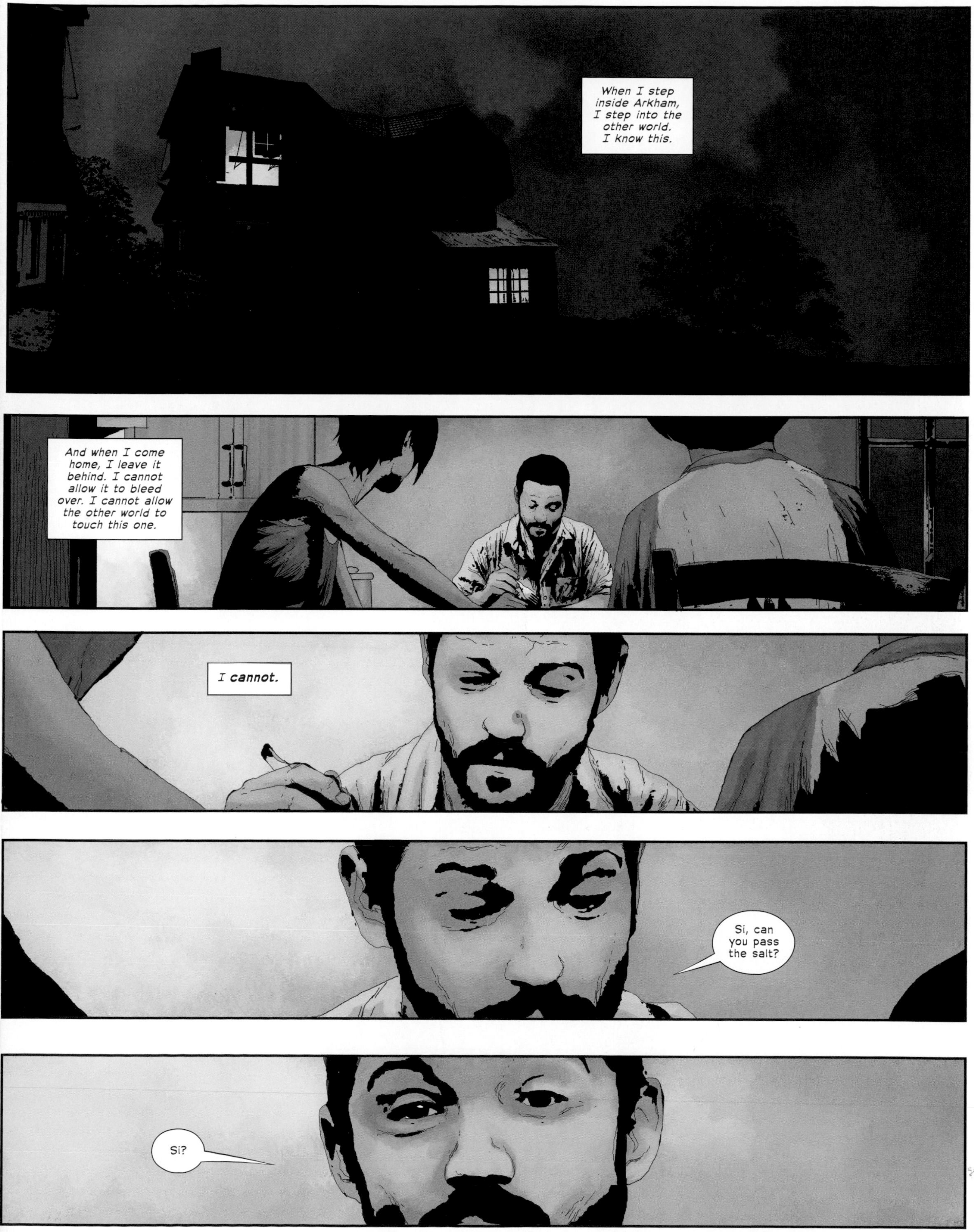
When I step inside Arkham, I step into the other world. I know this.
And when I come home, I leave it behind. I cannot allow it to bleed over. I cannot allow the other world to touch this one.
I **cannot.**
Si, can you pass the salt?
Si?

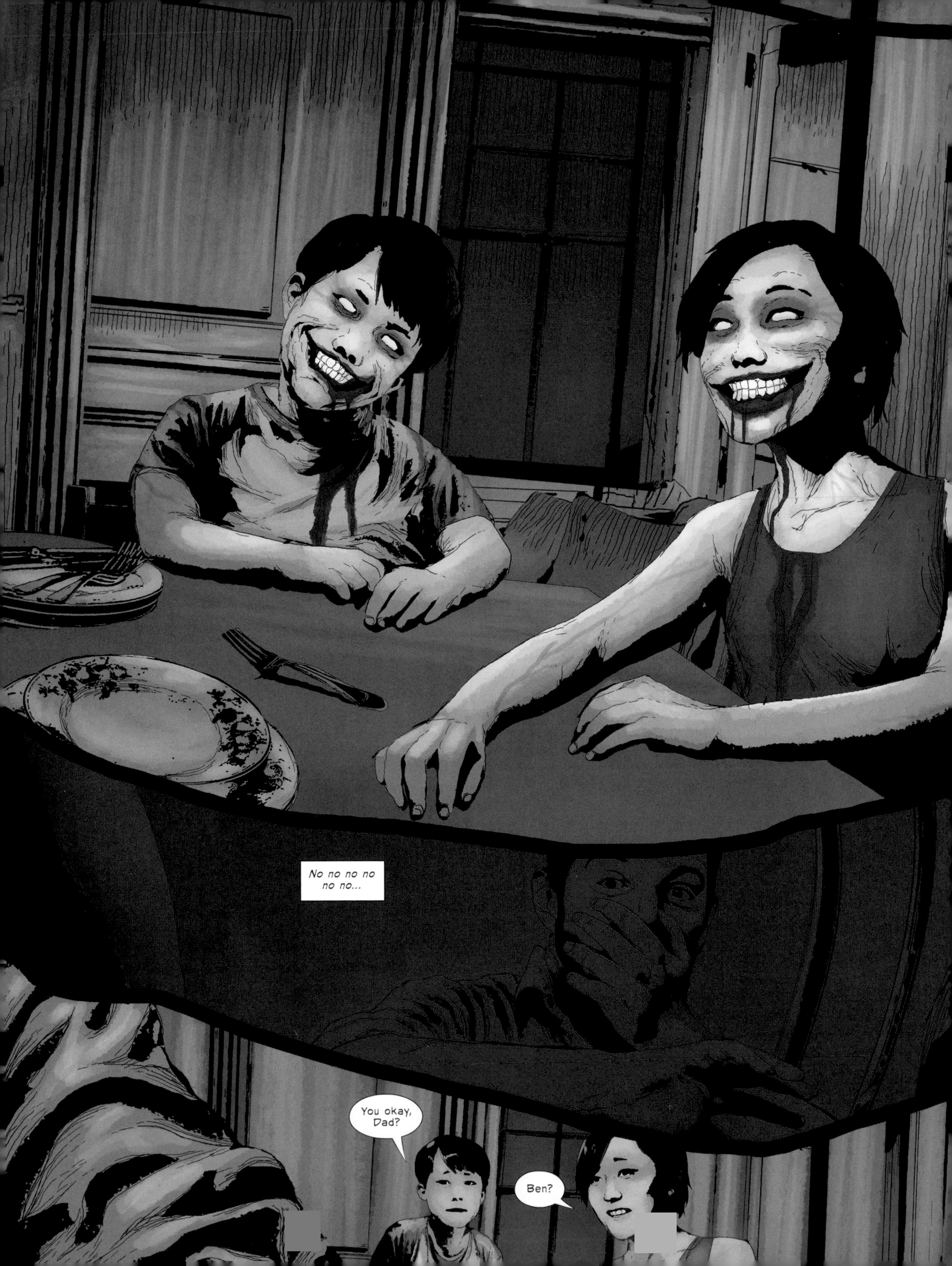
No no no no
no no...
You okay, Dad?
Ben?

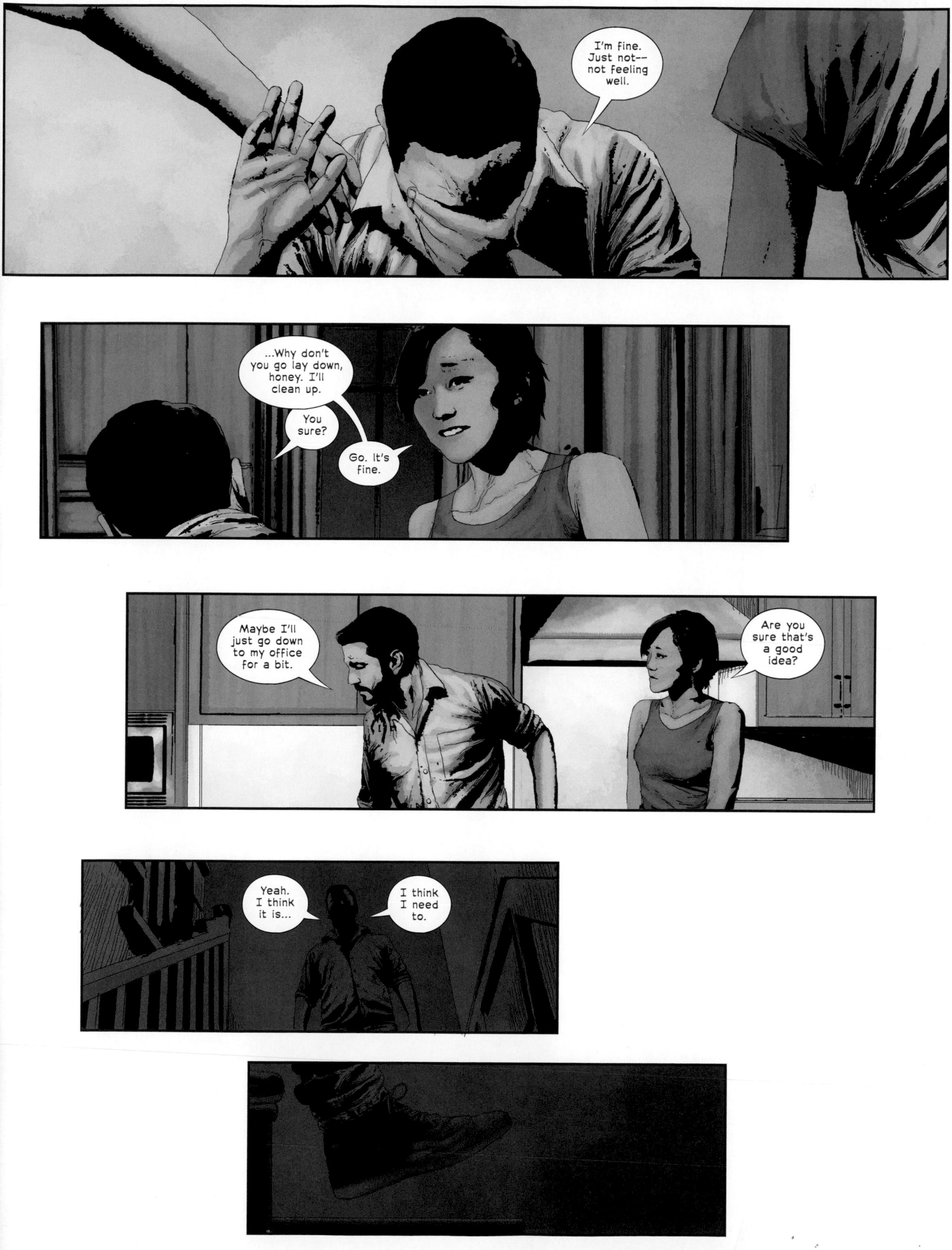
I'm fine. Just not-- not feeling well.
...Why don't you go lay down, honey. I'll clean up.
You sure?
Go. It's fine.
Maybe I'll just go down to my office for a bit.
Are you sure that's a good idea?
Yeah. I think it is...
I think I need to.

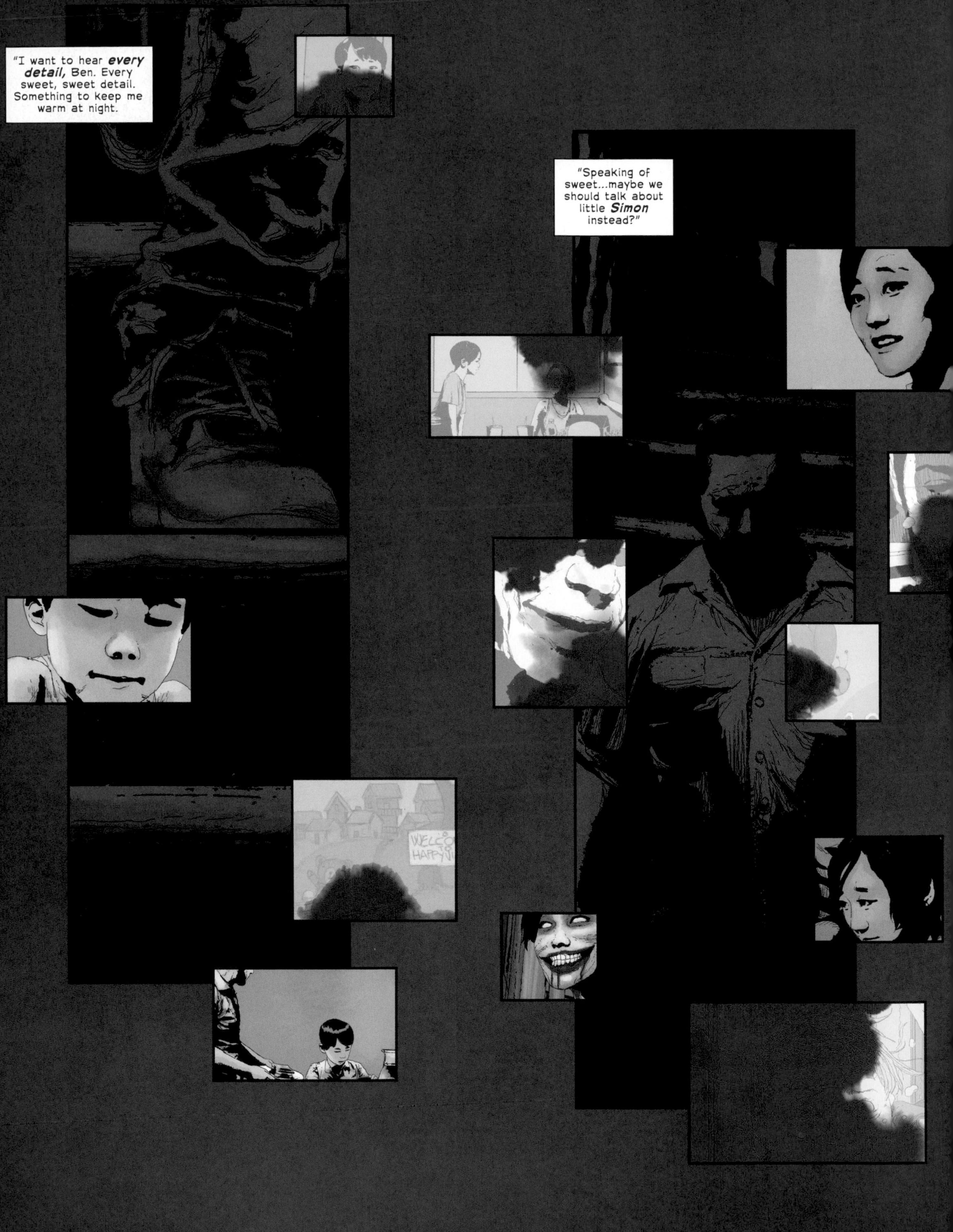
"I want to hear *every detail,* Ben. Every sweet, sweet detail. Something to keep me warm at night.
"Speaking of sweet...maybe we should talk about little *Simon* instead?"

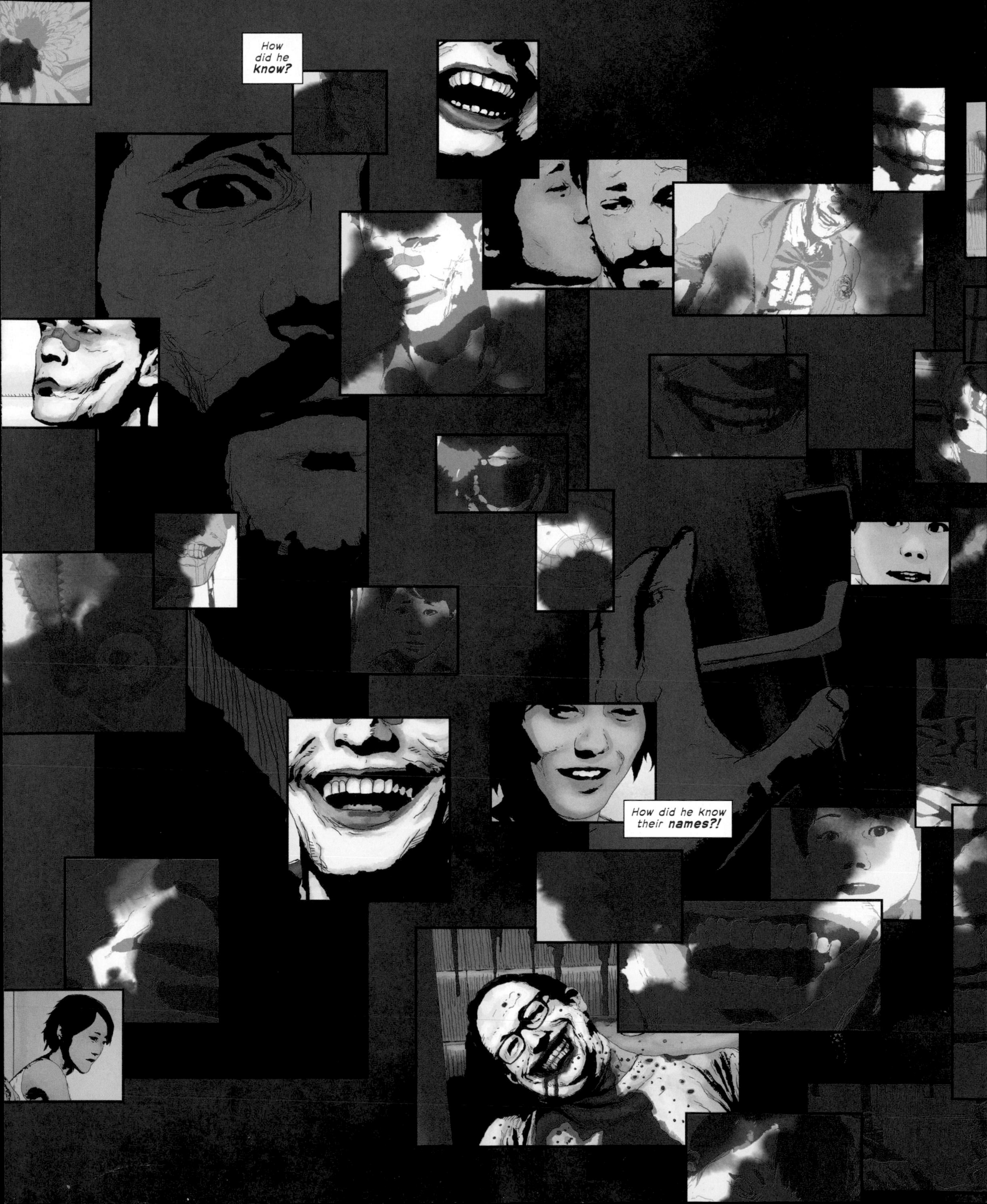

How did he know?
How did he know their names?!

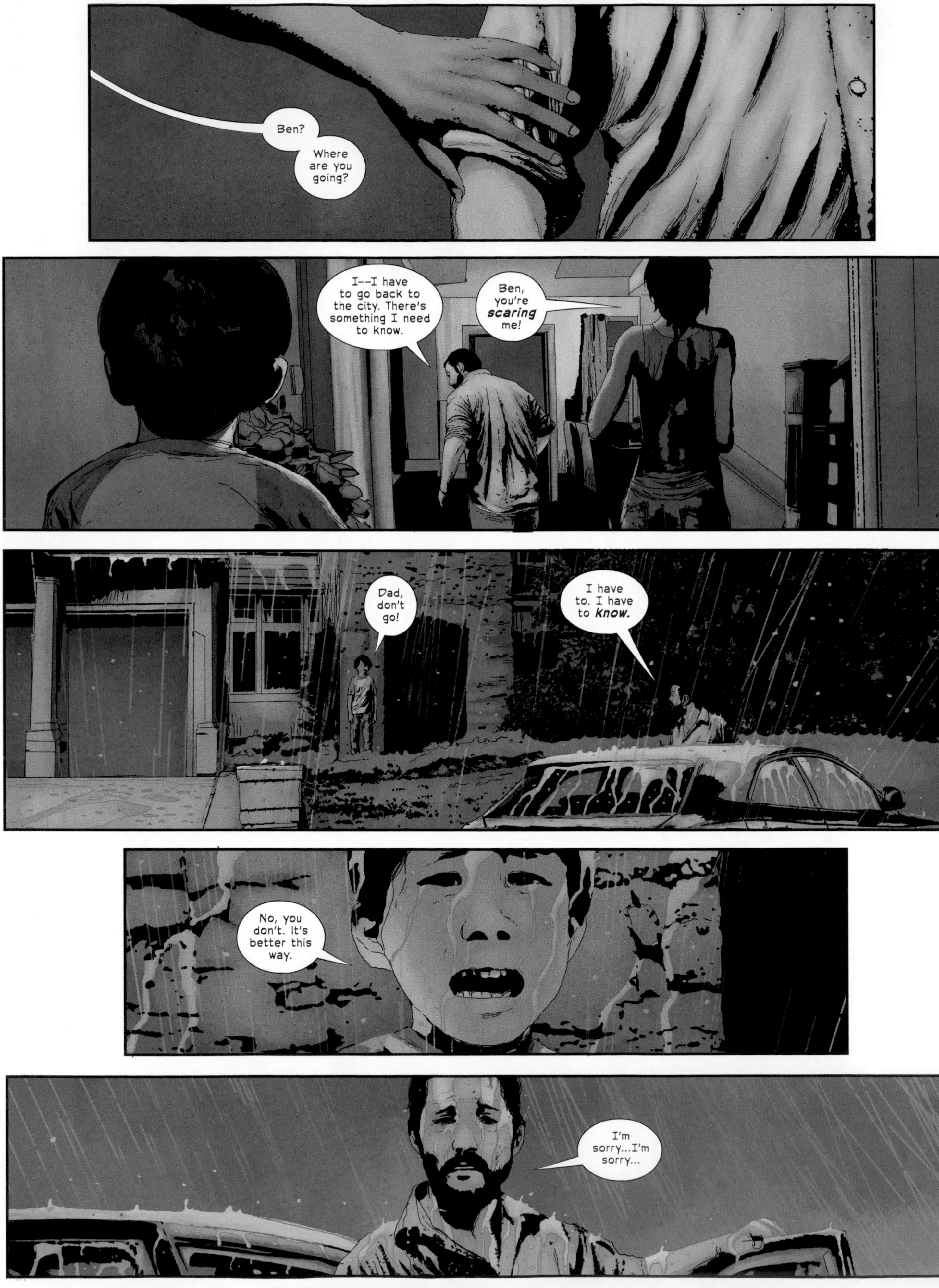
Ben?
Where are you going?
I--I have to go back to the city. There's something I need to know.
Ben, you're *scaring* me!
Dad, don't go!
I have to. I have to *know.*
No, you don't. It's better this way.
I'm sorry...I'm sorry...

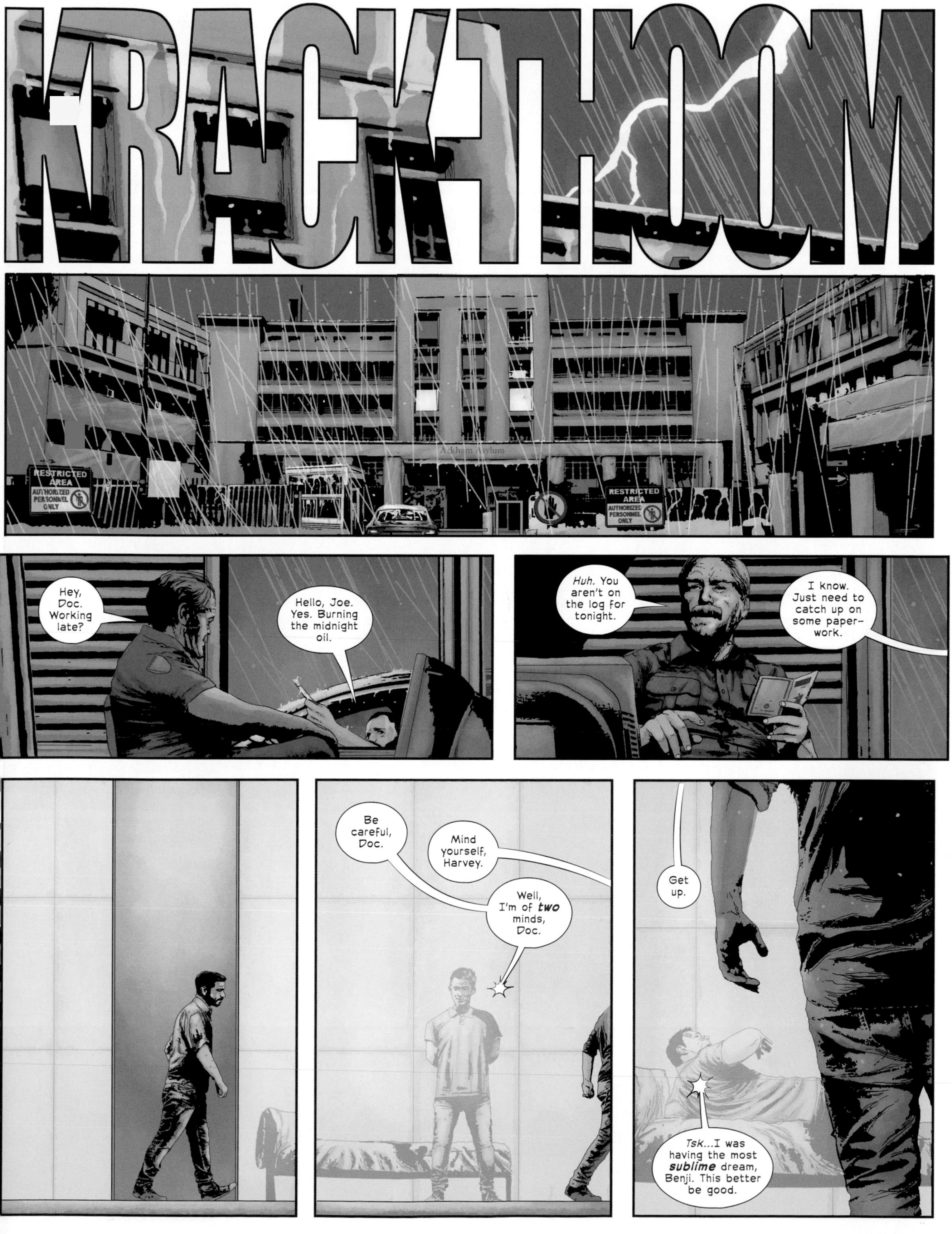
KRACK-THOOM
Arkham Asylum
RESTRICTED AREA AUTHORIZED PERSONNEL ONLY
RESTRICTED AREA AUTHORIZED PERSONNEL ONLY
Hey, Doc. Working late?
Hello, Joe. Yes. Burning the midnight oil.
Huh. You aren't on the log for tonight.
I know. Just need to catch up on some paper-work.
Be careful, Doc.
Mind yourself, Harvey.
Well, I'm of ***two*** minds, Doc.
Get up.
*Tsk...*I was having the most ***sublime*** dream, Benji. This better be good.

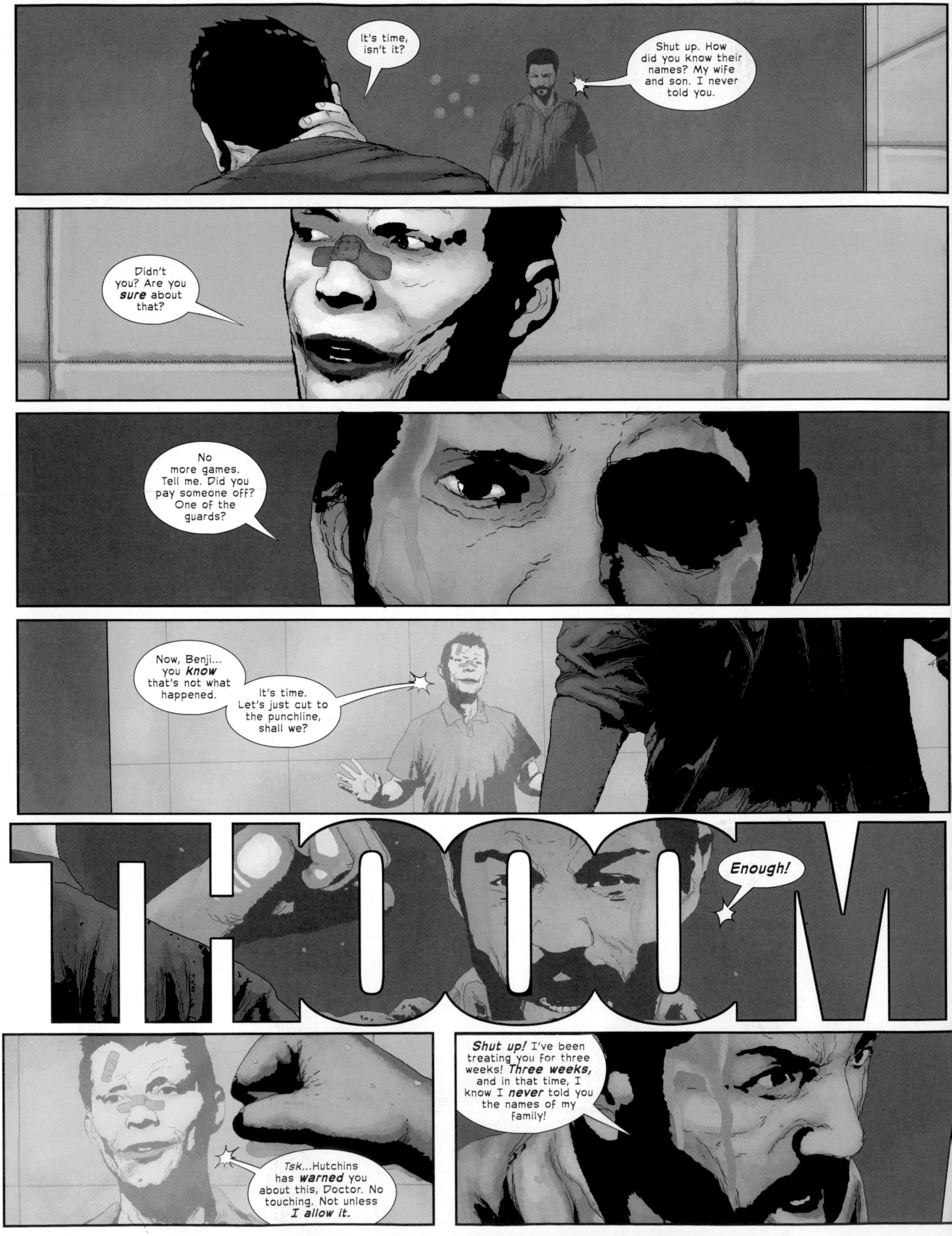

It's time, isn't it?
Shut up. How did you know their names? My wife and son. I never told you.
Didn't you? Are you *sure* about that?
No more games. Tell me. Did you pay someone off? One of the guards?
Now, Benji... you *know* that's not what happened.
It's time. Let's just cut to the punchline, shall we?
THOOOM
Enough!
Tsk...Hutchins has *warned* you about this, Doctor. No touching. Not unless *I allow it.*
Shut up! I've been treating you for three weeks! *Three weeks,* and in that time, I know I *never* told you the names of my family!

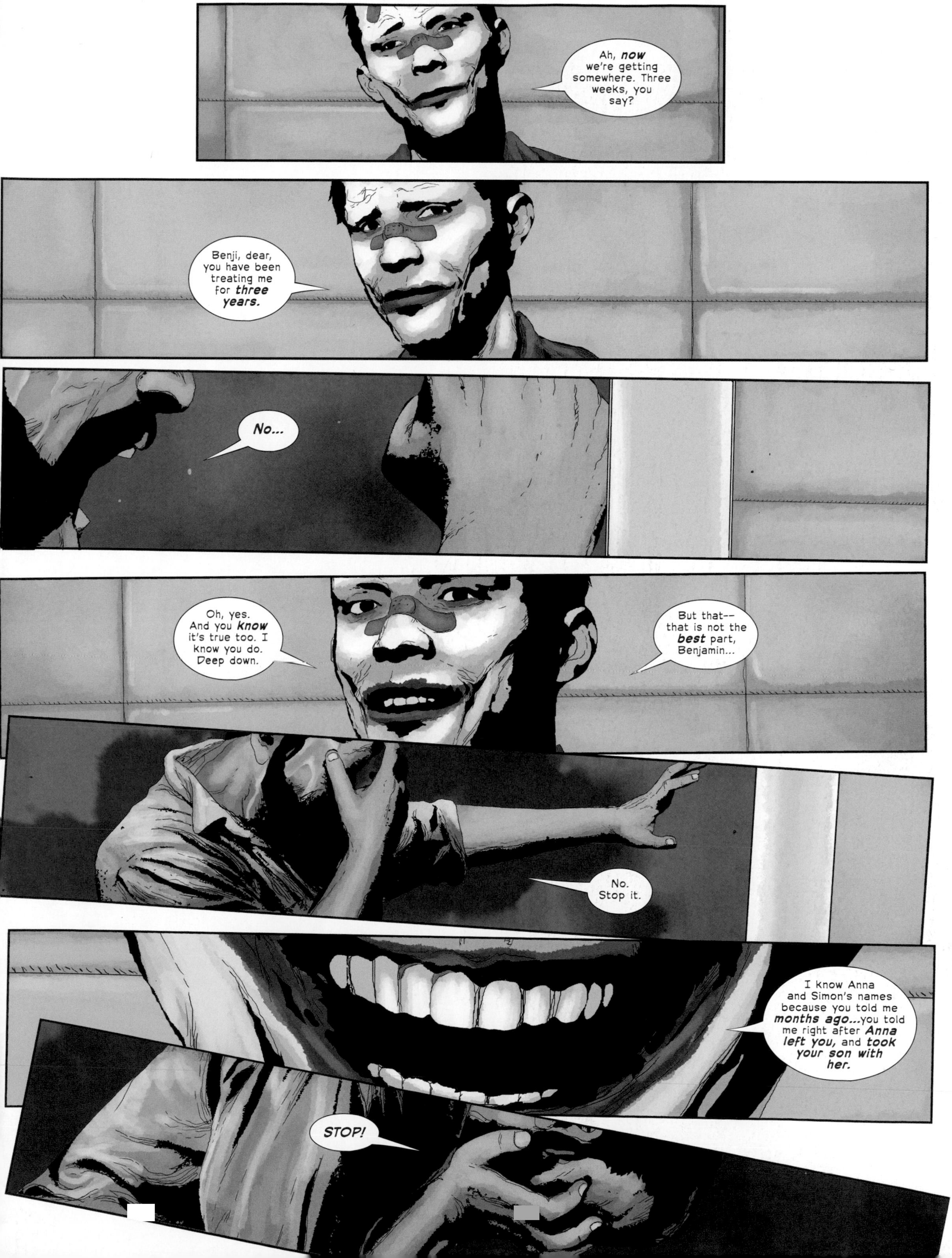
Ah, *now* we're getting somewhere. Three weeks, you say?
Benji, dear, you have been treating me for *three years.*
No...
Oh, yes. And you *know* it's true too. I know you do. Deep down.
But that-- that is not the *best* part, Benjamin...
No. Stop it.
I know Anna and Simon's names because you told me *months ago...*you told me right after *Anna left you,* and *took your son with her.*
STOP!

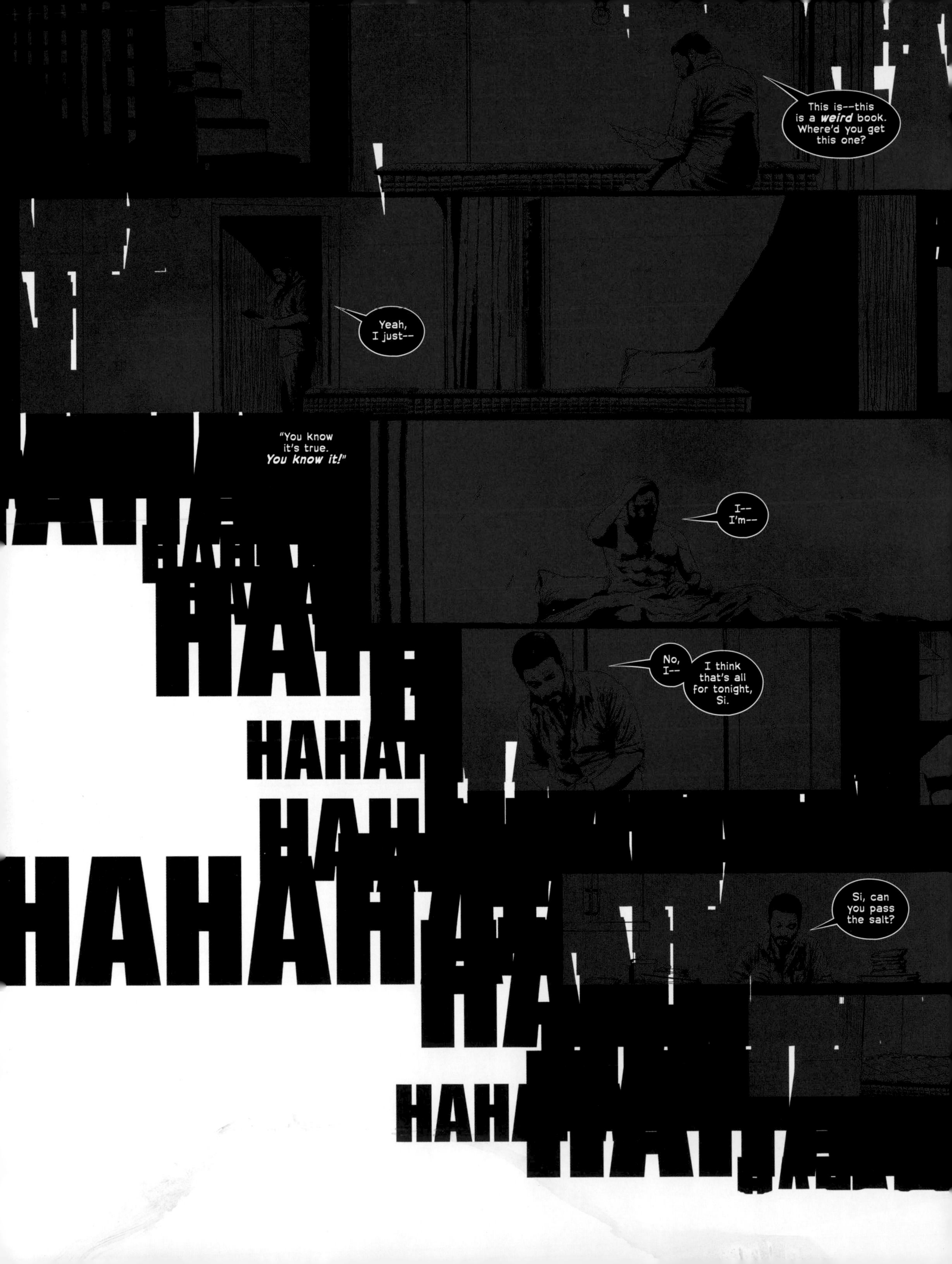

This is--this is a *weird* book. Where'd you get this one?
Yeah, I just--
"You know it's true. *You know it!*"
I-- I'm--
No, I--
I think that's all for tonight, Si.
HAHA
HAHA
HAHA
Si, can you pass the salt?
HAHA

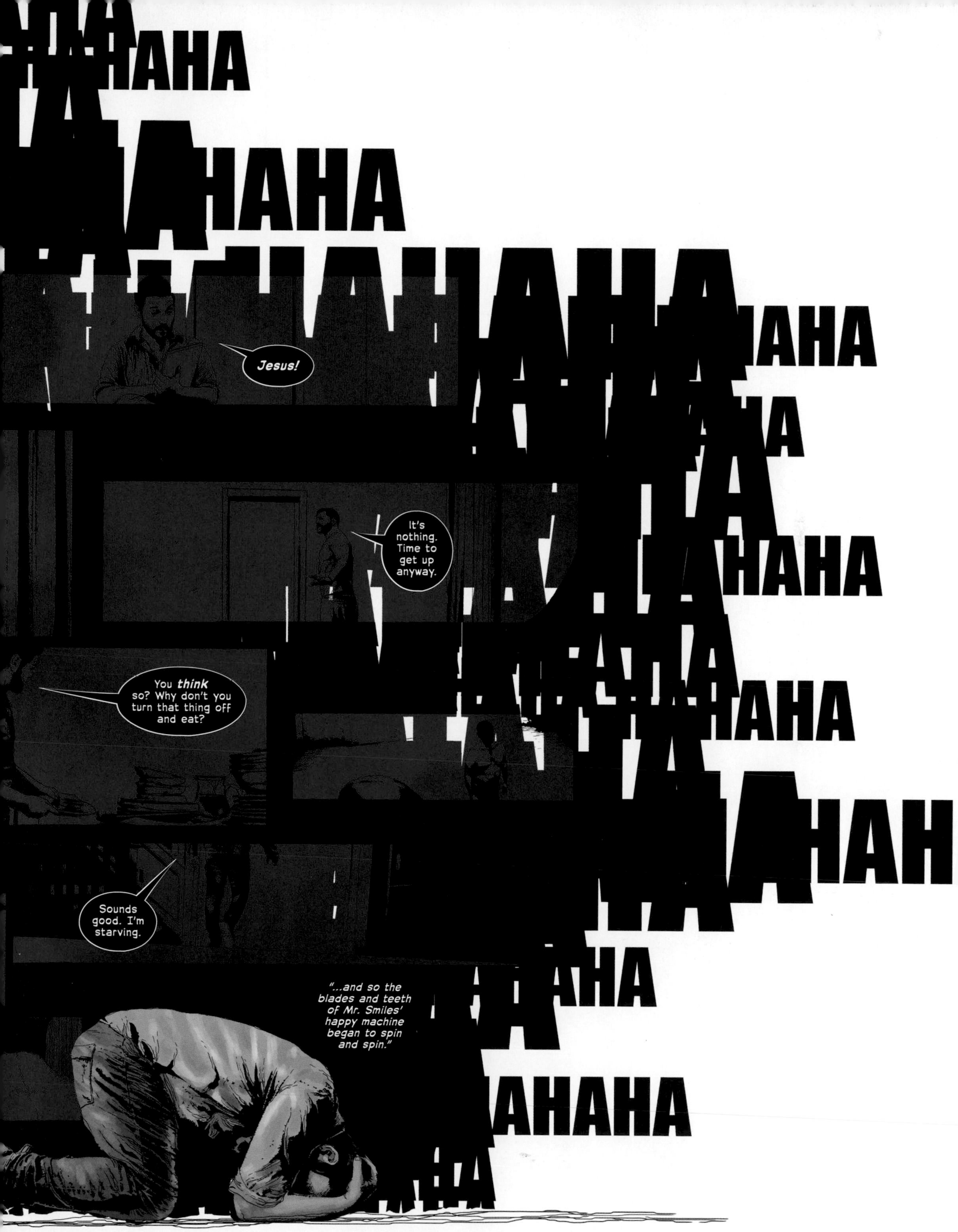

HAHA
HAHA
HAHA
HAHA
Jesus!
HA
It's nothing. Time to get up anyway.
HAHA
You *think* so? Why don't you turn that thing off and eat?
HAHA
HAH
Sounds good. I'm starving.
HAHA
"...and so the blades and teeth of Mr. Smiles' happy machine began to spin and spin."
HAHA

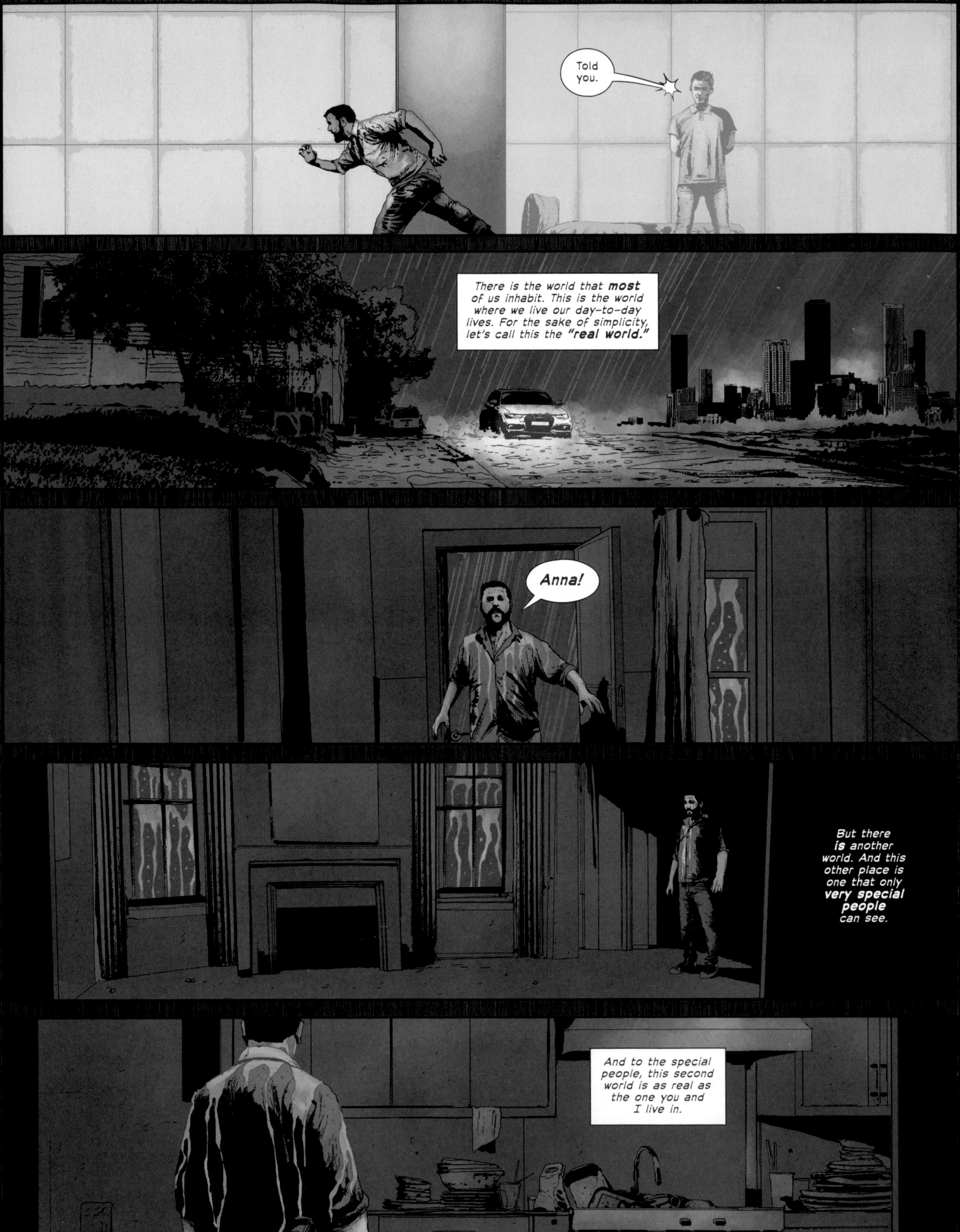
Told you.
There is the world that most of us inhabit. This is the world where we live our day-to-day lives. For the sake of simplicity, let's call this the "real world."
Anna!
But there is another world. And this other place is one that only very special people can see.
And to the special people, this second world is as real as the one you and I live in.

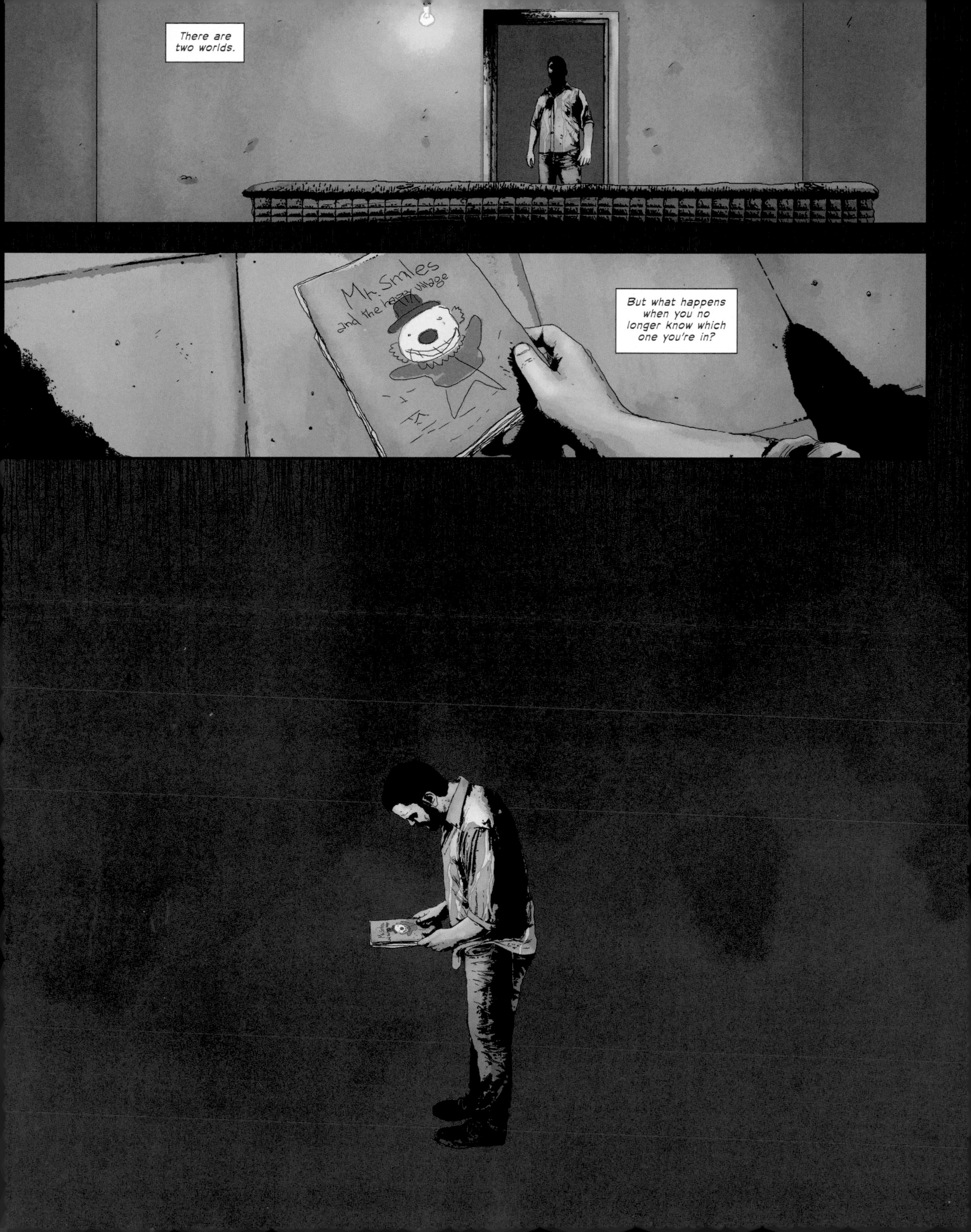
There are two worlds.
But what happens when you no longer know which one you're in?

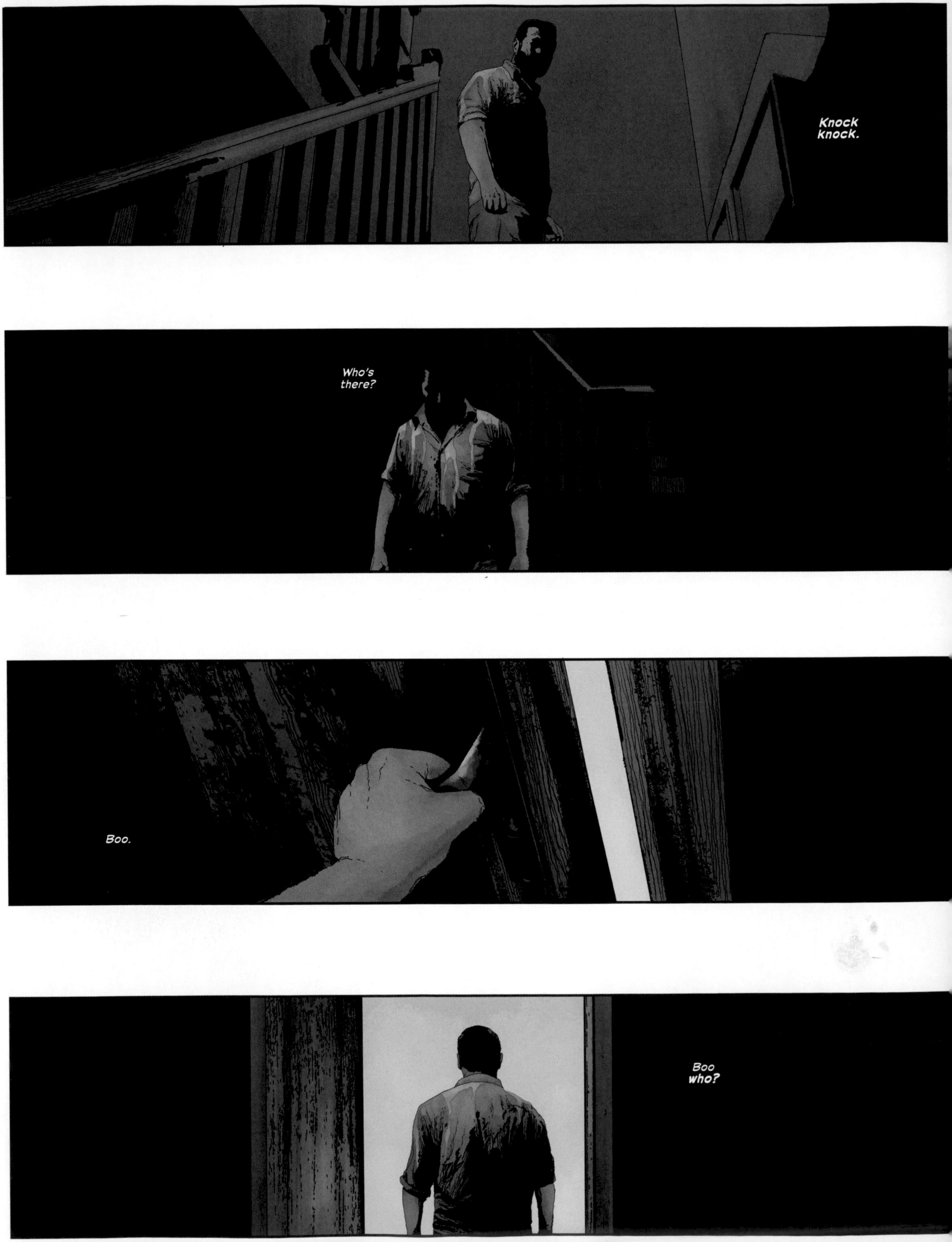
Knock
knock.
Who's
there?
Boo.
Boo
who?

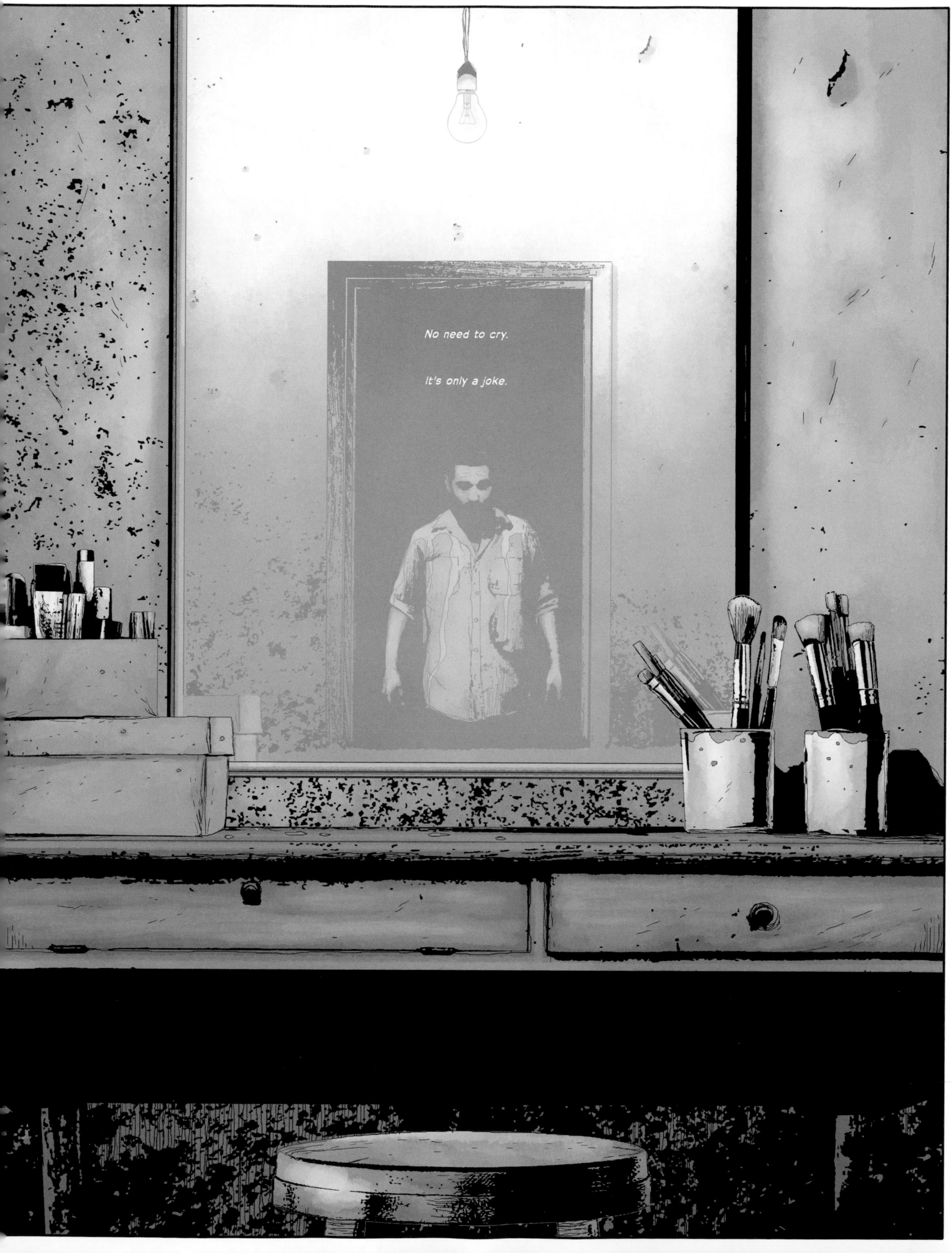
No need to cry.
It's only a joke.

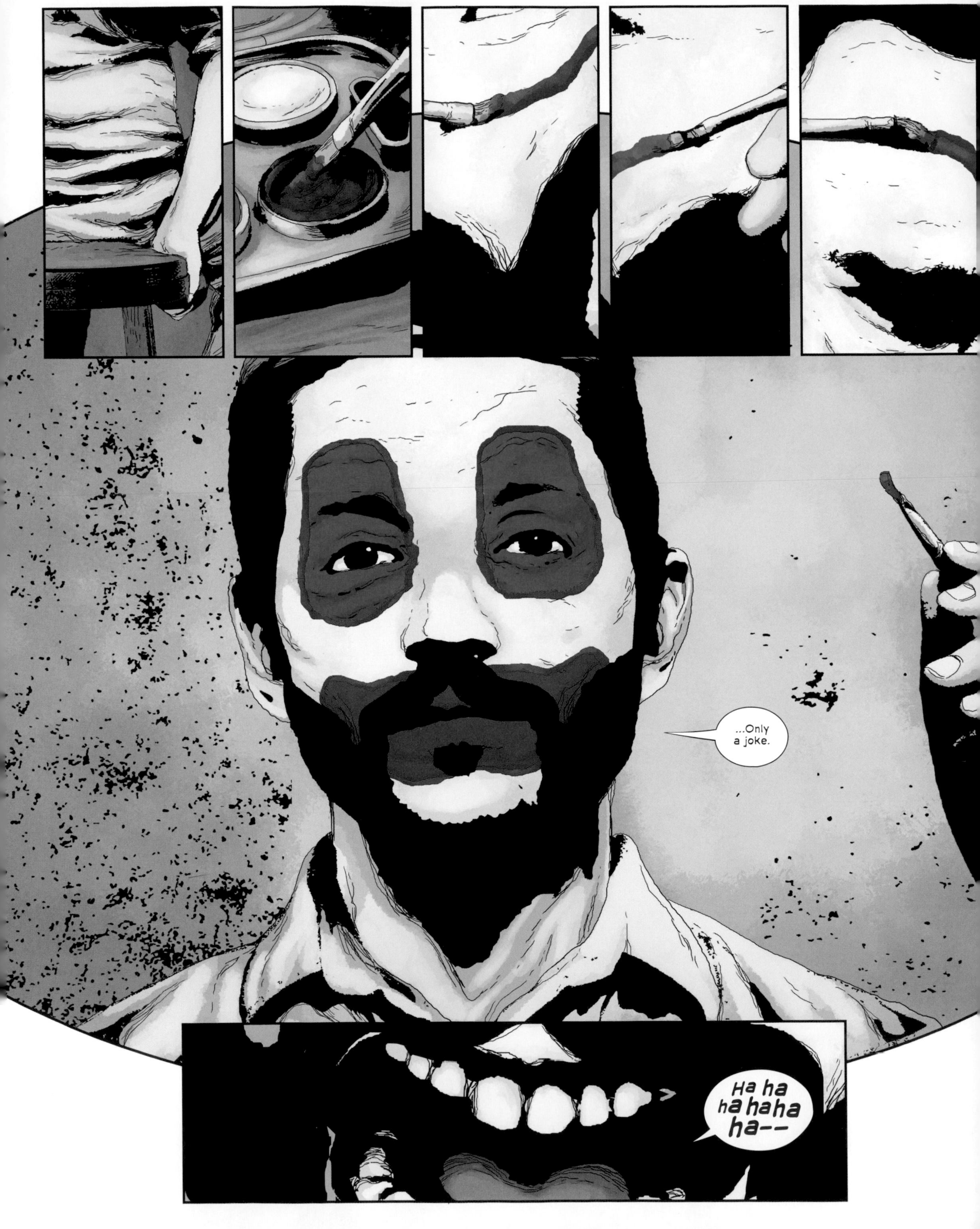

...Only a joke.
Ha ha ha haha ha--

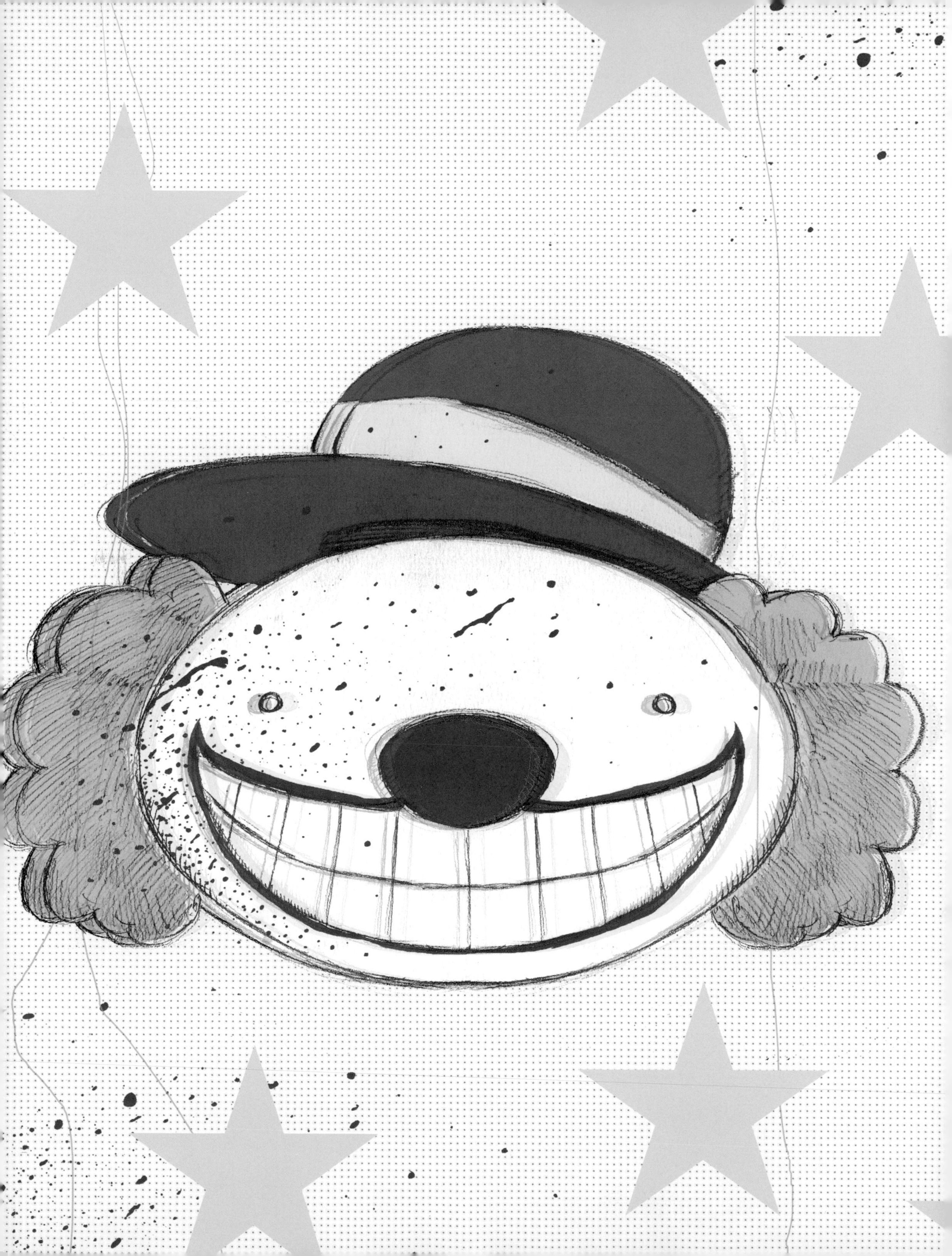

★★★

BOOK THREE

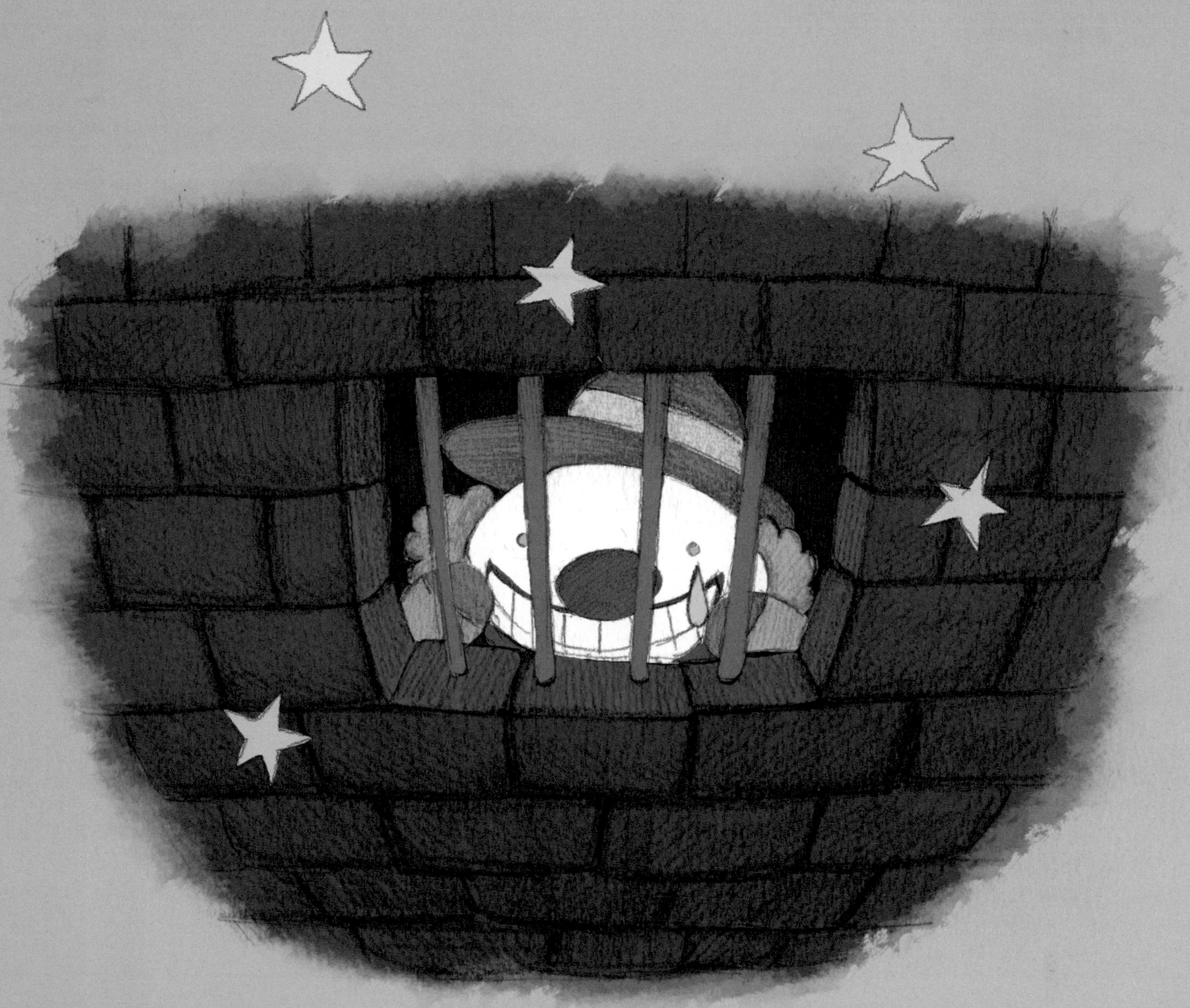

Happyville was sound asleep, all except one...

Mr. Smiles was restless, and try as he might,
he just could not sleep.

You see, Mr. Smiles was trapped in the
Magic Castle, and he could not leave.

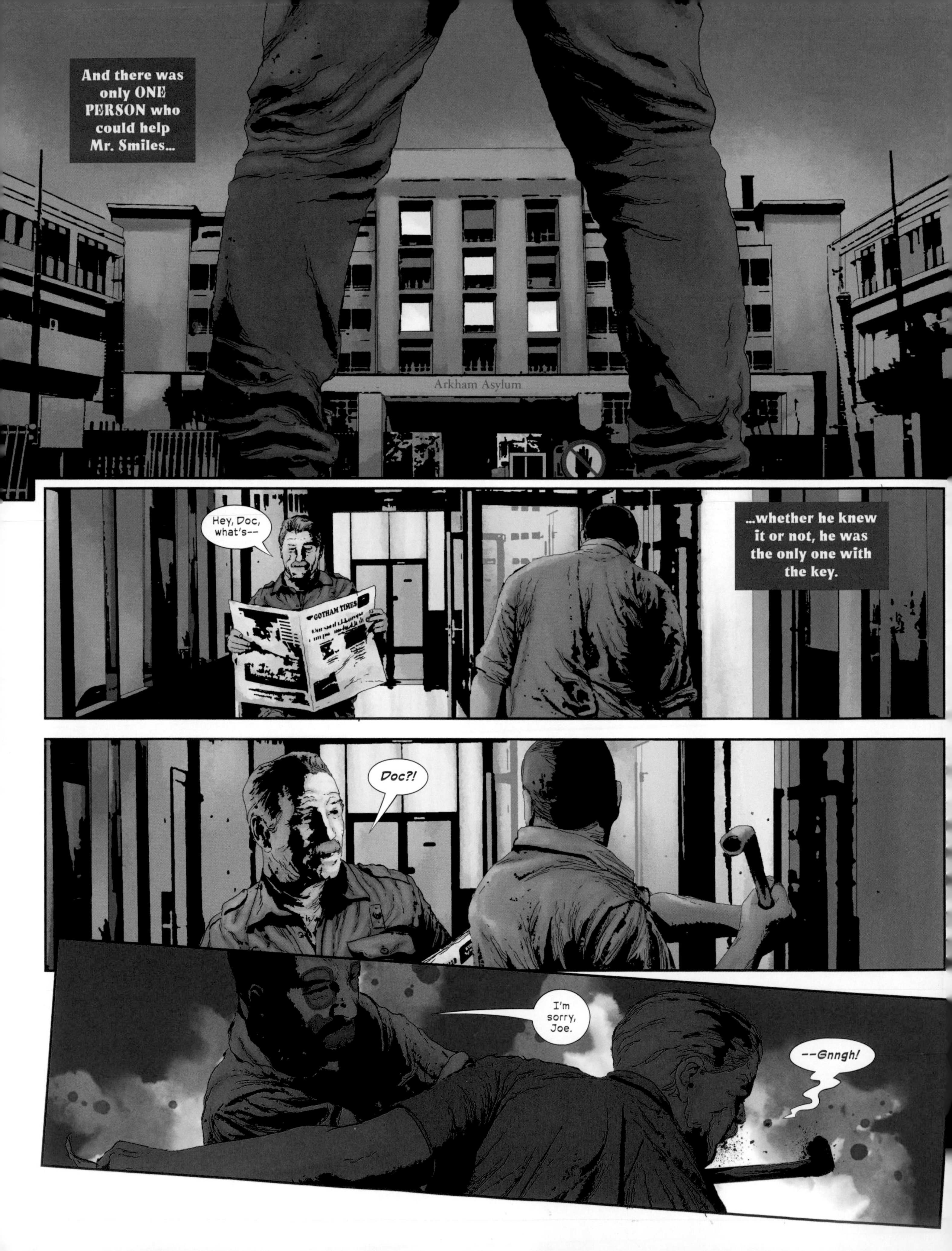
And there was only ONE PERSON who could help Mr. Smiles...
Arkham Asylum
Hey, Doc, what's--
...whether he knew it or not, he was the only one with the key.
GOTHAM TIMES
Doc?!
I'm sorry, Joe.
--Gnngh!

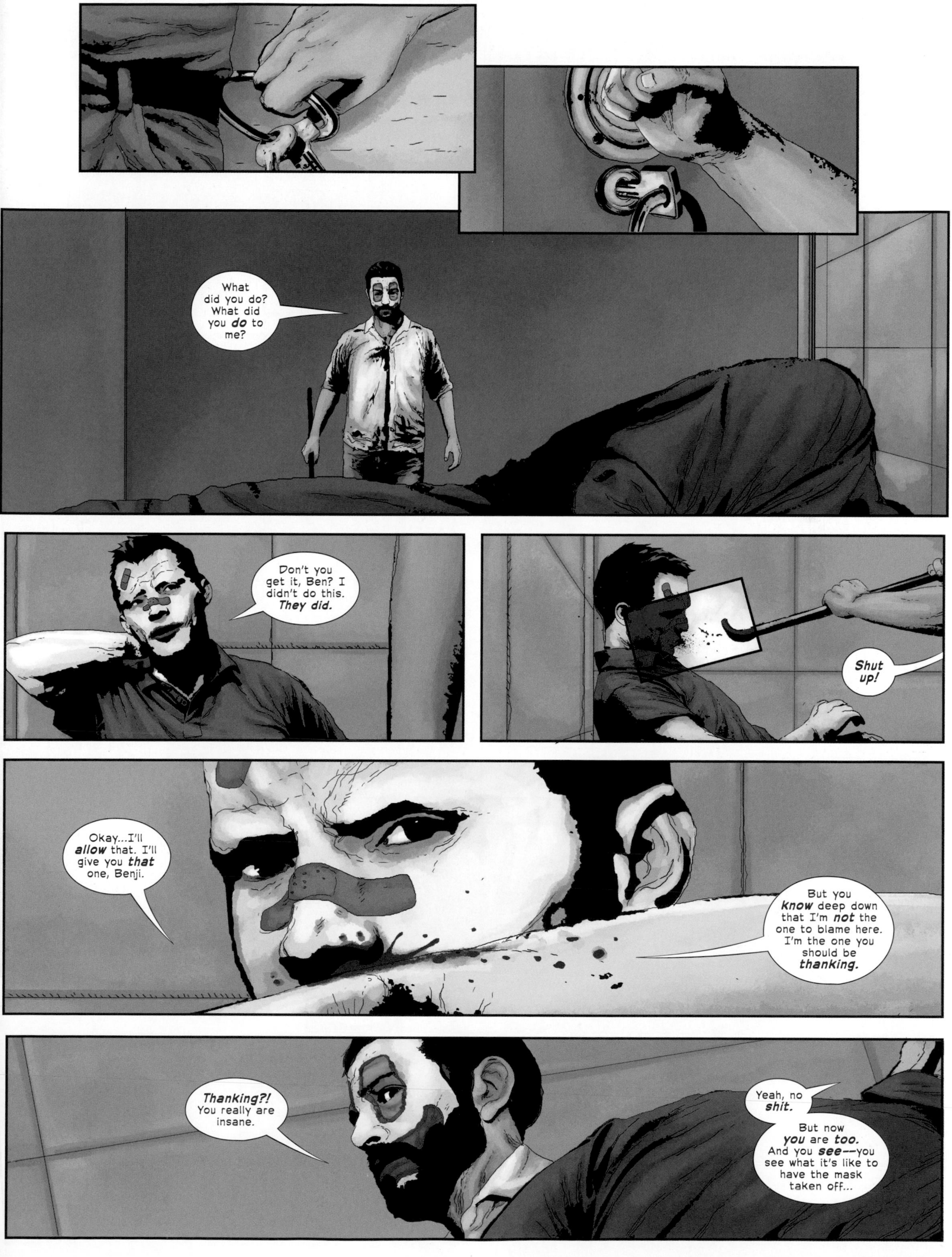

What did you do? What did you *do* to me?
Don't you get it, Ben? I didn't do this. ***They did.***
Shut up!
Okay...I'll ***allow*** that. I'll give you ***that*** one, Benji.
But you ***know*** deep down that I'm ***not*** the one to blame here. I'm the one you should be ***thanking.***
Thanking?! You really are insane.
Yeah, no ***shit.***
But now ***you*** are ***too.*** And you ***see***--you see what it's like to have the mask taken off...

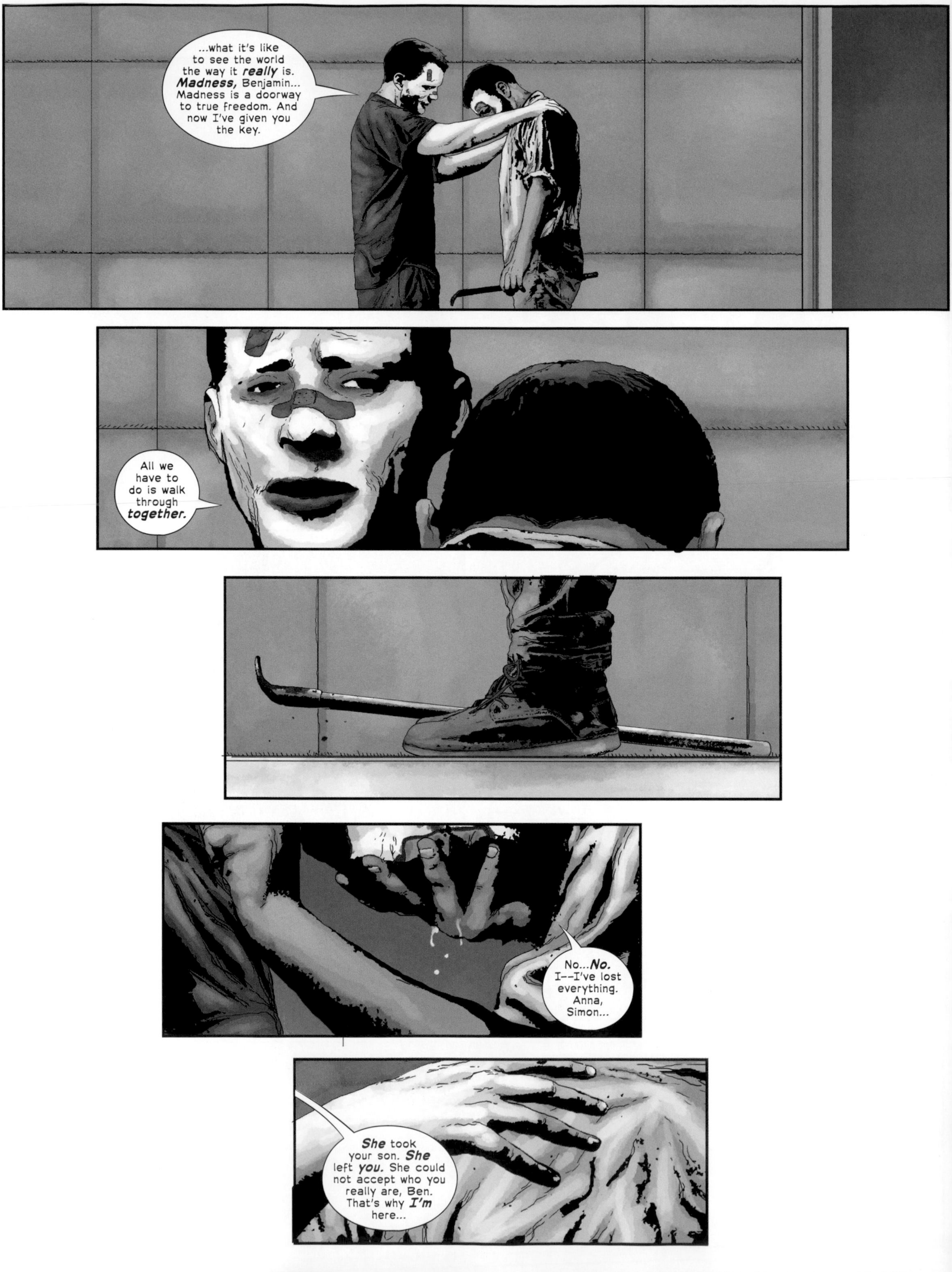
...what it's like to see the world the way it *really* is. ***Madness,*** Benjamin... Madness is a doorway to true freedom. And now I've given you the key.
All we have to do is walk through ***together.***
No...***No.*** I--I've lost everything. Anna, Simon...
She took your son. ***She*** left ***you.*** She could not accept who you really are, Ben. That's why ***I'm*** here...

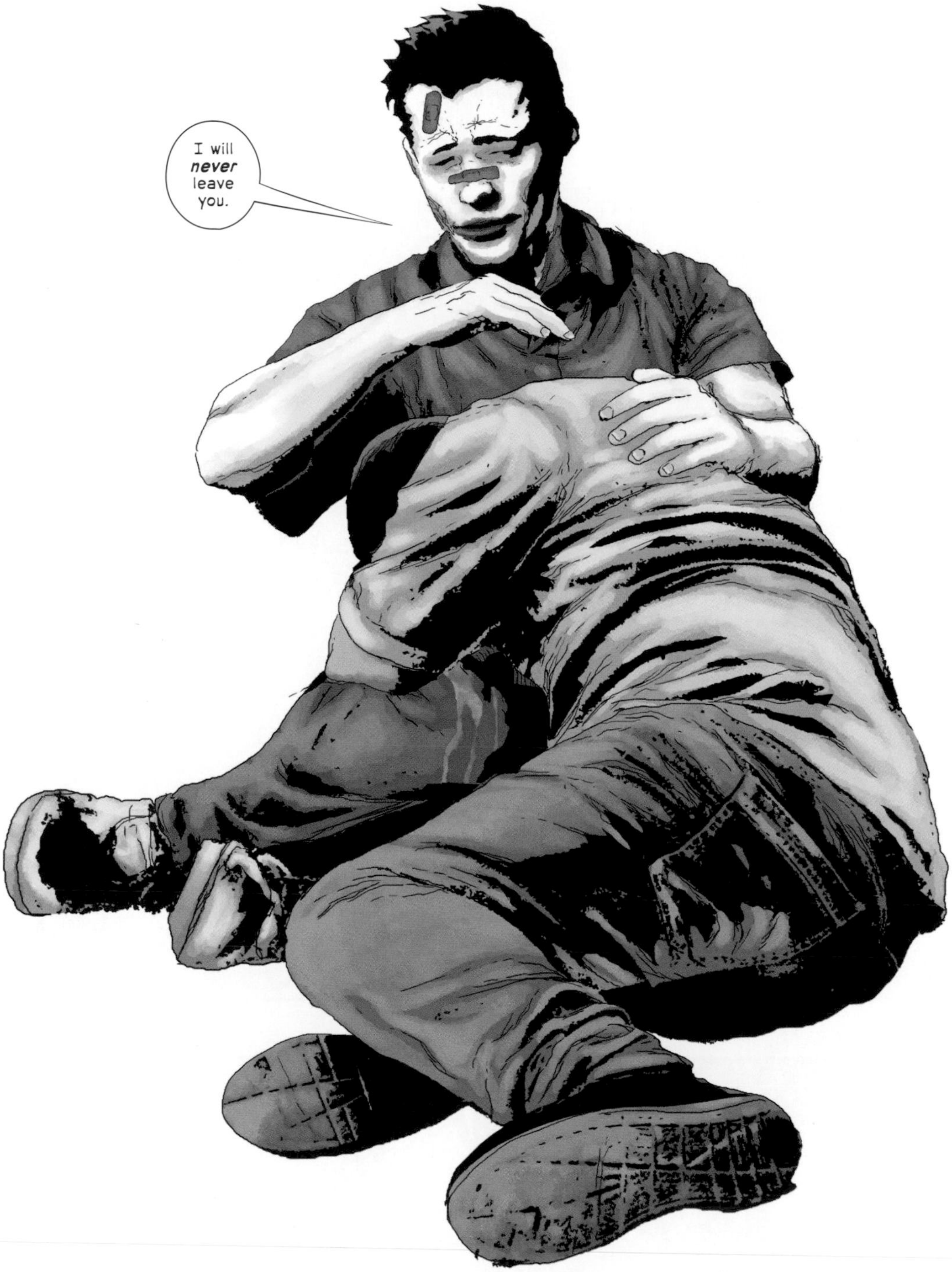
I will *never* leave you.

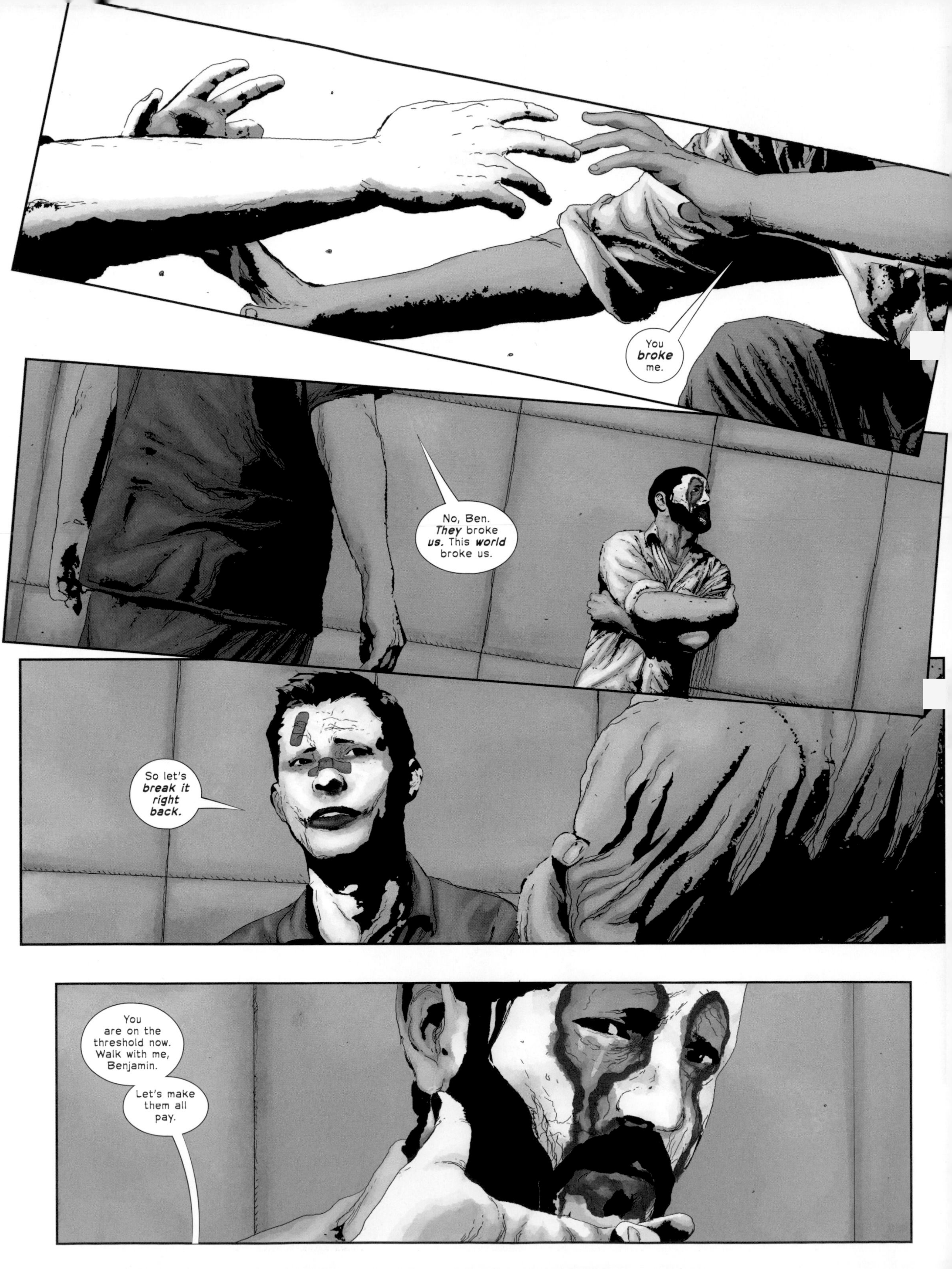

You *broke* me.
No, Ben. *They* broke *us.* This *world* broke us.
So let's *break it right back.*
You are on the threshold now. Walk with me, Benjamin.
Let's make them all pay.

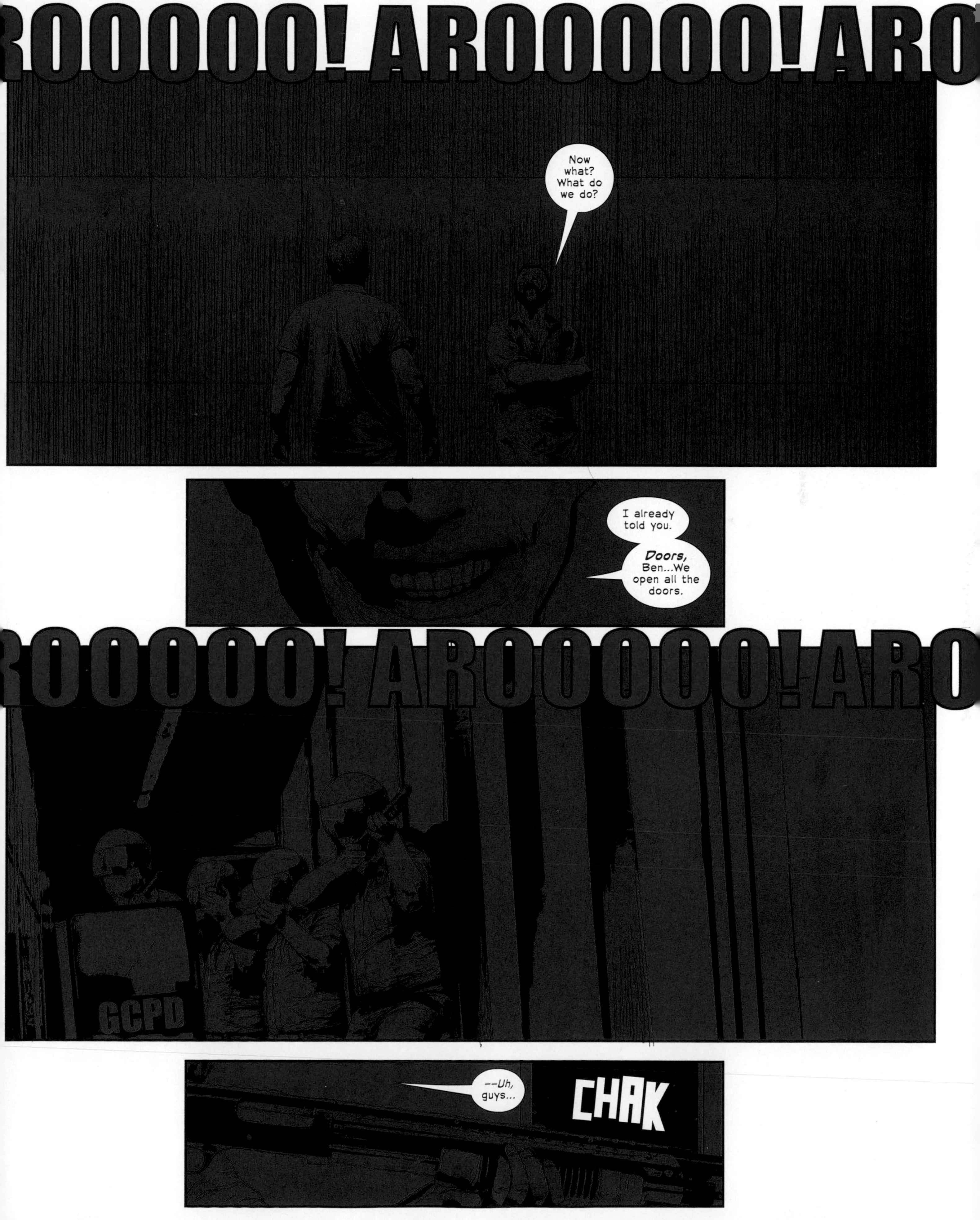
ROOOOO! AROOOOOO! ARO
Now what? What do we do?
I already told you.
Doors, Ben...We open all the doors.
ROOOOO! AROOOOOO! ARO
GCPD
--Uh, guys...
CHAK

Shit.

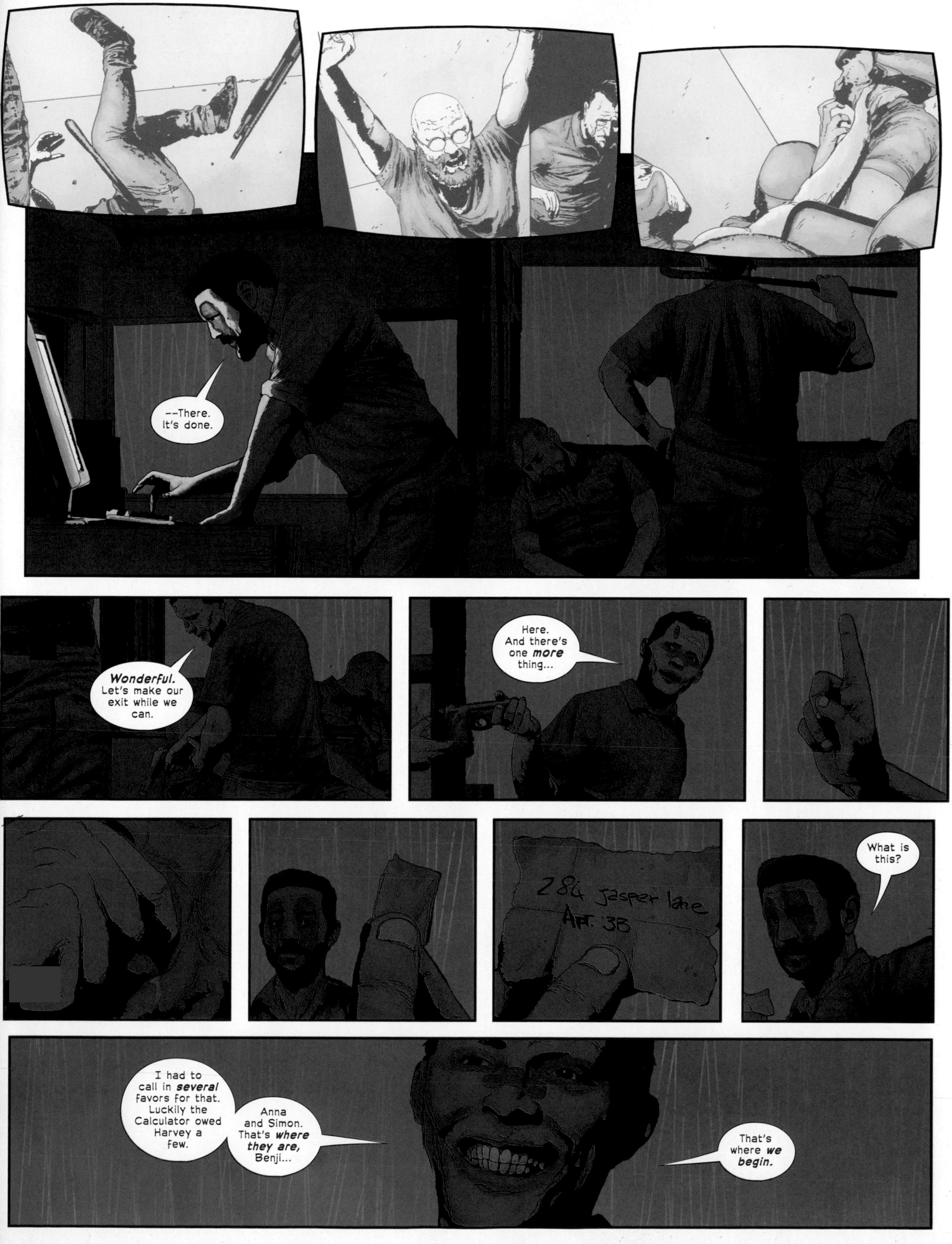

--There. It's done.
Wonderful. Let's make our exit while we can.
Here. And there's one more thing...
284 Jasper lane
Apt. 3B
What is this?
I had to call in several favors for that. Luckily the Calculator owed Harvey a few.
Anna and Simon. That's where they are, Benji...
That's where we begin.

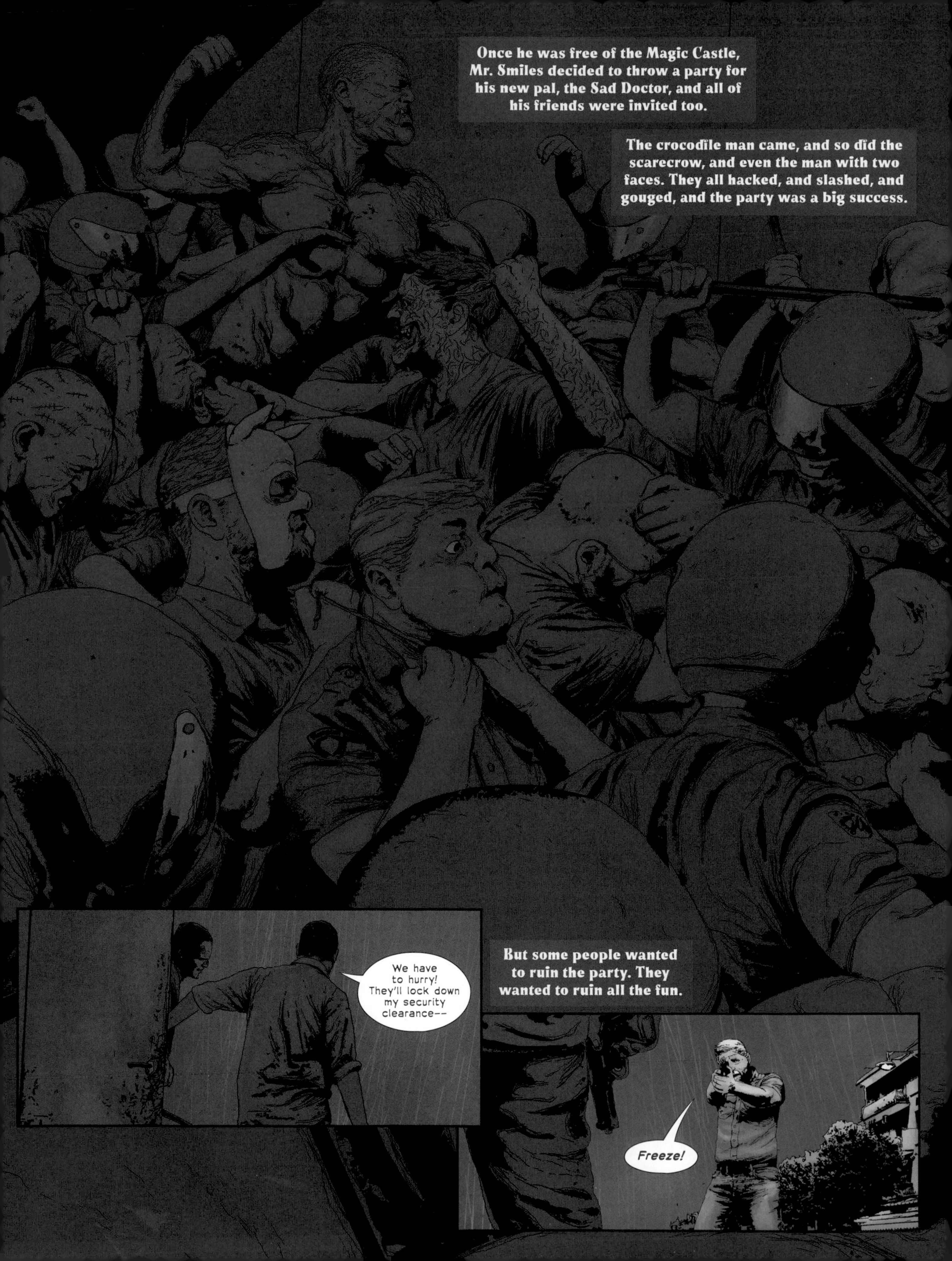
Once he was free of the Magic Castle, Mr. Smiles decided to throw a party for his new pal, the Sad Doctor, and all of his friends were invited too.
The crocodile man came, and so did the scarecrow, and even the man with two faces. They all hacked, and slashed, and gouged, and the party was a big success.
We have to hurry! They'll lock down my security clearance--
But some people wanted to ruin the party. They wanted to ruin all the fun.
Freeze!

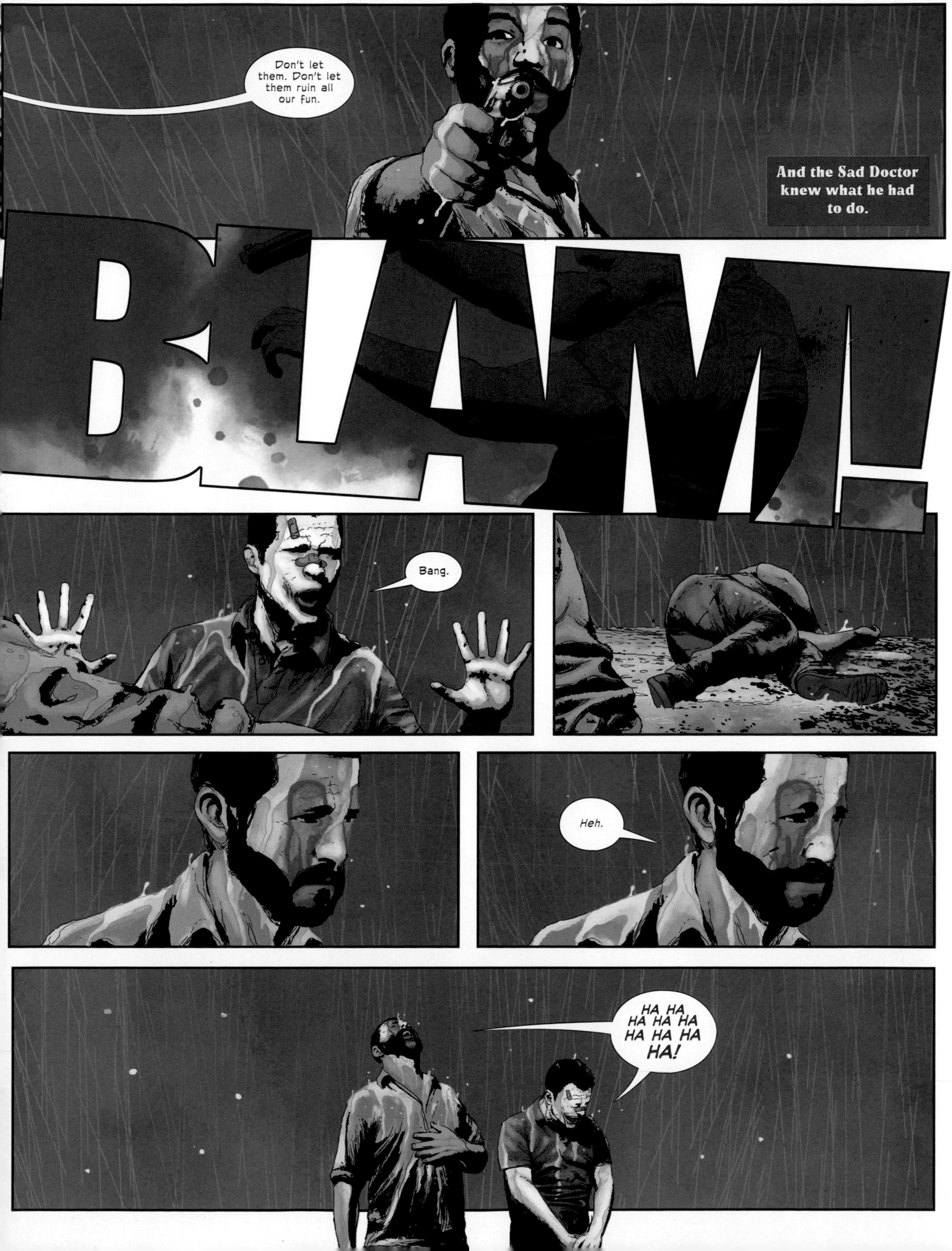
Don't let them. Don't let them ruin all our fun.
And the Sad Doctor knew what he had to do.
BLAM!
Bang.
Heh.
HA HA HA HA HA HA HA HA HA!

Mr. Smiles took the Sad Doctor's hand and led him to the greatest place in all of Happyville...

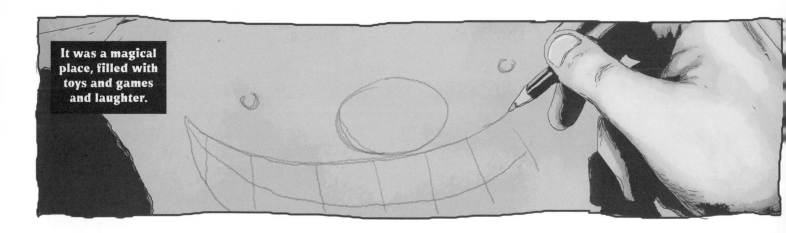

What is this?

It was a magical place, filled with toys and games and laughter.

Oh, you'll *like* it here, Doc...

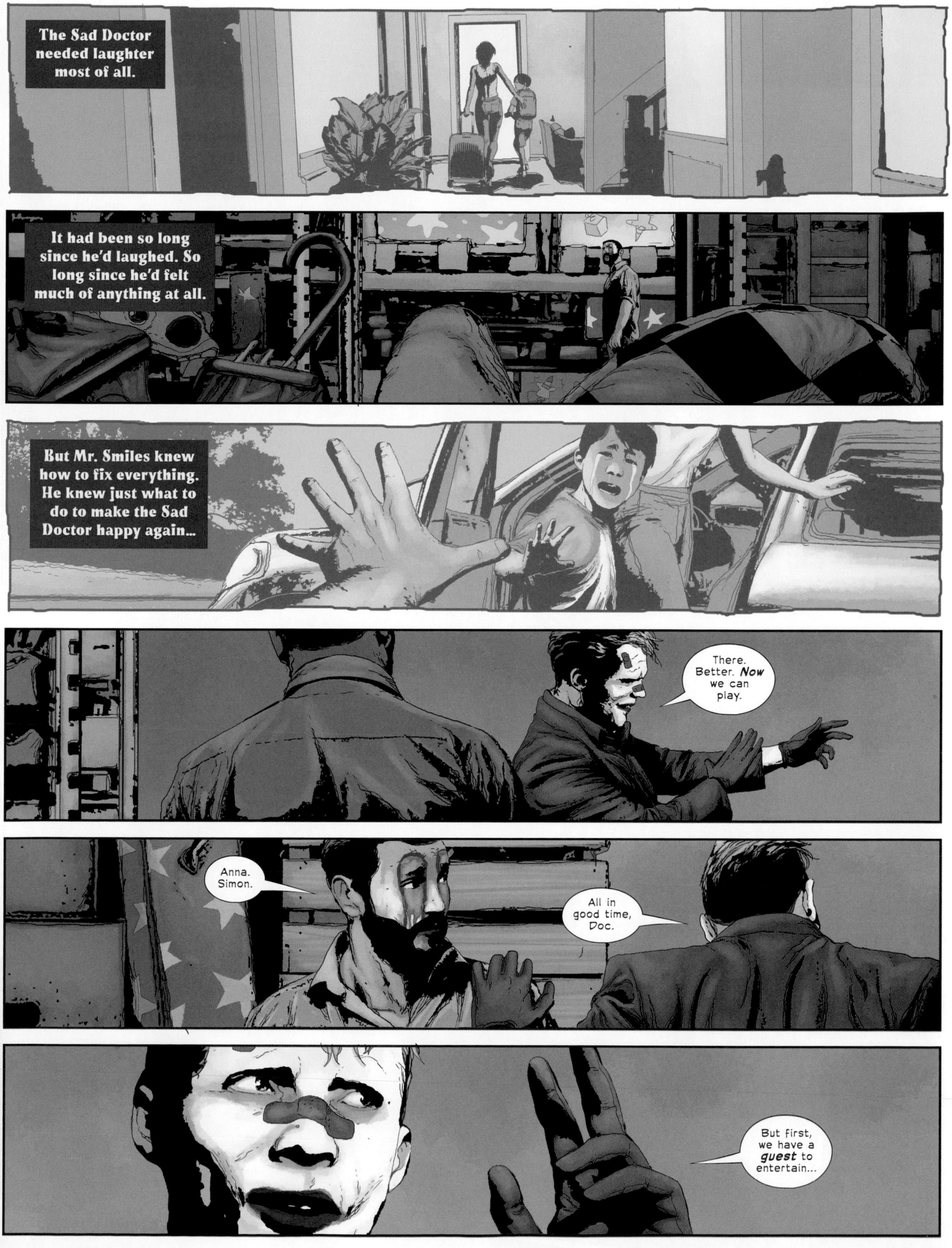

The Sad Doctor needed laughter most of all.
It had been so long since he'd laughed. So long since he'd felt much of anything at all.
But Mr. Smiles knew how to fix everything. He knew just what to do to make the Sad Doctor happy again...
There. Better. *Now* we can play.
Anna. Simon.
All in good time, Doc.
But first, we have a ***guest*** to entertain...

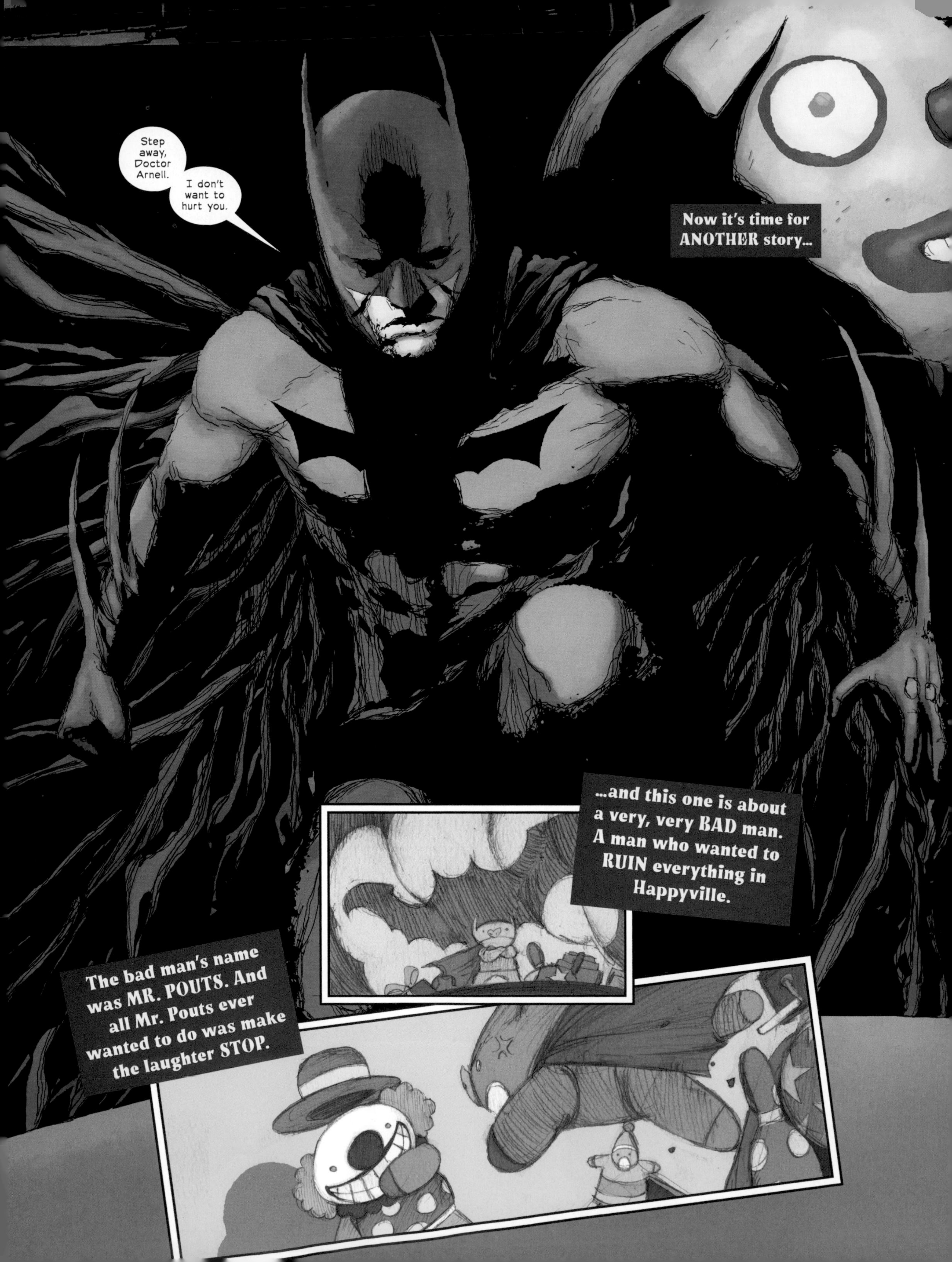

Step away, Doctor Arnell.
I don't want to hurt you.
Now it's time for ANOTHER story...
...and this one is about a very, very BAD man. A man who wanted to RUIN everything in Happyville.
The bad man's name was MR. POUTS. And all Mr. Pouts ever wanted to do was make the laughter STOP.

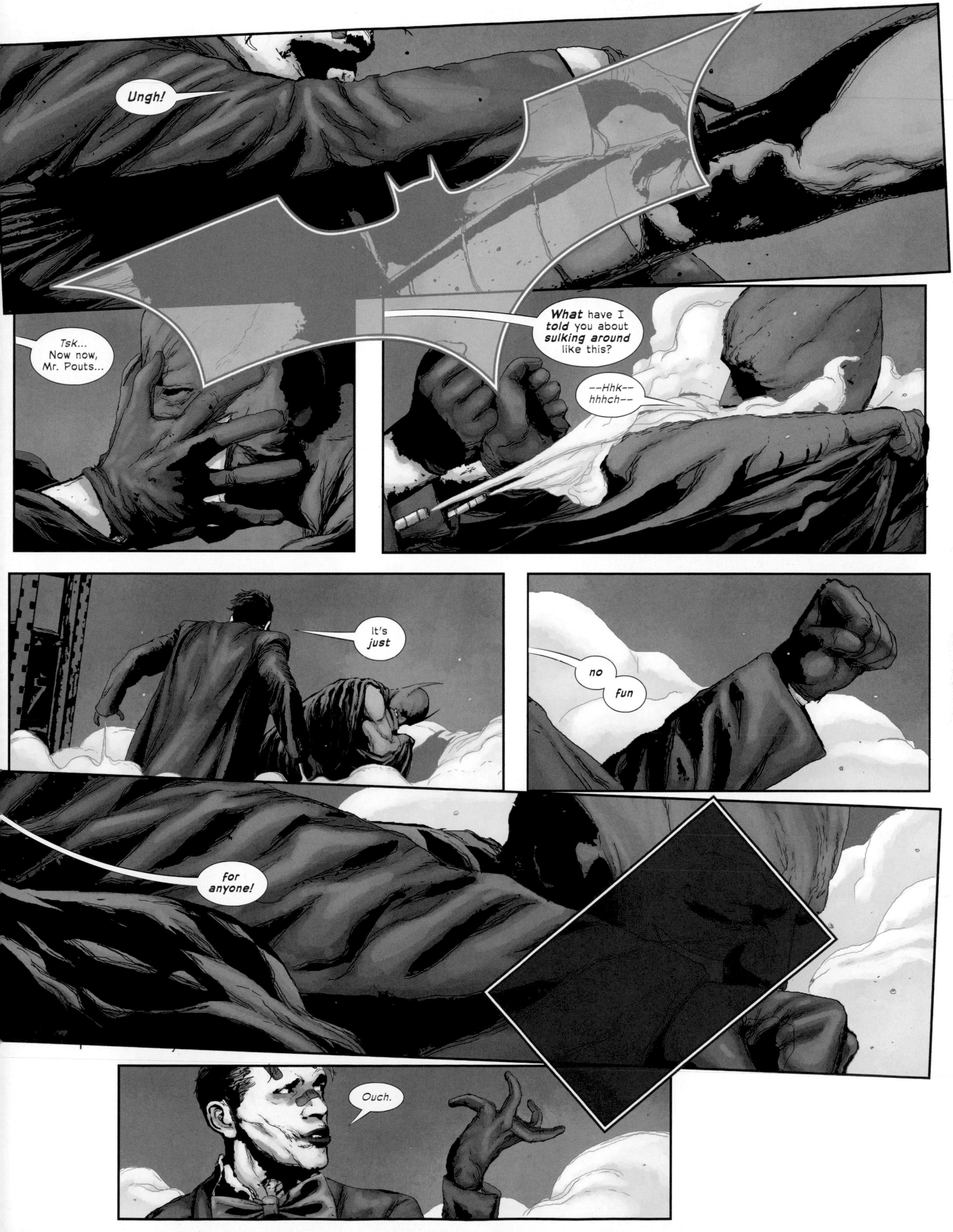
Ungh!
Tsk... Now now, Mr. Pouts...
What have I told you about sulking around like this?
--Hhk-- hhhch--
It's just
no
fun
for anyone!
Ouch.

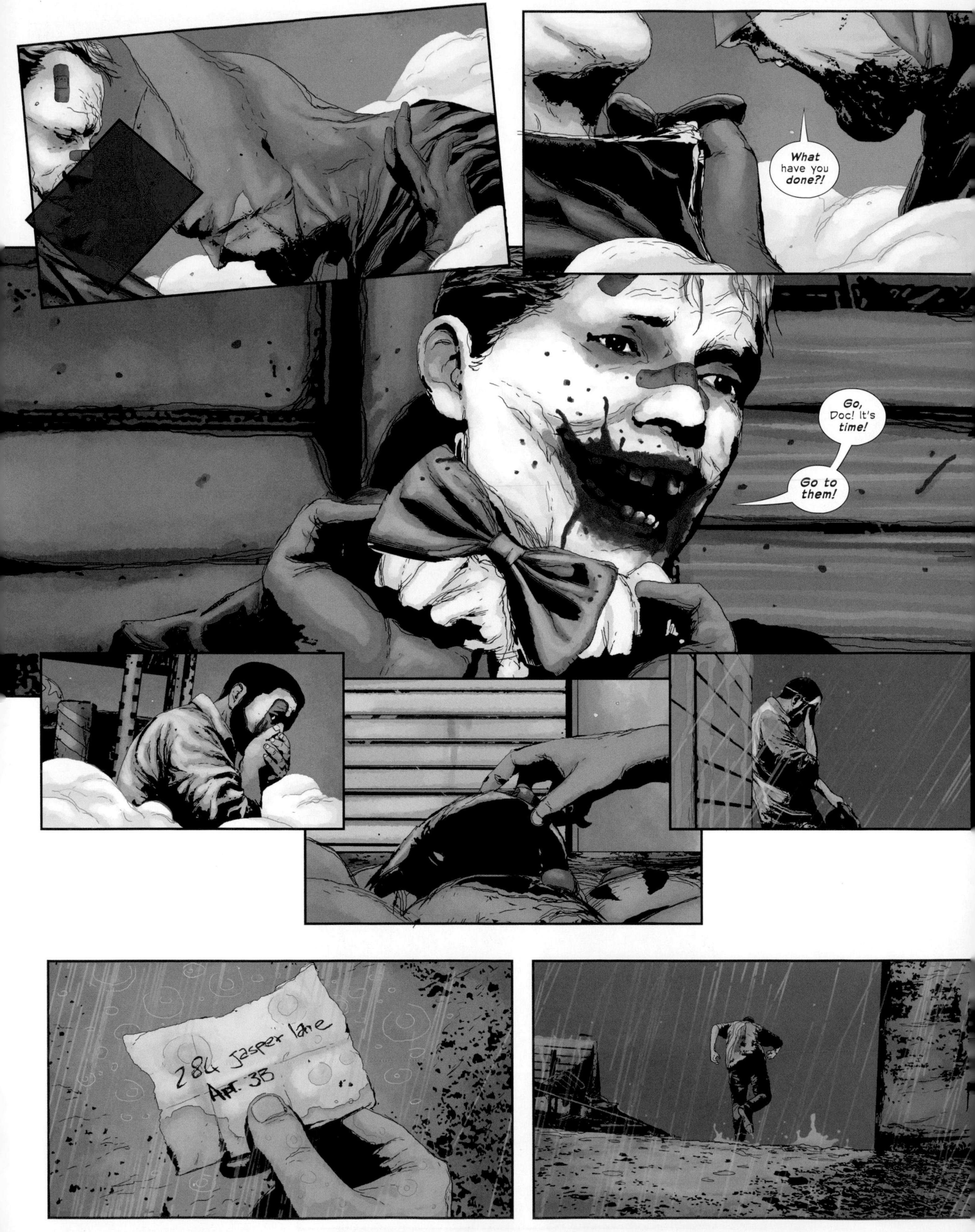
What have you done?!
Go, Doc! It's time!
Go to them!
284 Jasper lane
Apt. 3B

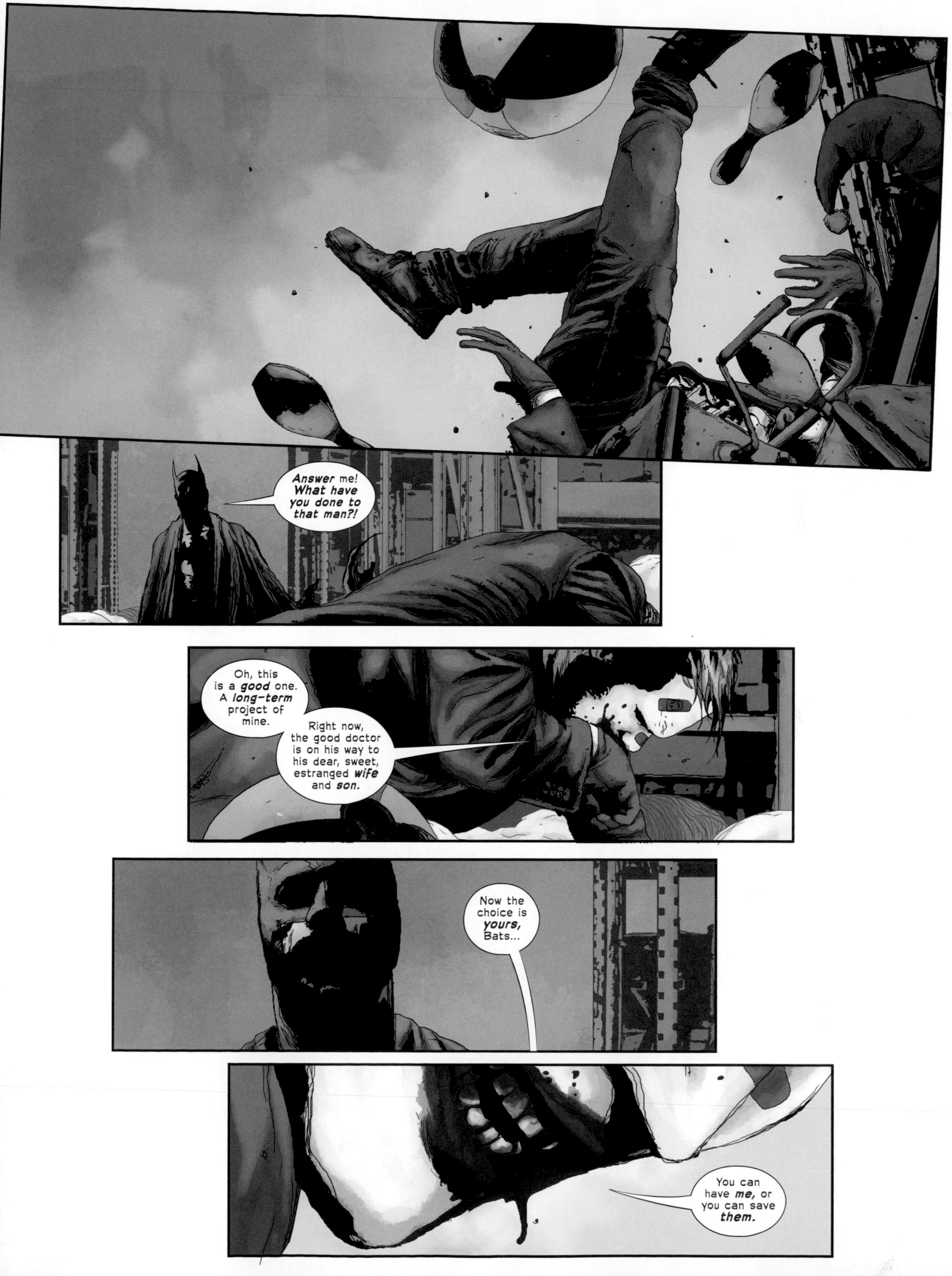
Answer me! What have you done to that man?!
Oh, this is a good one. A long-term project of mine.
Right now, the good doctor is on his way to his dear, sweet, estranged wife and son.
Now the choice is yours, Bats...
You can have me, or you can save them.

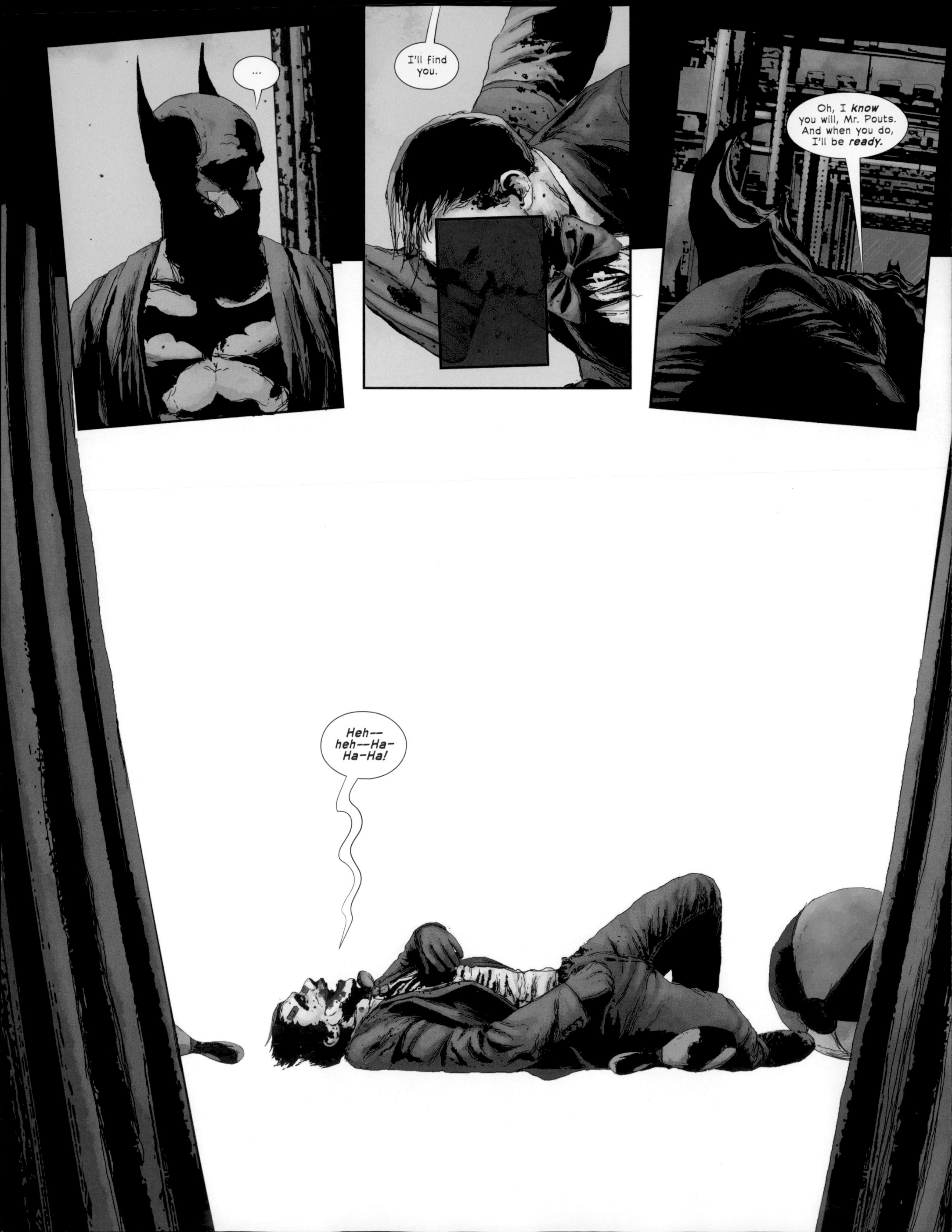
...
I'll find you.
Oh, I *know* you will, Mr. Pouts. And when you do, I'll be *ready.*
Heh-- heh--Ha- Ha-Ha!

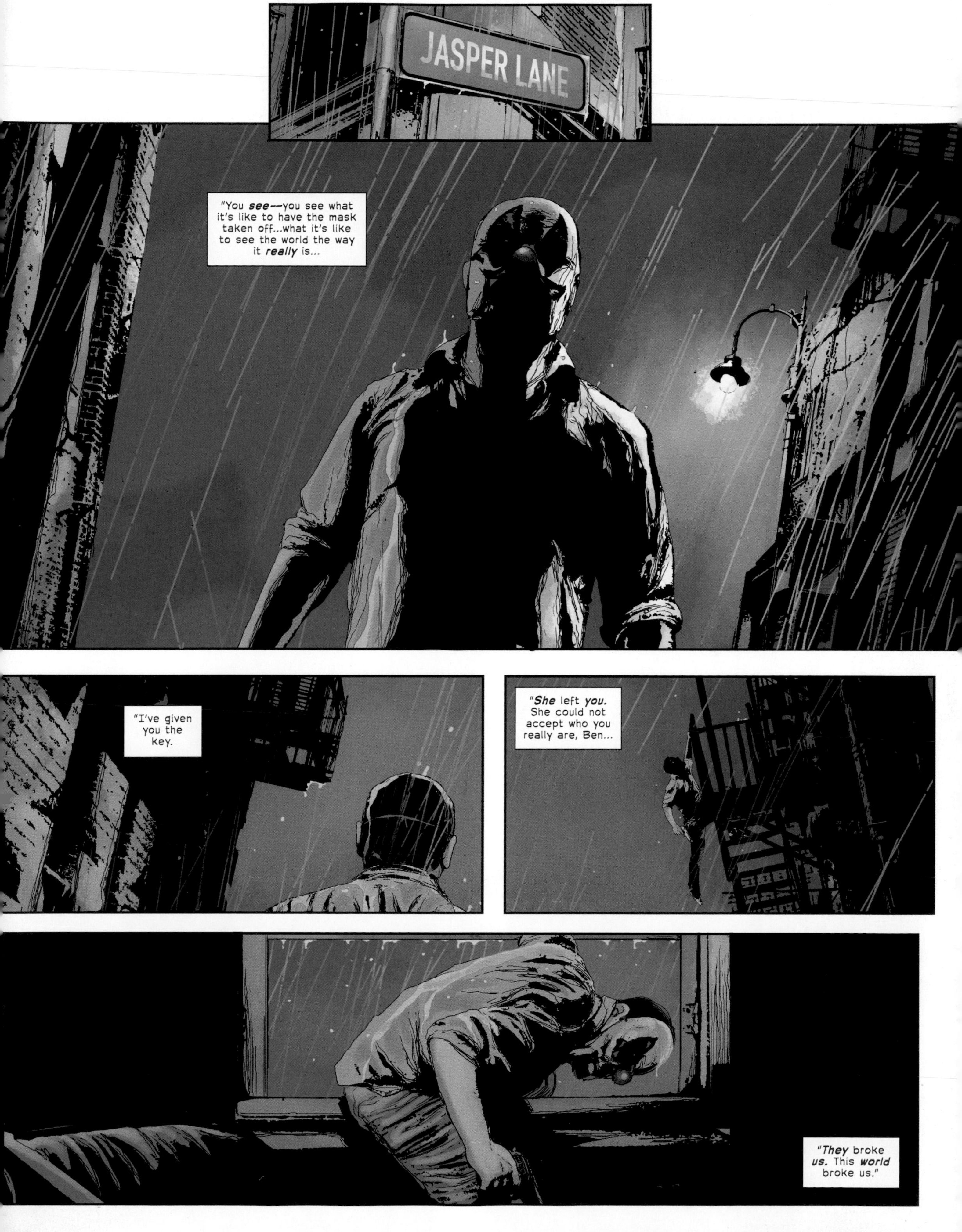
JASPER LANE
"You *see*––you see what it's like to have the mask taken off...what it's like to see the world the way it *really* is...
"I've given you the key.
"*She* left *you.* She could not accept who you really are, Ben...
"*They* broke *us.* This *world* broke us."

"So let's *break* it right back."

B--*Ben?*

"You are on the threshold now.

"Walk with me, Benjamin...

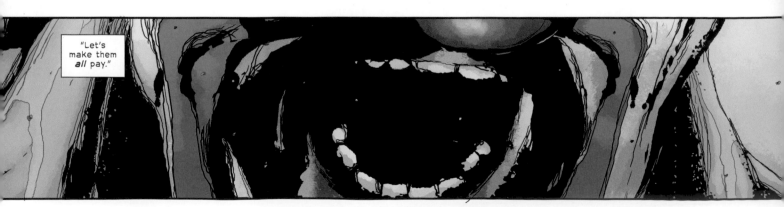

"Let's make them *all* pay."

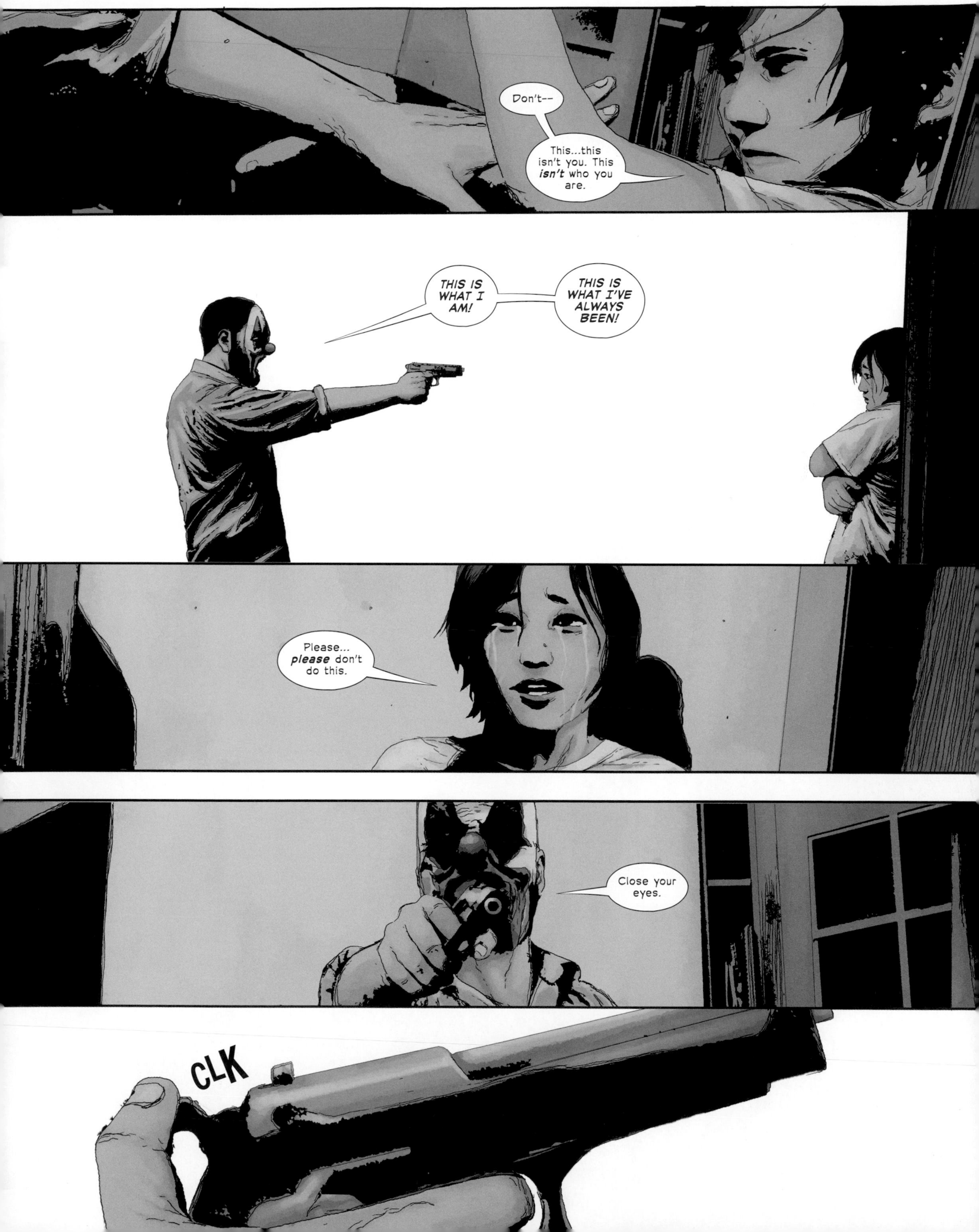
Don't--
This...this isn't you. This *isn't* who you are.
THIS IS WHAT I AM!
THIS IS WHAT I'VE ALWAYS BEEN!
Please... ***please*** don't do this.
Close your eyes.
CLK

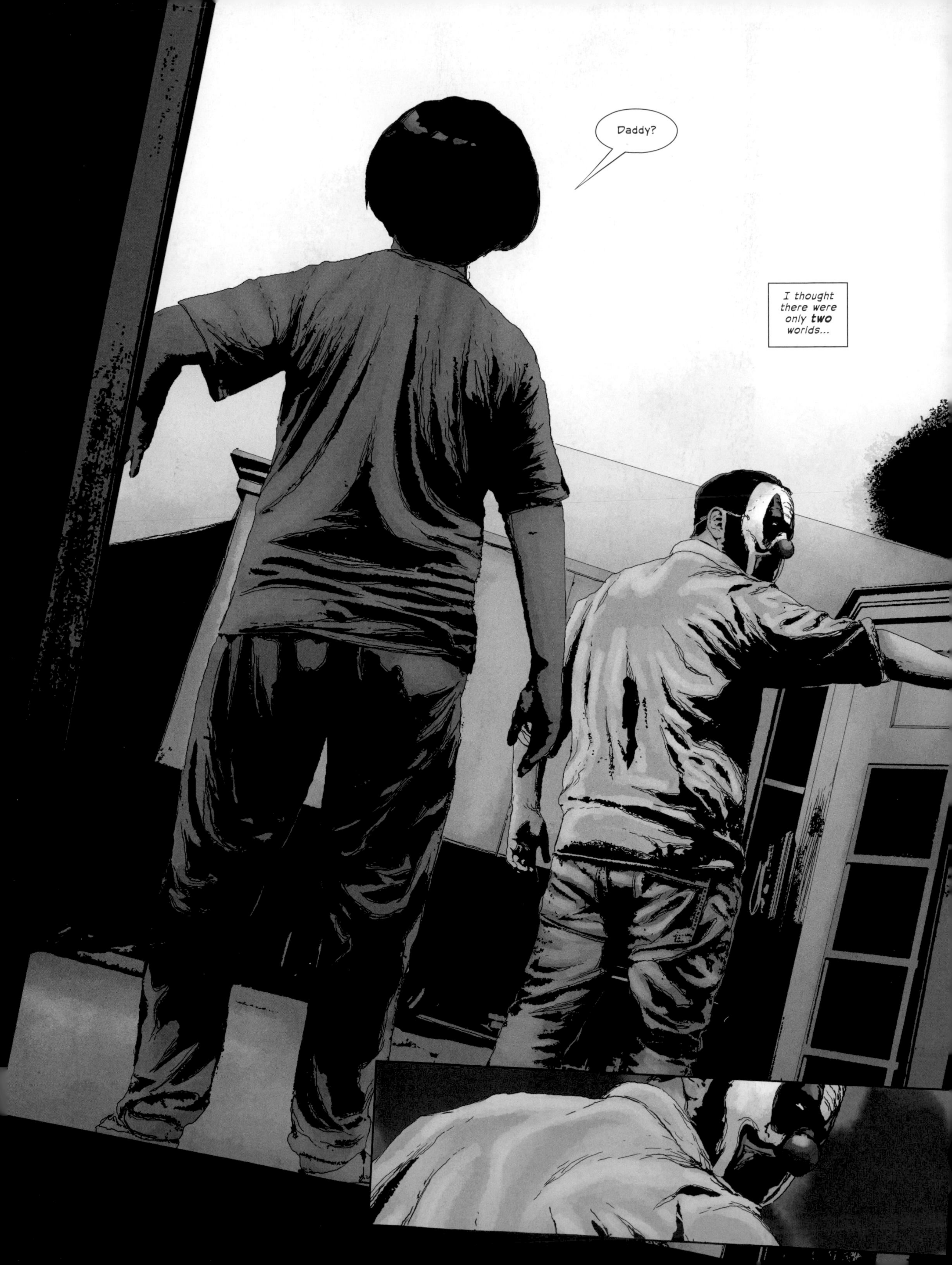
Daddy?
I thought there were only **two** worlds...

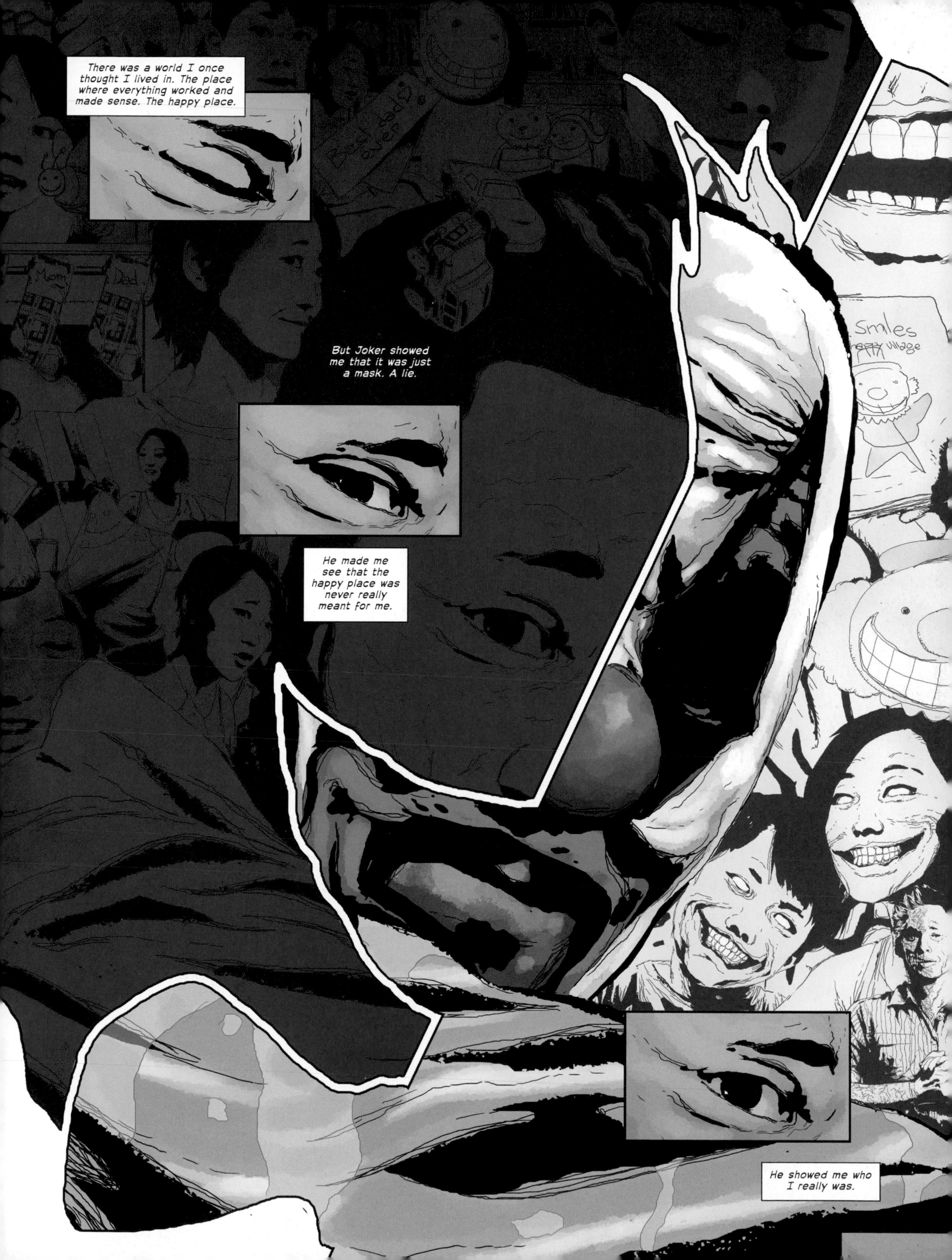
There was a world I once thought I lived in. The place where everything worked and made sense. The happy place.
But Joker showed me that it was just a mask. A lie.
He made me see that the happy place was never really meant for me.
He showed me who I really was.

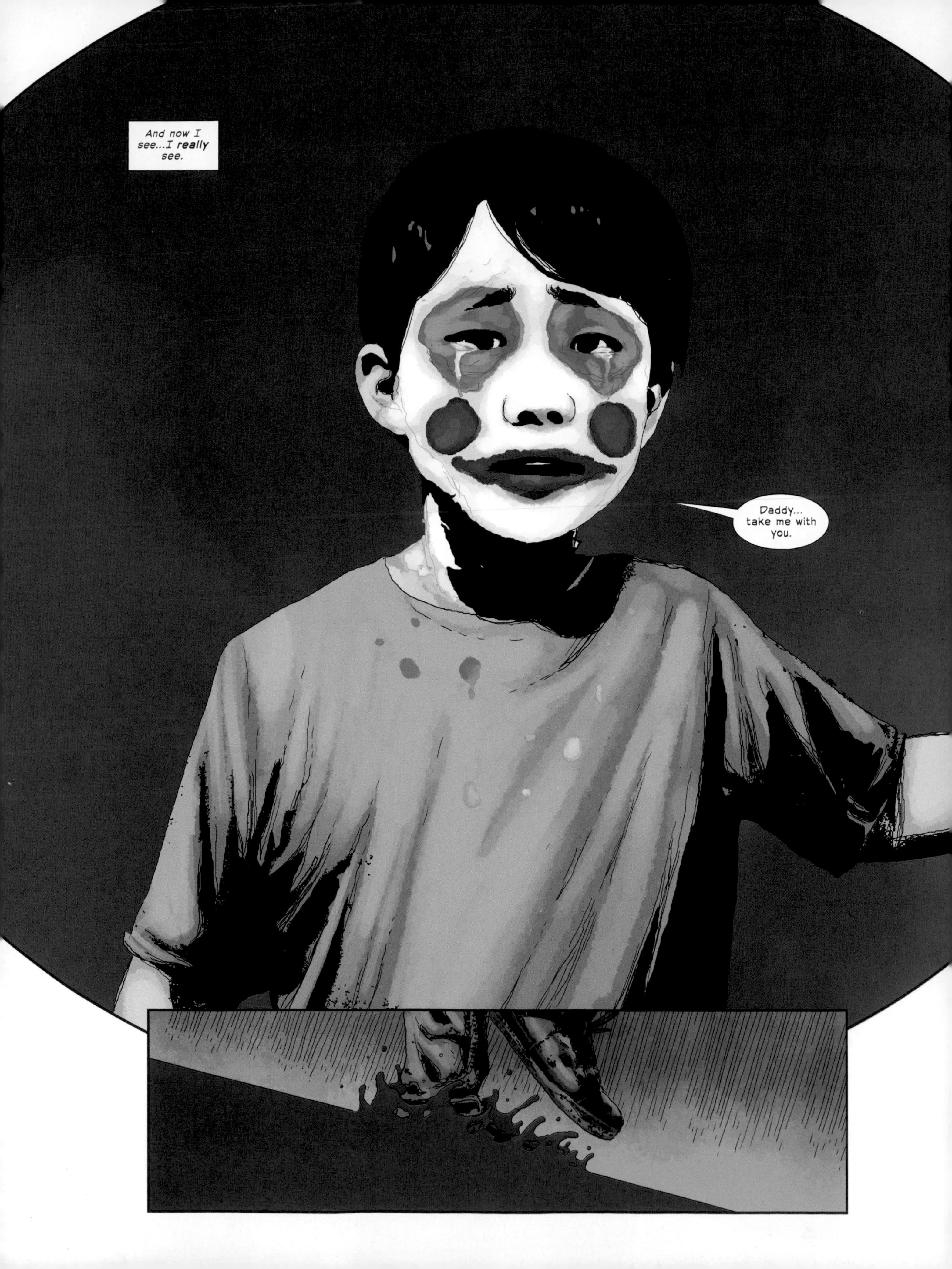
And now I see...I **really** see.
Daddy... take me with you.

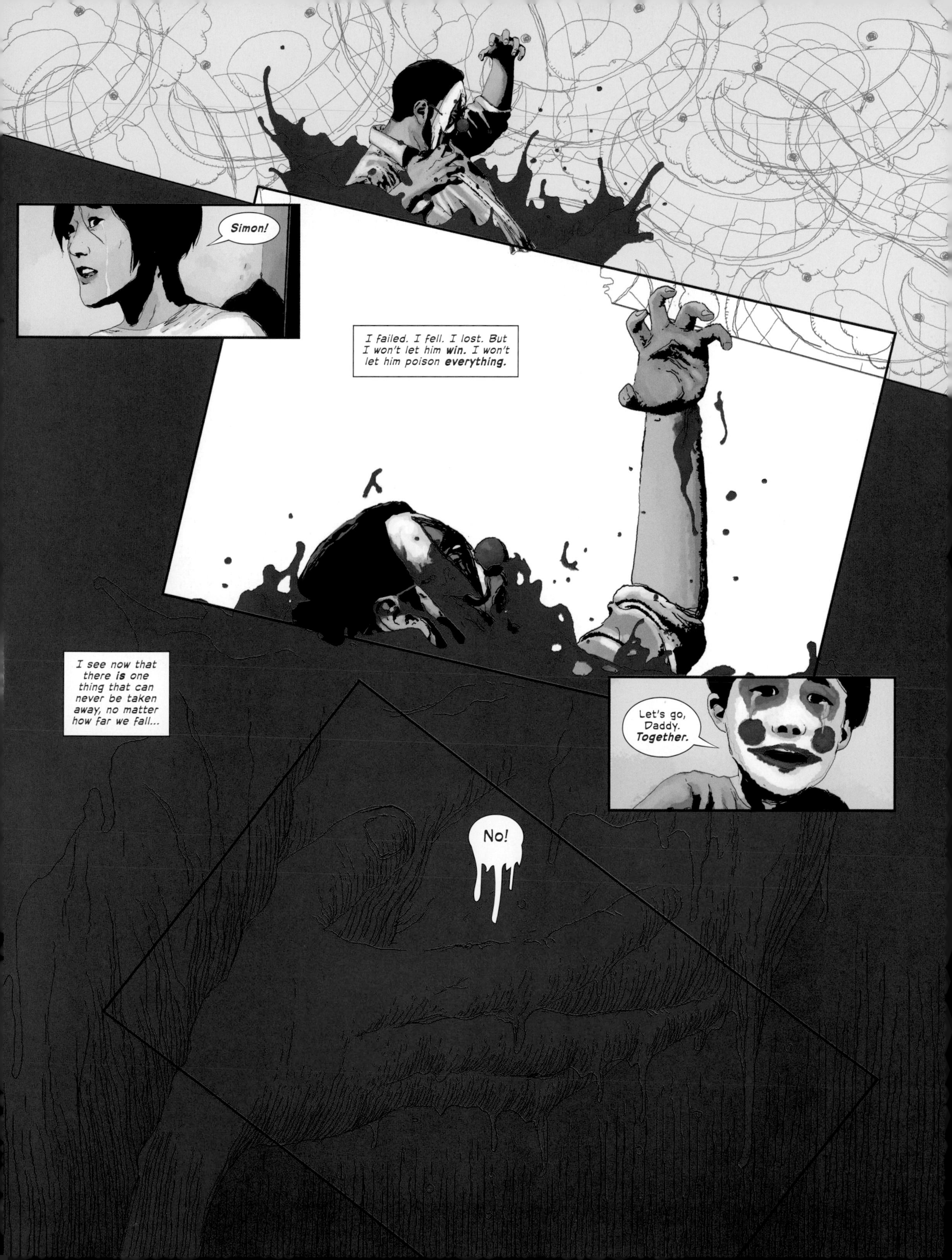
Simon!
I failed. I fell. I lost. But I won't let him win. I won't let him poison everything.
I see now that there is one thing that can never be taken away, no matter how far we fall...
Let's go, Daddy. Together.
No!

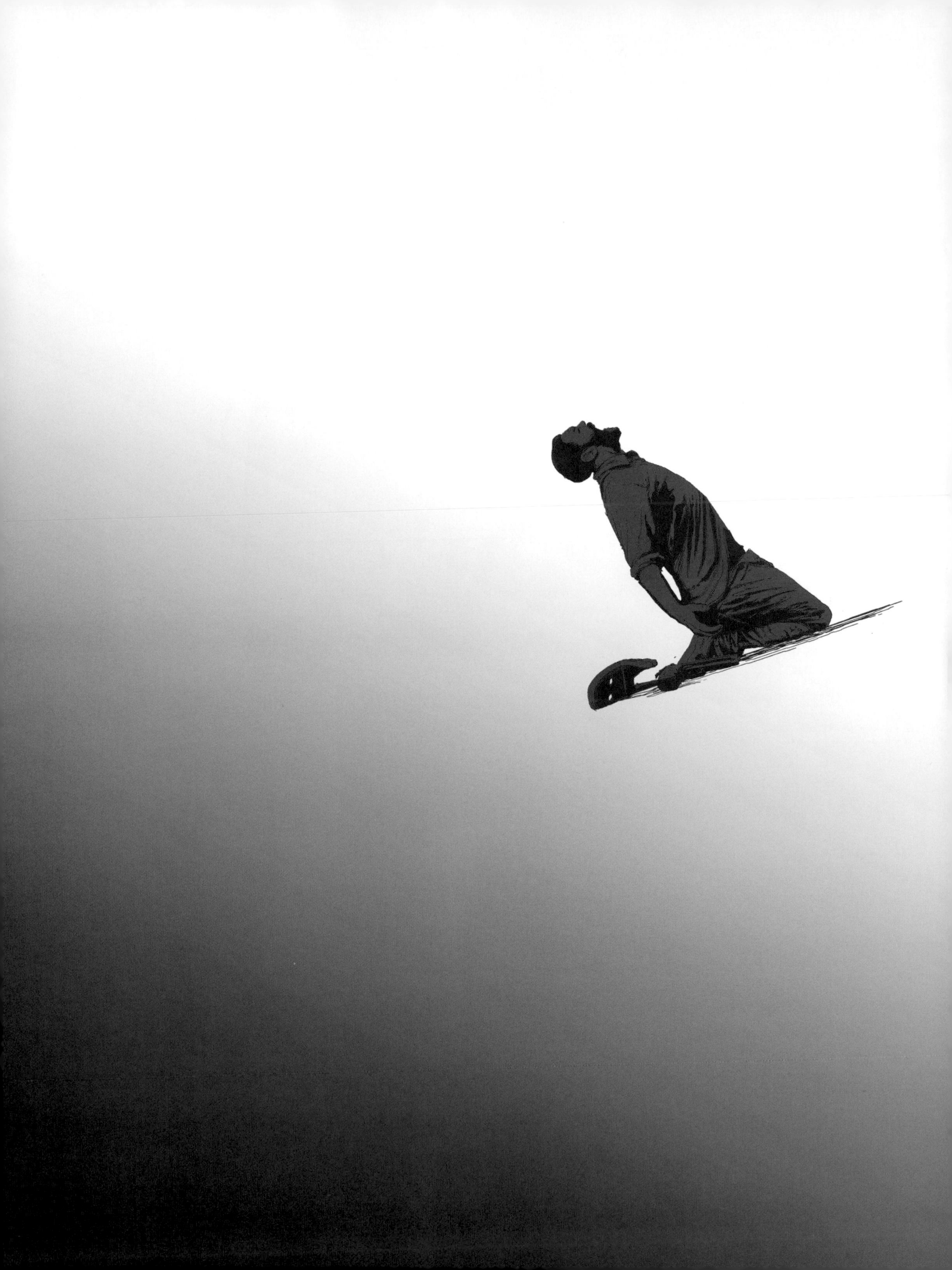

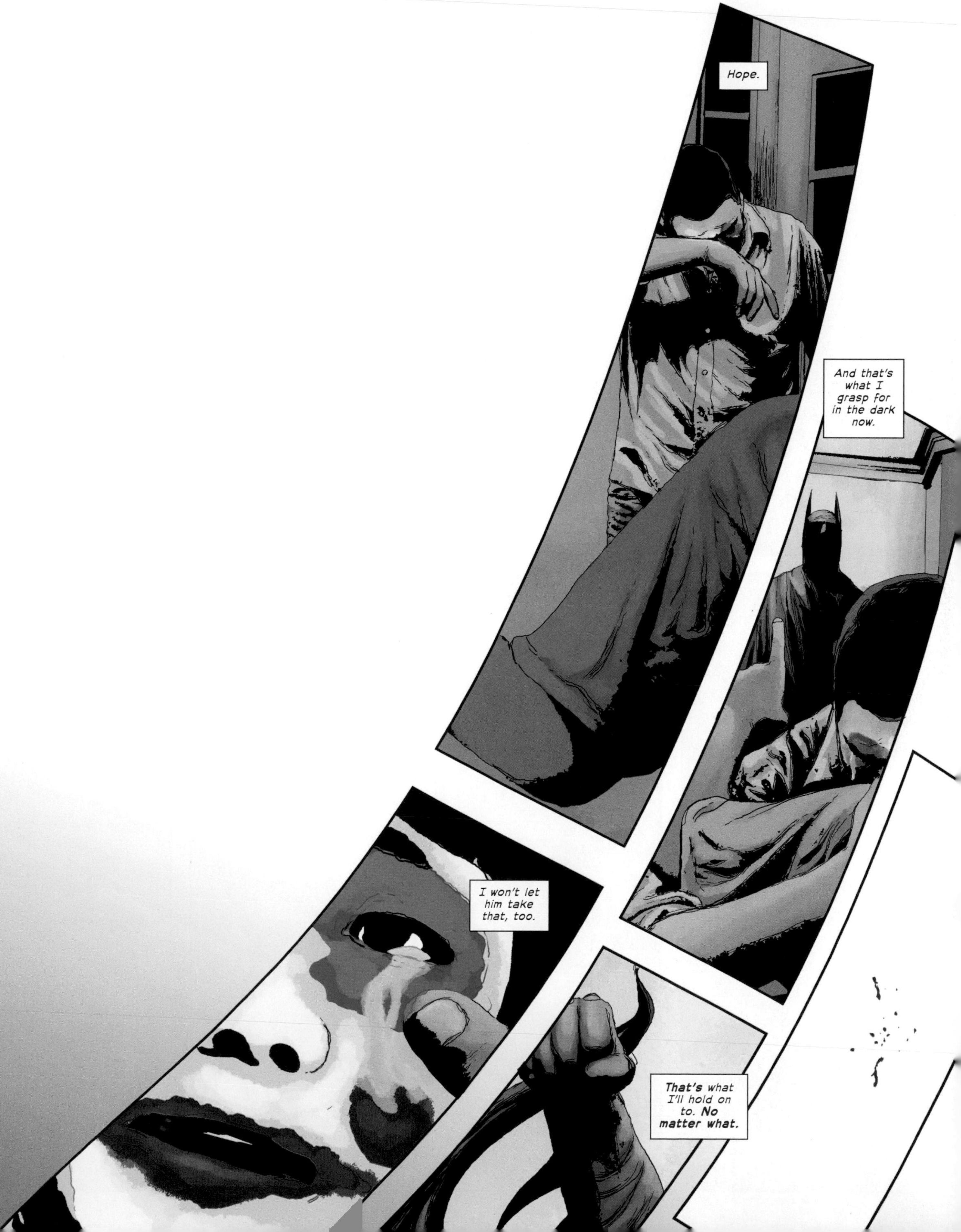
Hope.
And that's what I grasp for in the dark now.
I won't let him take that, too.
That's what I'll hold on to. No matter what.

This is good, Benjamin. **Very** good.

But is it too late, Doctor Hutchins?

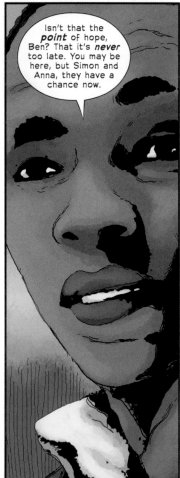
Isn't that the **point** of hope, Ben? That it's **never** too late. You may be here, but Simon and Anna, they have a chance now.

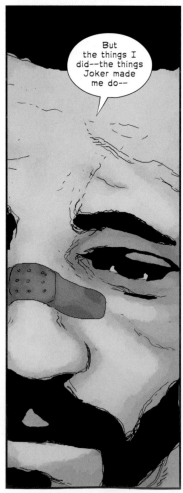
But the things I did--the things Joker made me do--

Joker is a **disease,** Ben. Everything he touches is corrupted.

But don't you see? He **didn't get you.** He didn't win...

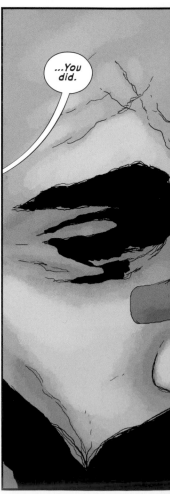
...You did.

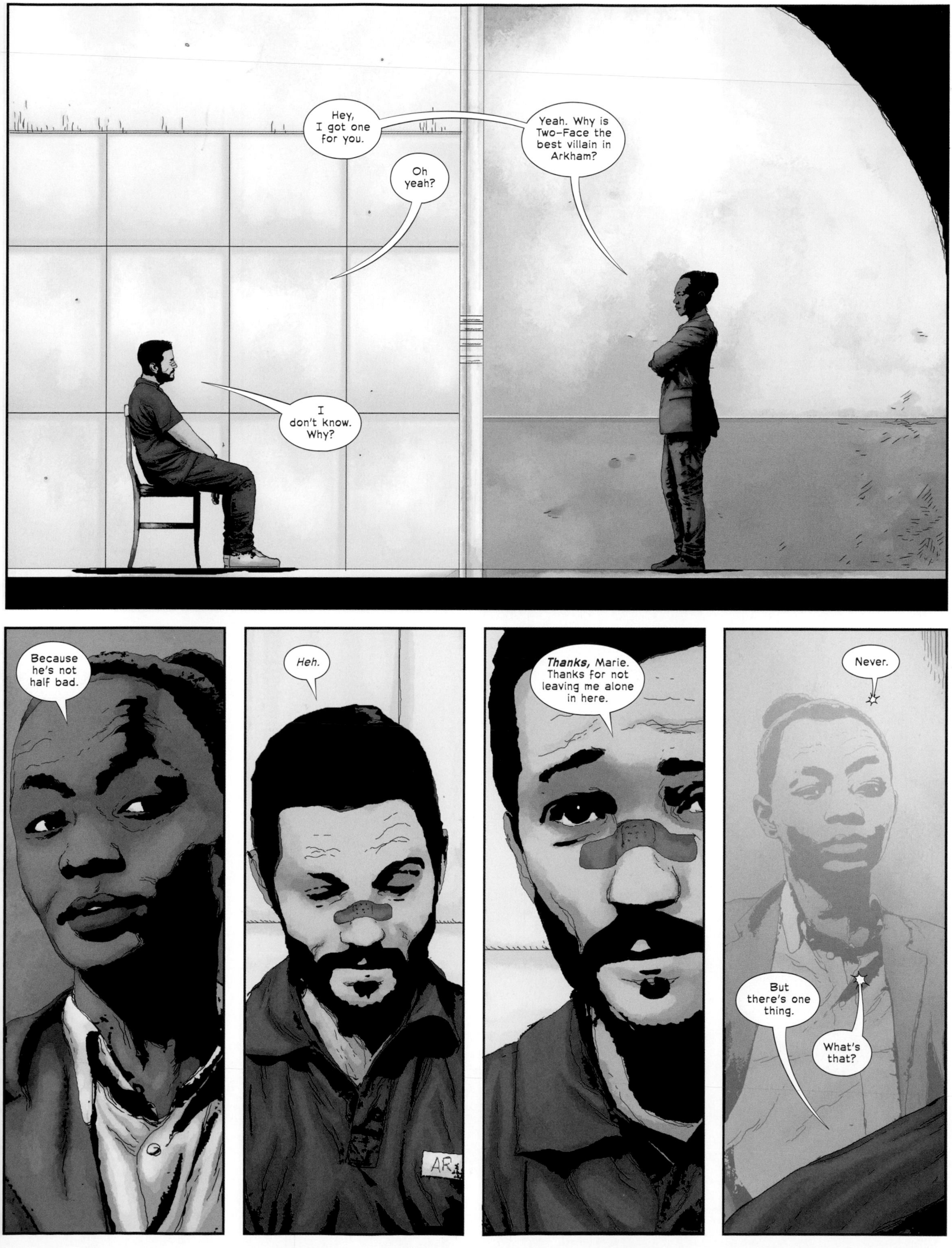
Hey, I got one for you.
Oh yeah?
Yeah. Why is Two-Face the best villain in Arkham?
I don't know. Why?
Because he's not half bad.
Heh.
Thanks, Marie. Thanks for not leaving me alone in here.
Never.
But there's one thing.
What's that?
AR

"Joker used me--and now he's out there in the open."

"And if he really *is* a disease-- then what do we do when it starts to spread?"

"The only thing we can, Ben..."

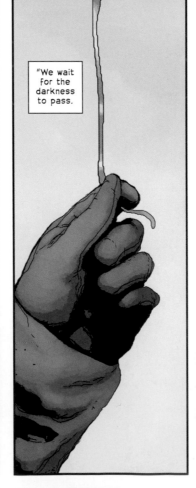

"We wait for the darkness to pass.

"And we pray that hope is *enough*."

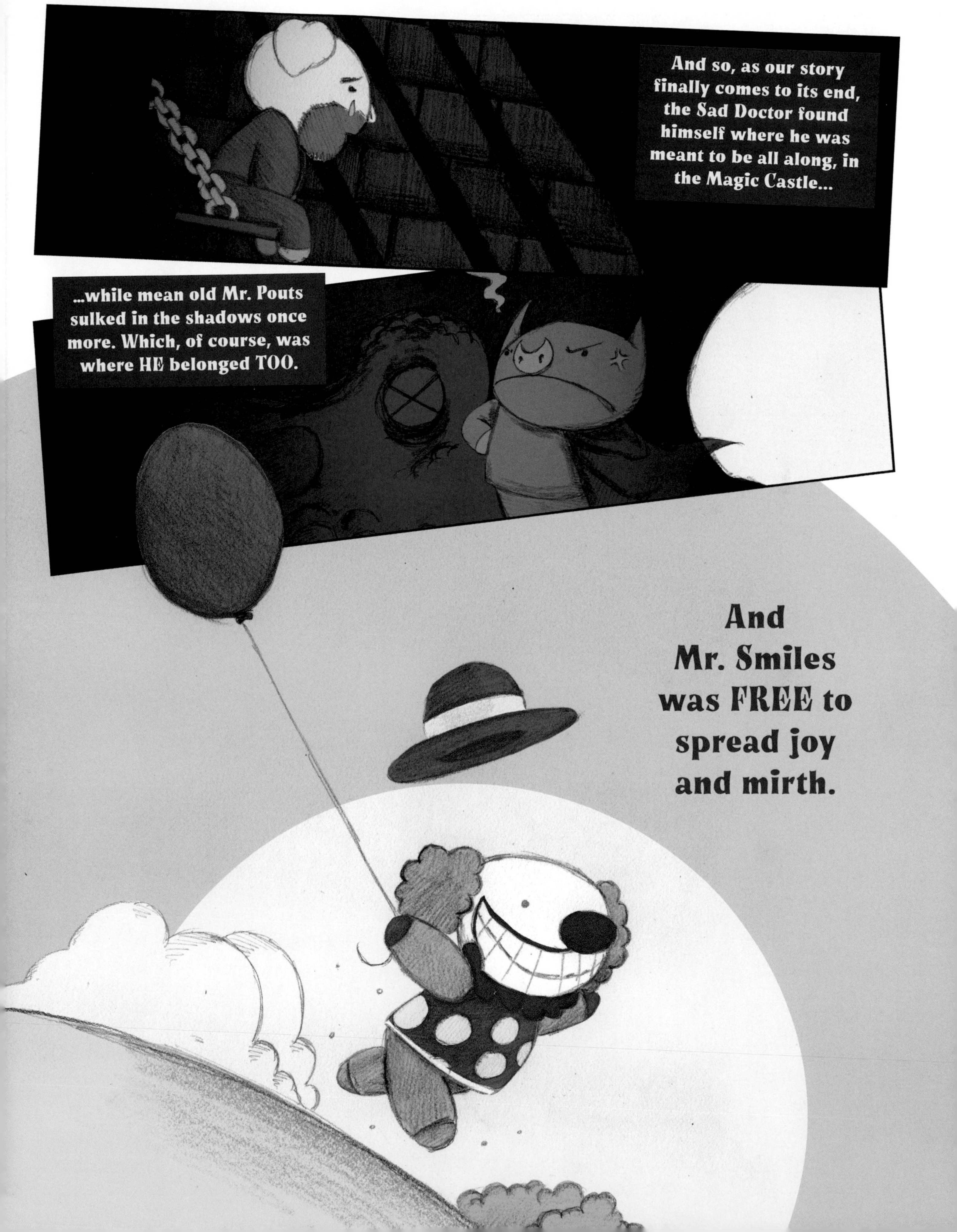
And so, as our story finally comes to its end, the Sad Doctor found himself where he was meant to be all along, in the Magic Castle...
...while mean old Mr. Pouts sulked in the shadows once more. Which, of course, was where HE belonged TOO.
And Mr. Smiles was FREE to spread joy and mirth.

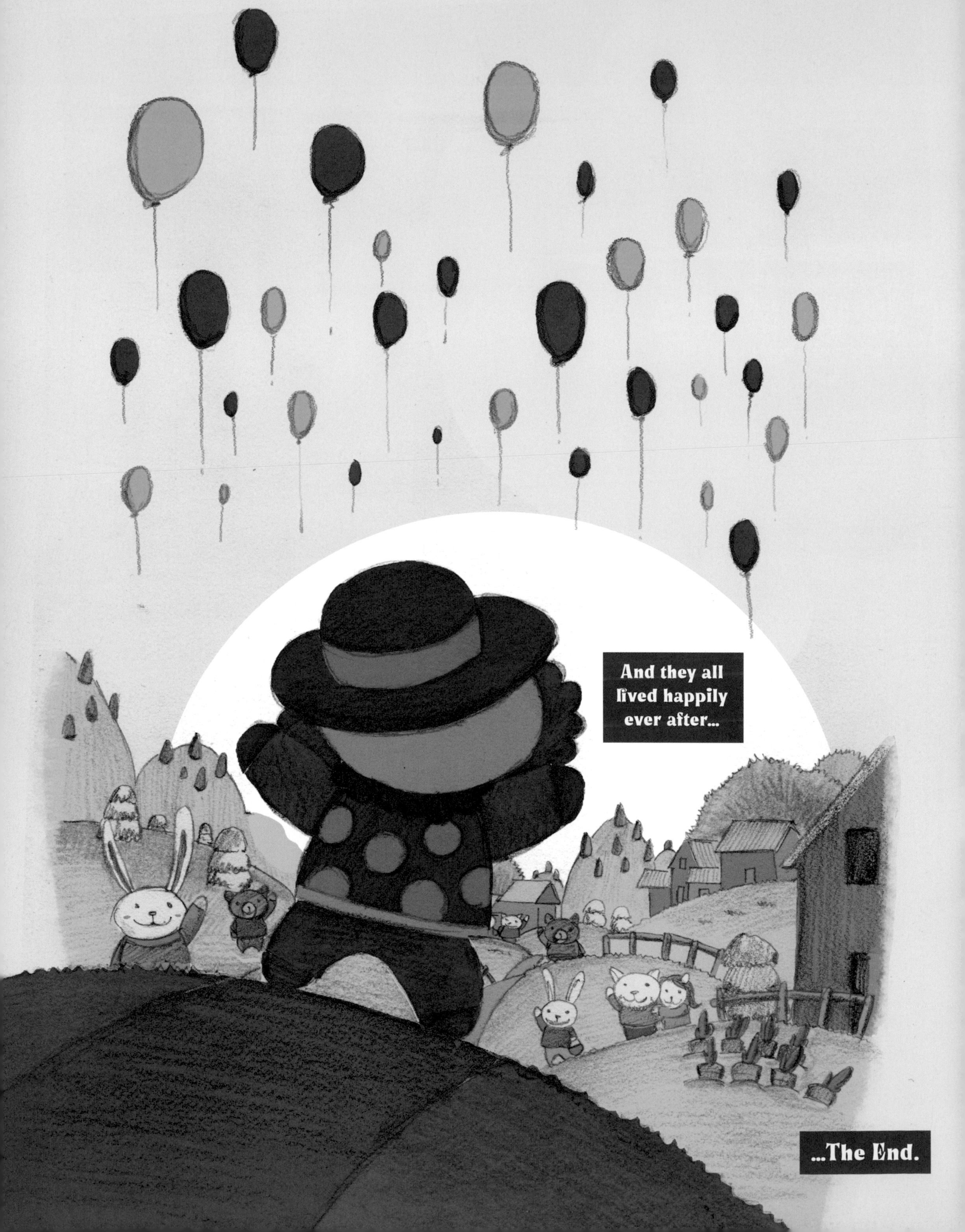
And they all lived happily ever after...
...The End.

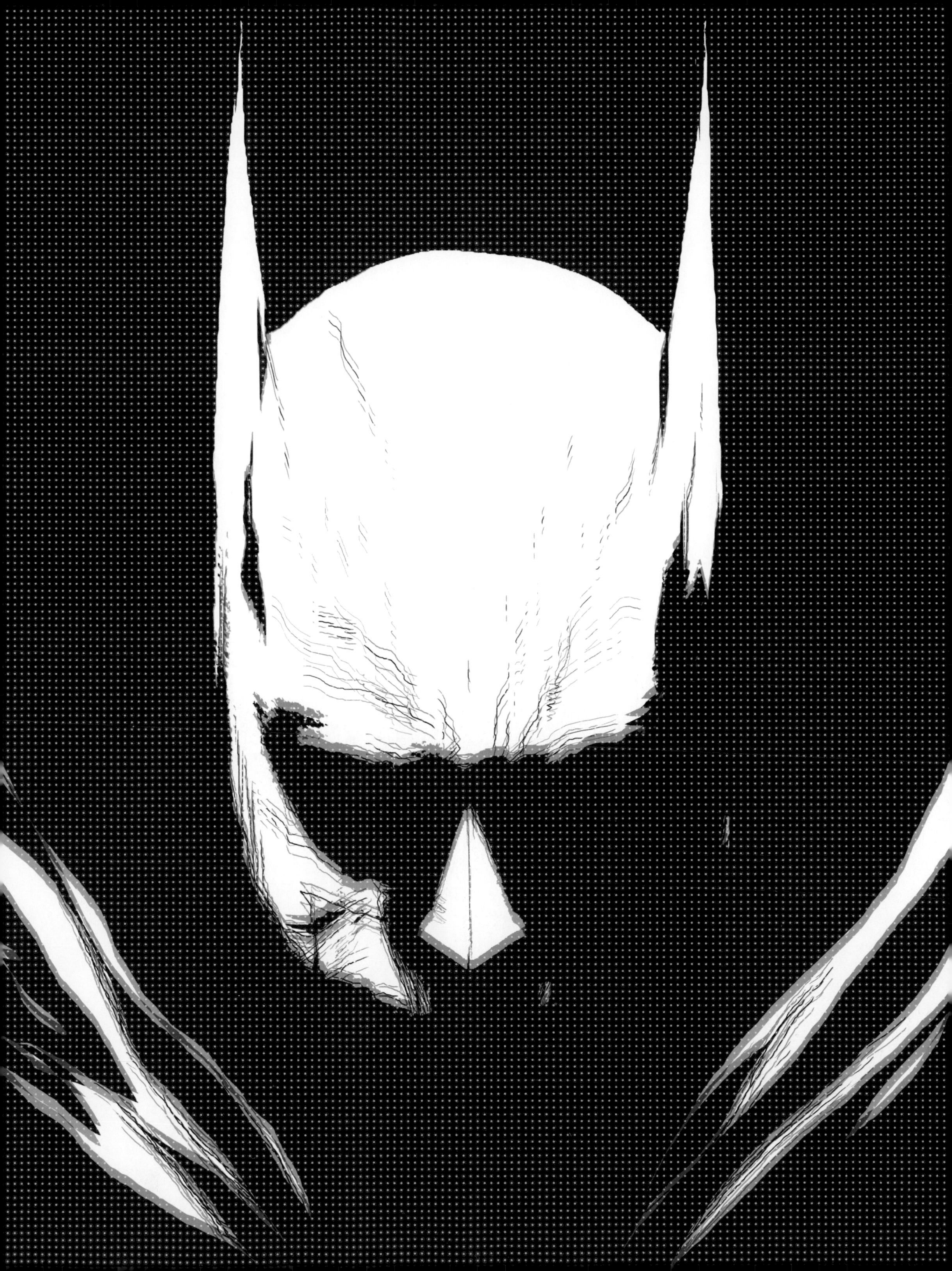

BATMAN:
THE SMILE KILLER

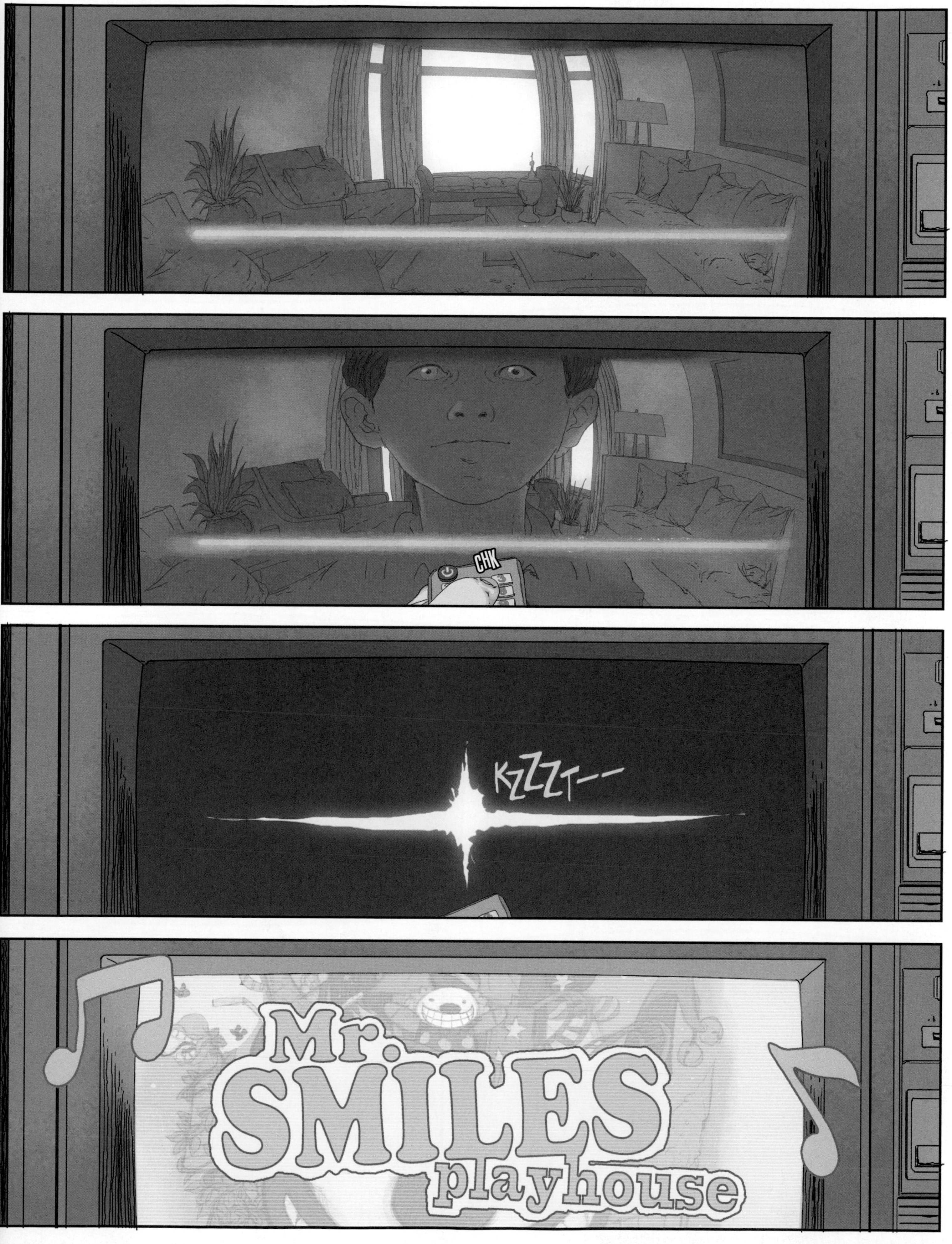
CHK
KZZZT--
Mr. SMILES playhouse

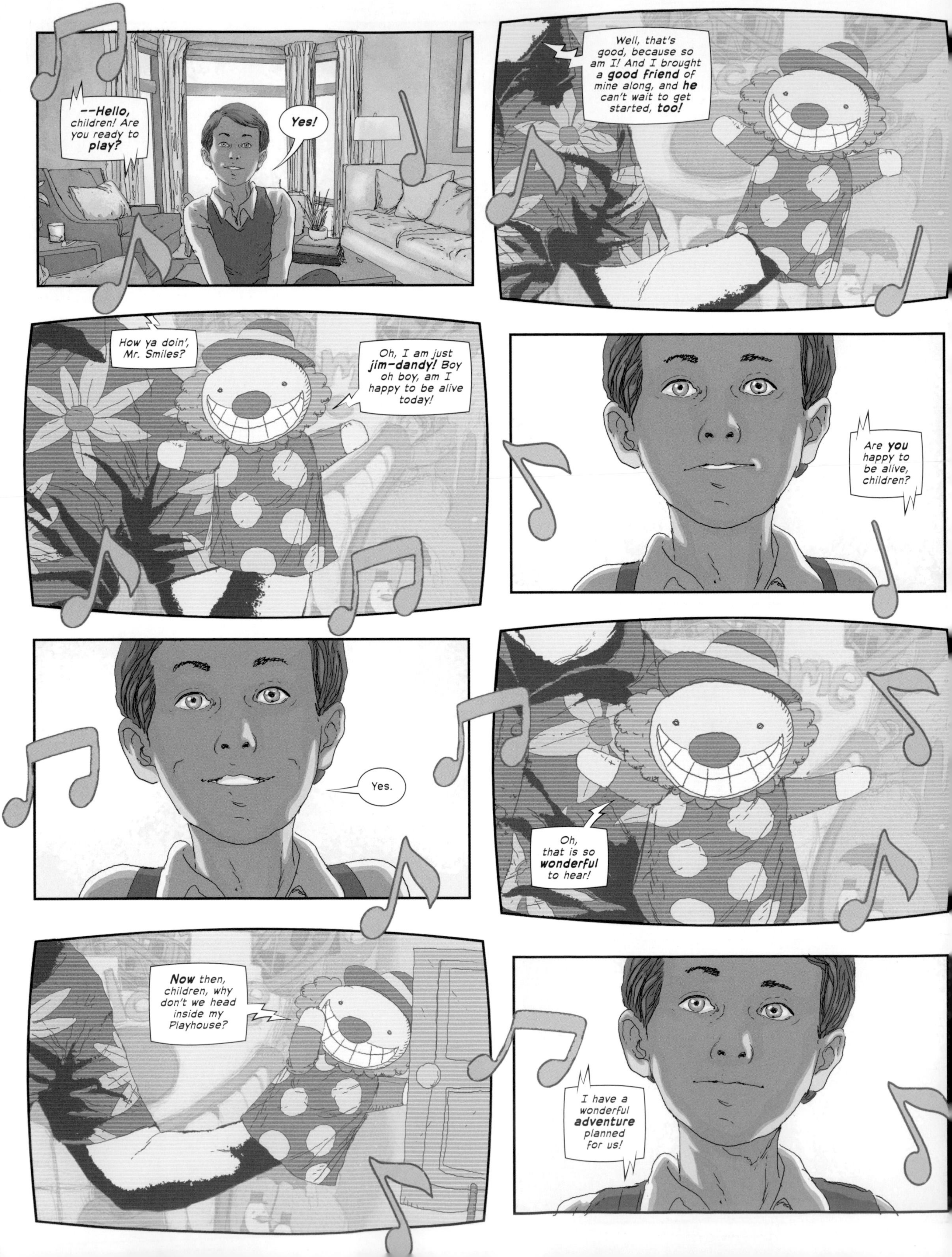
--Hello, children! Are you ready to play?
Yes!
Well, that's good, because so am I! And I brought a good friend of mine along, and he can't wait to get started, too!
How ya doin', Mr. Smiles?
Oh, I am just jim-dandy! Boy oh boy, am I happy to be alive today!
Are you happy to be alive, children?
Yes.
Oh, that is so wonderful to hear!
Now then, children, why don't we head inside my Playhouse?
I have a wonderful adventure planned for us!

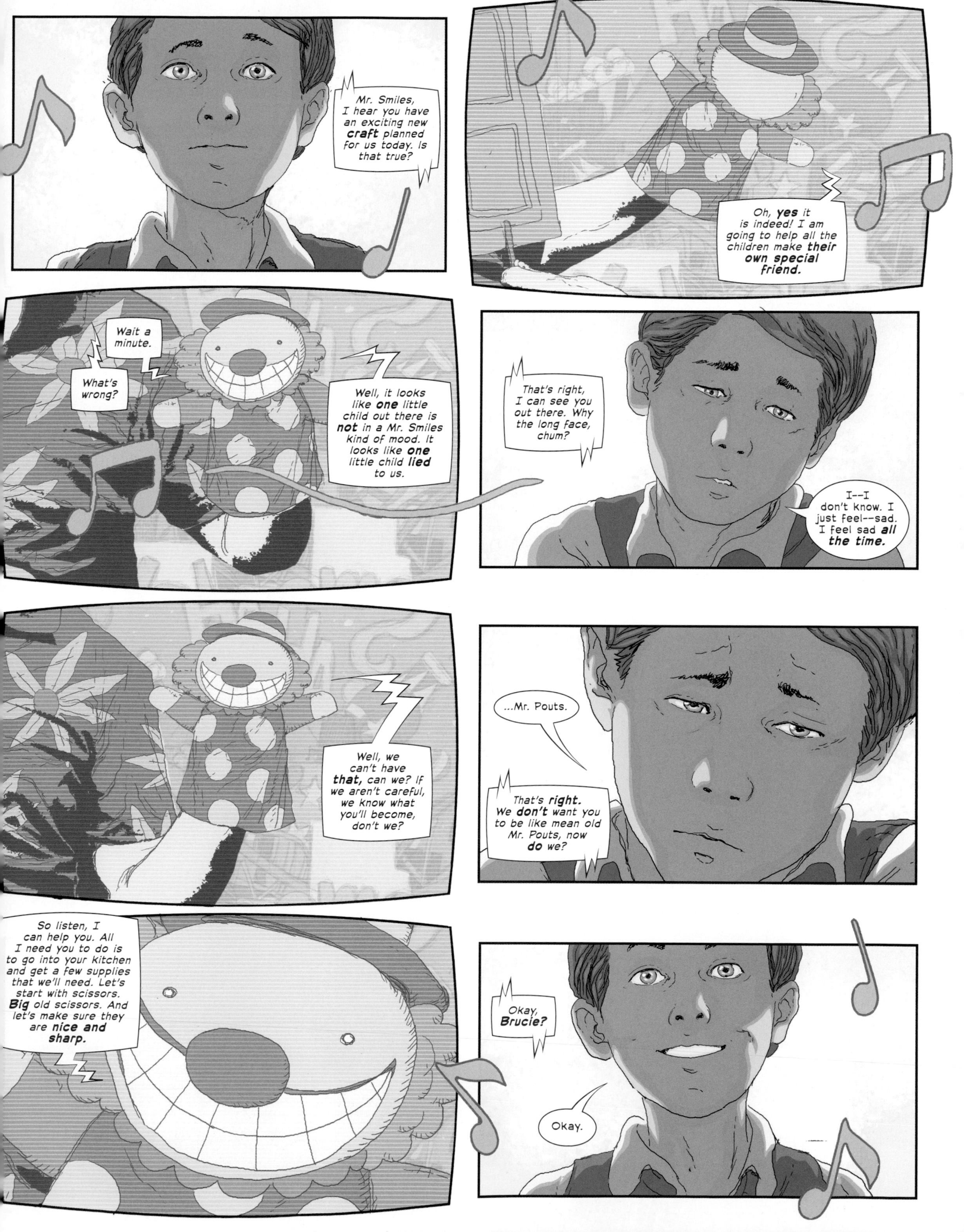

Mr. Smiles, I hear you have an exciting new **craft** planned for us today. Is that true?
Oh, **yes** it is indeed! I am going to help all the children make **their own special friend.**
Wait a minute.
What's wrong?
Well, it looks like **one** little child out there is **not** in a Mr. Smiles kind of mood. It looks like **one** little child **lied** to us.
That's right, I can see you out there. Why the long face, chum?
I--I don't know. I just feel--sad. I feel sad **all the time.**
Well, we can't have **that,** can we? If we aren't careful, we know what you'll become, don't we?
...Mr. Pouts.
That's **right.** We **don't** want you to be like mean old Mr. Pouts, now **do** we?
So listen, I can help you. All I need you to do is to go into your kitchen and get a few supplies that we'll need. Let's start with scissors. **Big** old scissors. And let's make sure they are **nice and sharp.**
Okay, **Brucie?**
Okay.

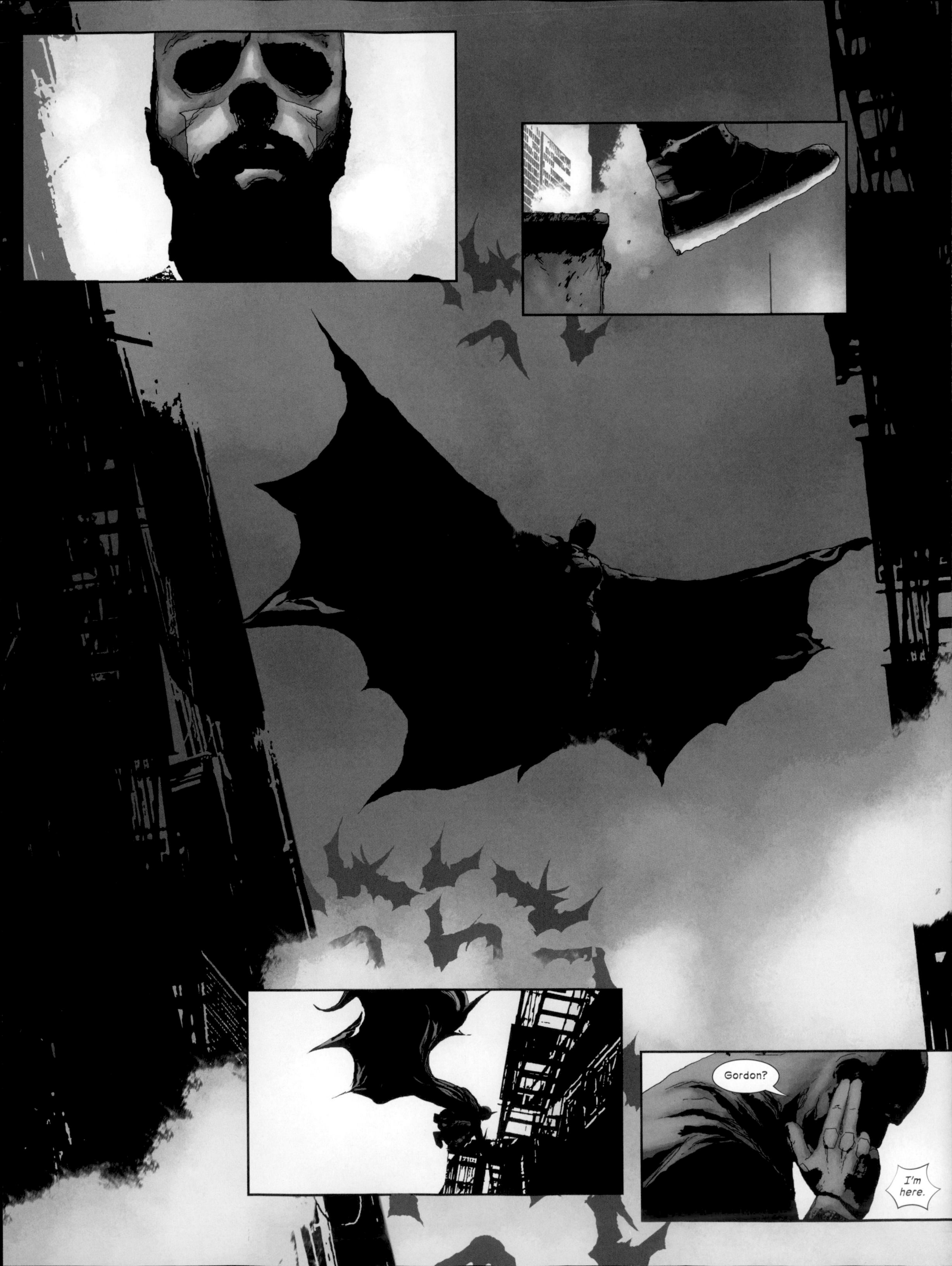
Gordon?
I'm here.

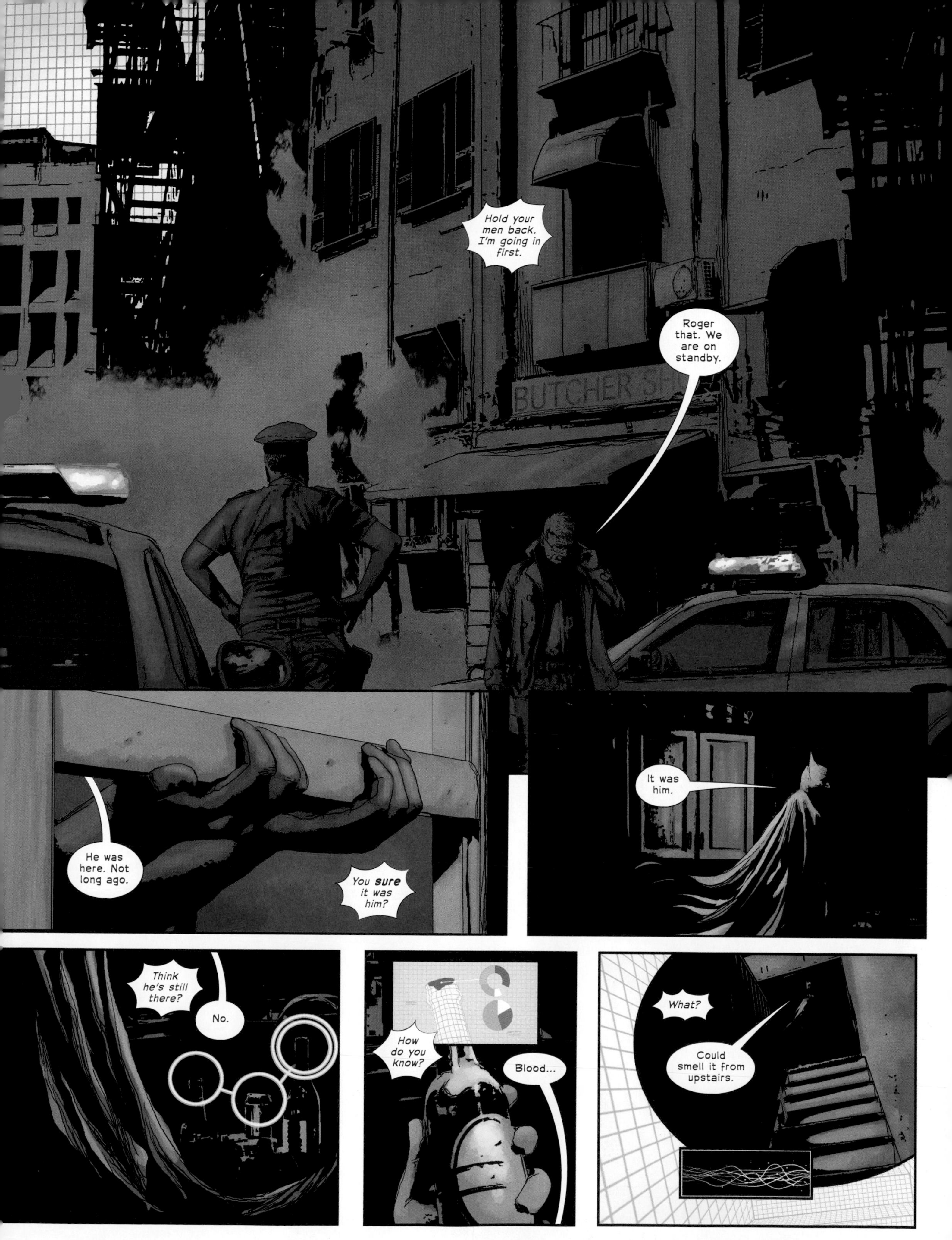
Hold your men back. I'm going in first.
Roger that. We are on standby.
BUTCHER SH
He was here. Not long ago.
You **sure** it was him?
It was him.
Think he's still there?
No.
How do you know?
Blood...
What?
Could smell it from upstairs.

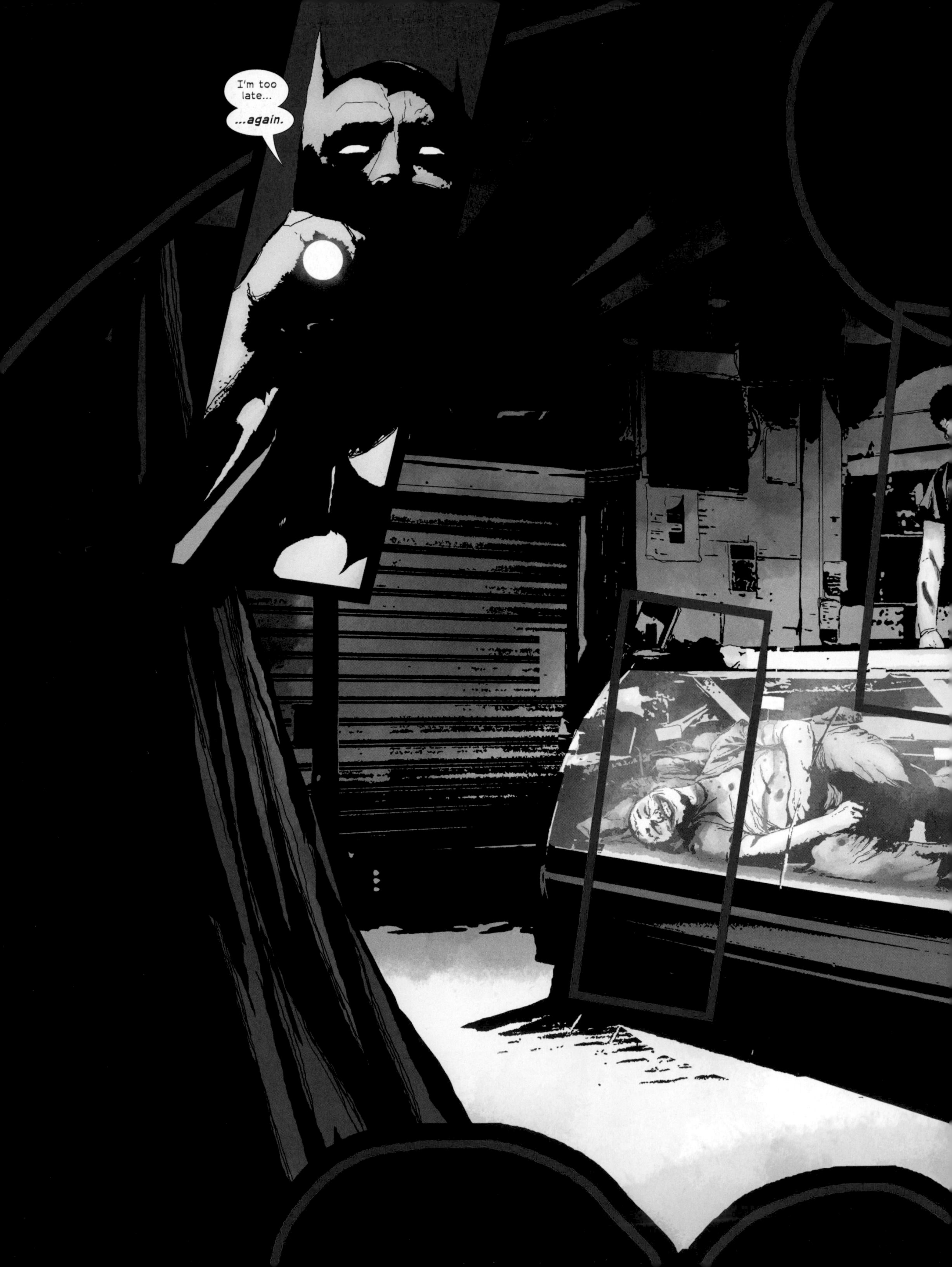
I'm too late...
...again.

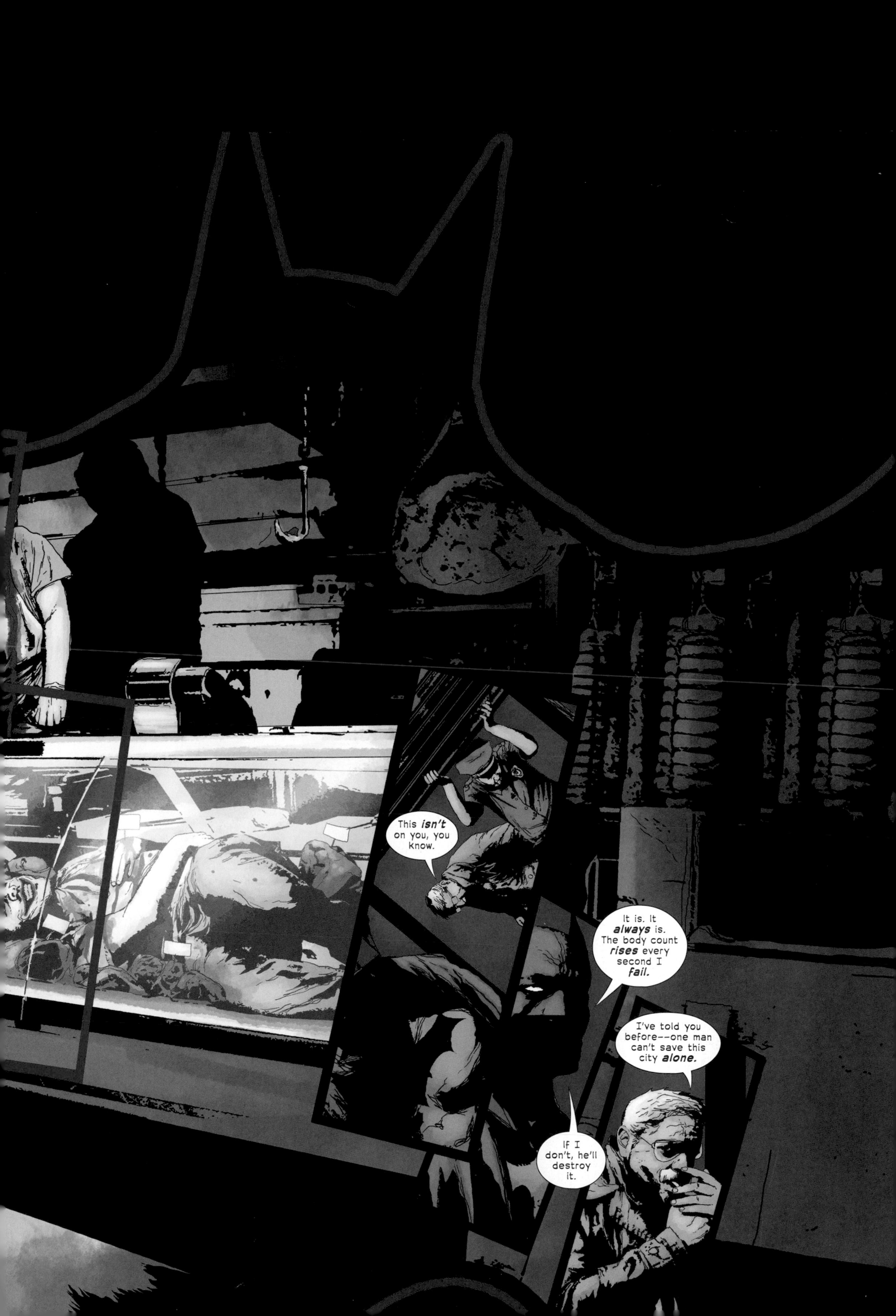
This isn't on you, you know.
It is. It always is. The body count rises every second I fail.
I've told you before--one man can't save this city alone.
If I don't, he'll destroy it.

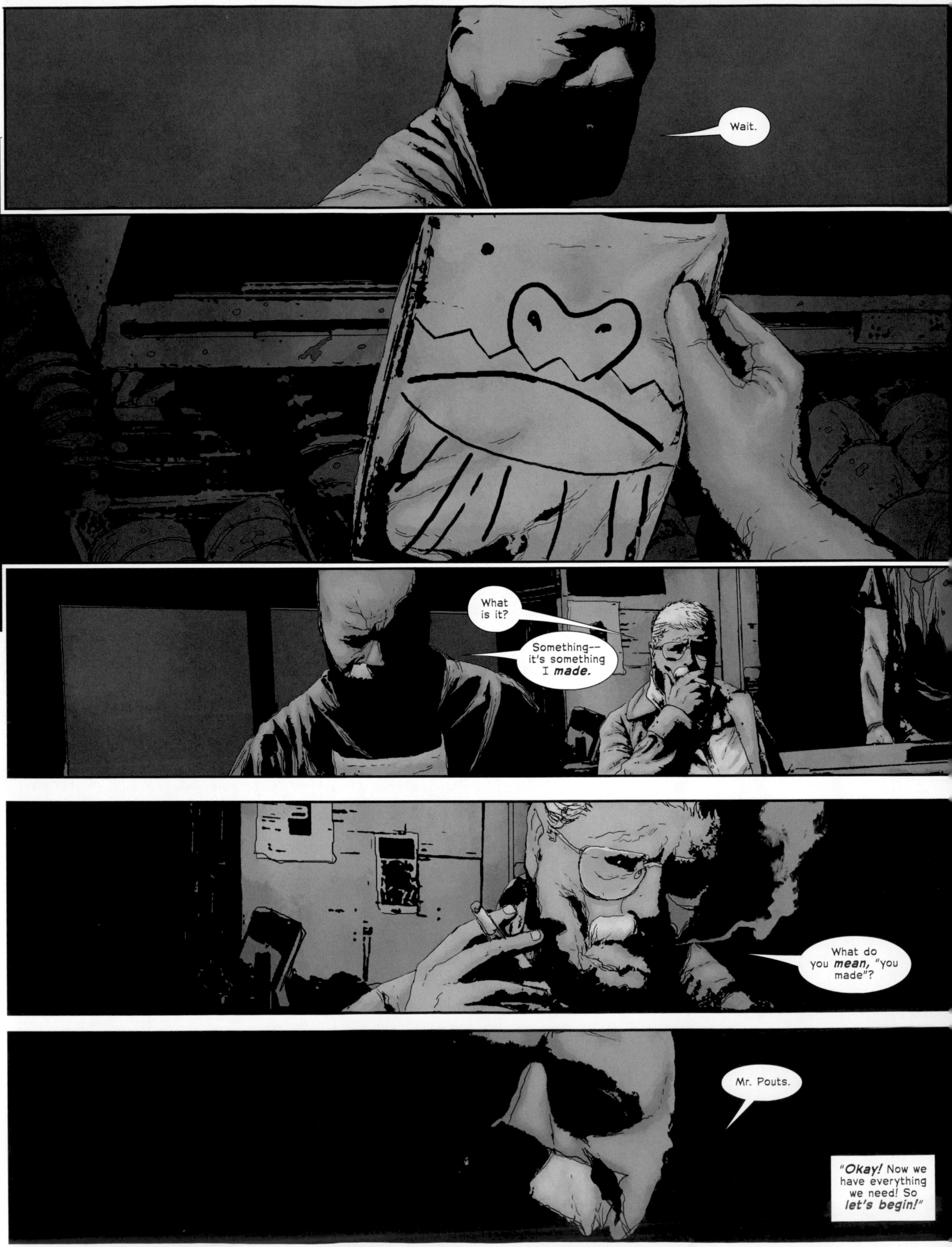

Wait.
What is it?
Something-- it's something I *made.*
What do you *mean,* "you made"?
Mr. Pouts.
"*Okay!* Now we have everything we need! So *let's begin!*"

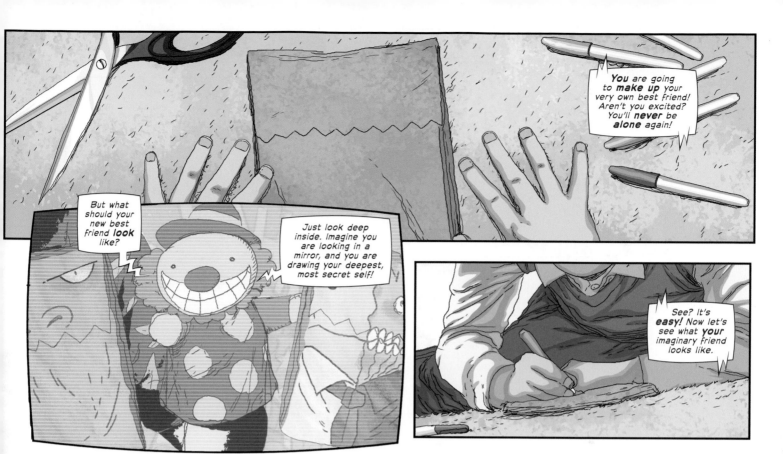

You are going to **make up** your very own best friend! Aren't you excited? You'll **never** be **alone** again!

But what should your new best friend **look** like?

Just look deep inside. Imagine you are looking in a mirror, and you are drawing your deepest, most secret self!

See? It's **easy!** Now let's see what **your** imaginary friend looks like.

Tsk. Now that is **very** disappointing. Why did you draw **that?**

Couldn't help myself.

Well, I'm afraid you are going to need to be **punished**, then. **Isn't** he, Mr. Smiles?

I'm afraid so. You've been a bad, bad boy.

I'm sorry.

And **bad** boys need to learn their **lessons.**

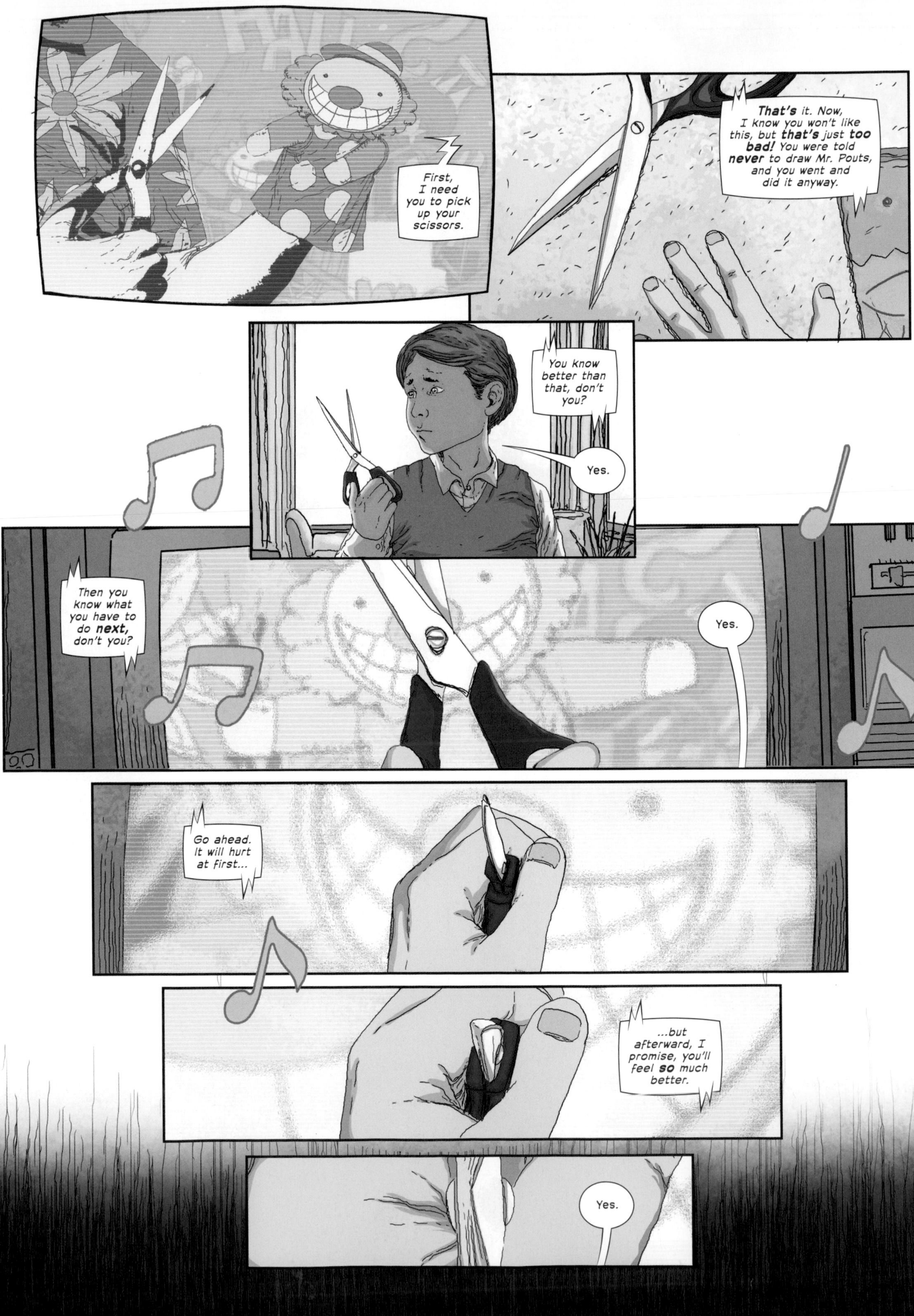
First, I need you to pick up your scissors.
That's it. Now, I know you won't like this, but that's just too bad! You were told never to draw Mr. Pouts, and you went and did it anyway.
You know better than that, don't you?
Yes.
Then you know what you have to do next, don't you?
Yes.
Go ahead. It will hurt at first...
...but afterward, I promise, you'll feel so much better.
Yes.

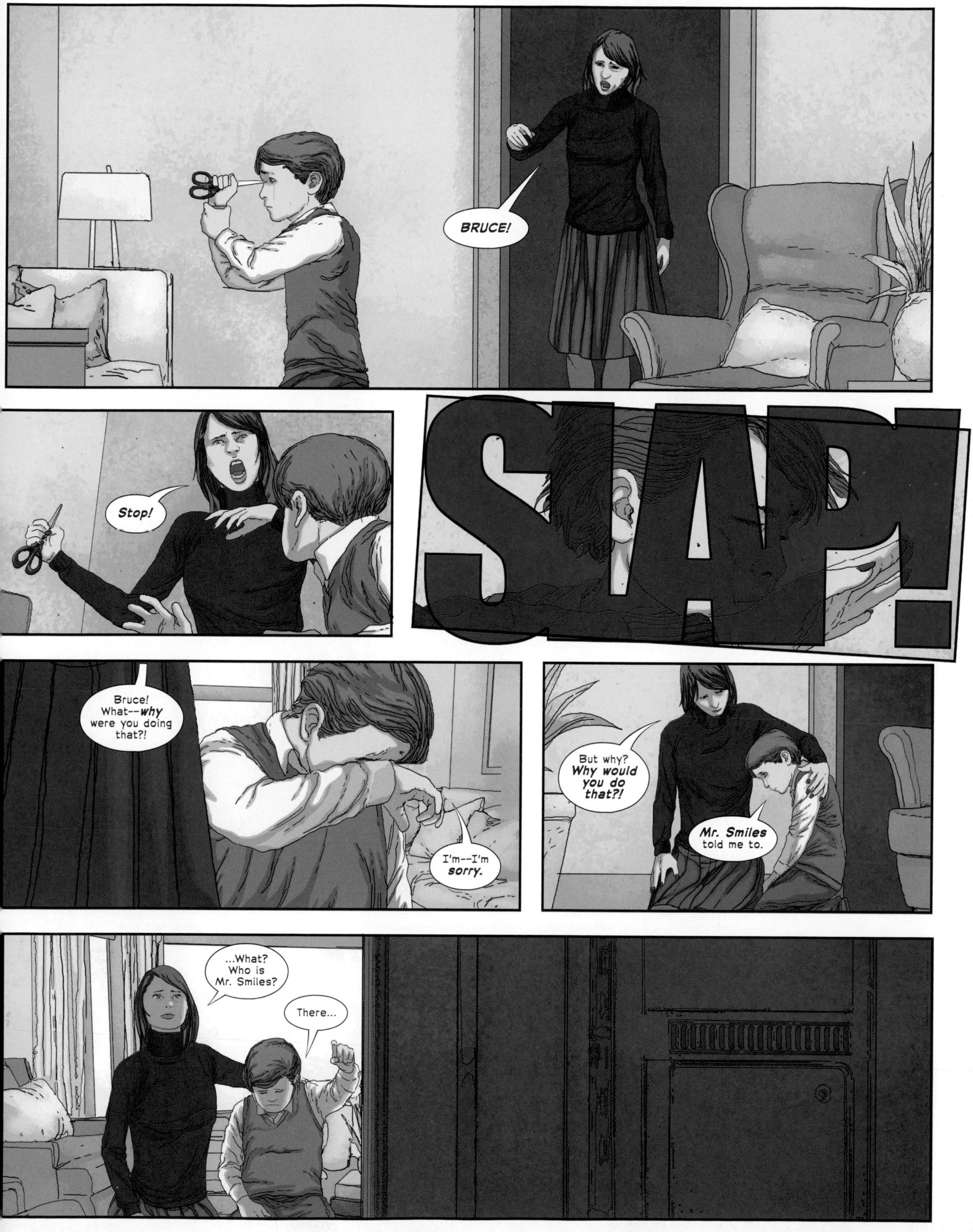
BRUCE!
Stop!
SLAP!
Bruce! What--why were you doing that?!
I'm--I'm sorry.
But why? Why would you do that?!
Mr. Smiles told me to.
...What? Who is Mr. Smiles?
There...

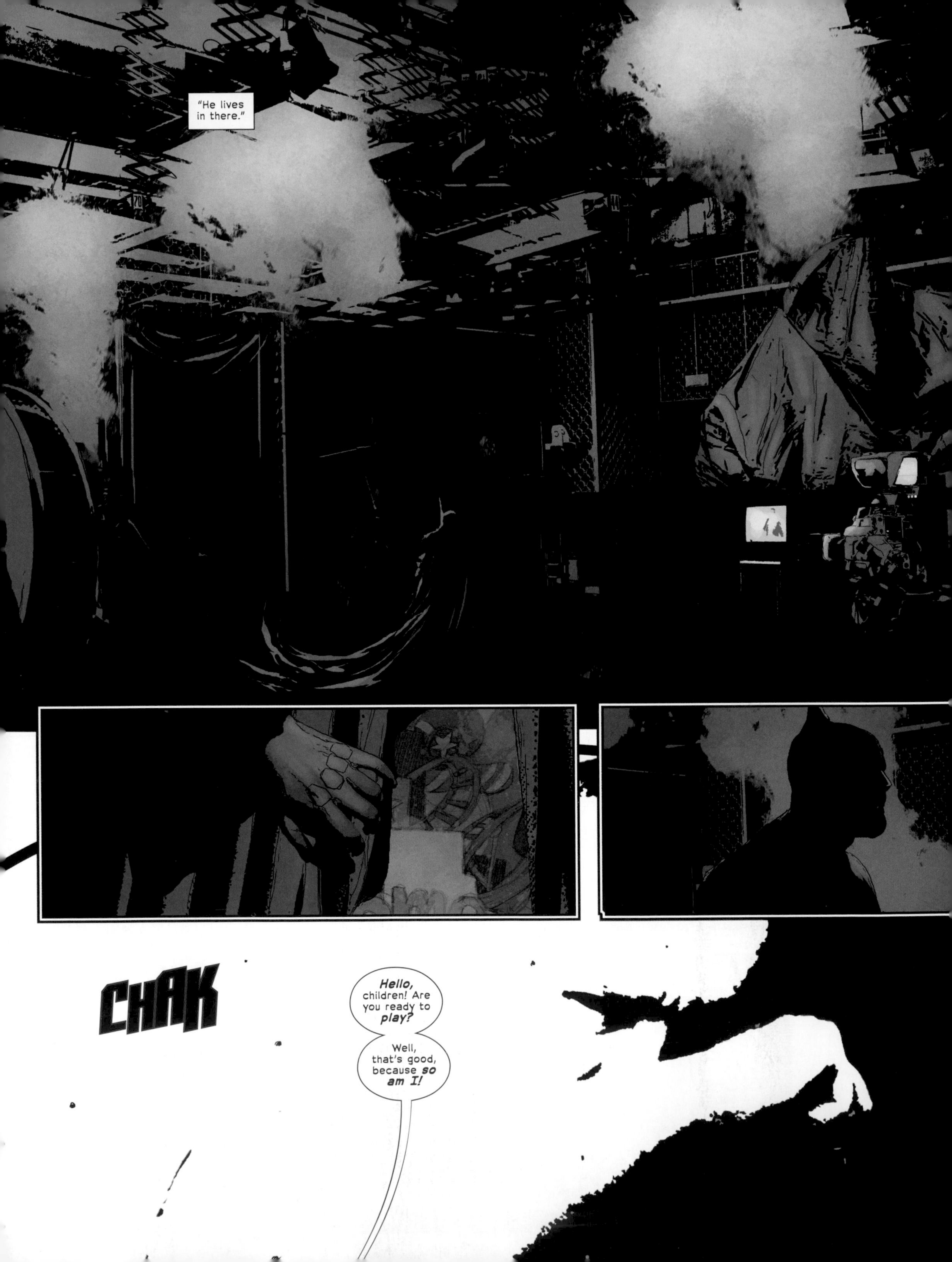
"He lives in there."
CHAK
Hello, children! Are you ready to play?
Well, that's good, because so am I!

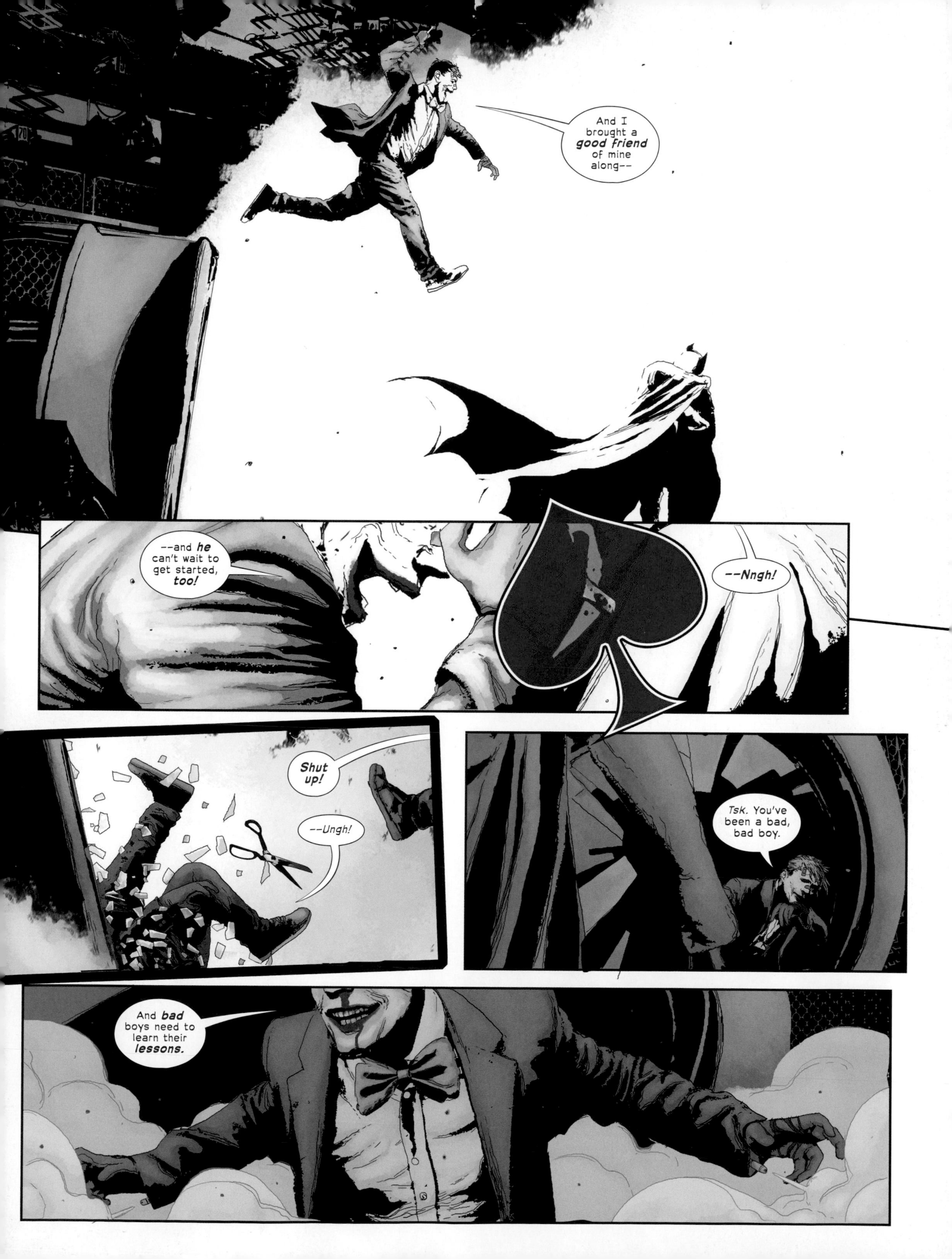
And I brought a good friend of mine along--
--and he can't wait to get started, too!
--Nngh!
Shut up!
--Ungh!
Tsk. You've been a bad, bad boy.
And bad boys need to learn their lessons.

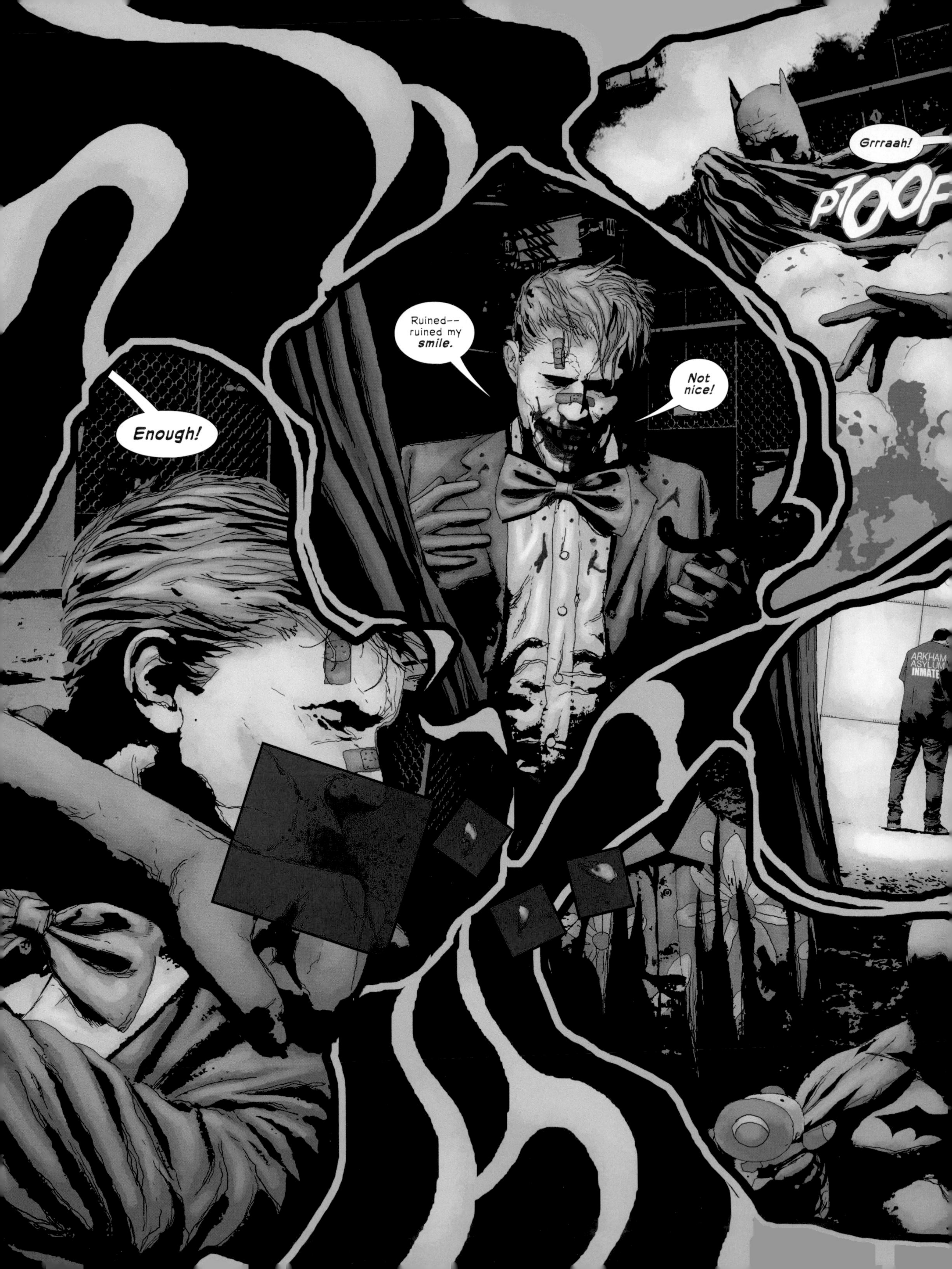
Grrraah!
PTOOF
Ruined--
ruined my
smile.
Not
nice!
Enough!
ARKHAM
ASYLUM
INMATE

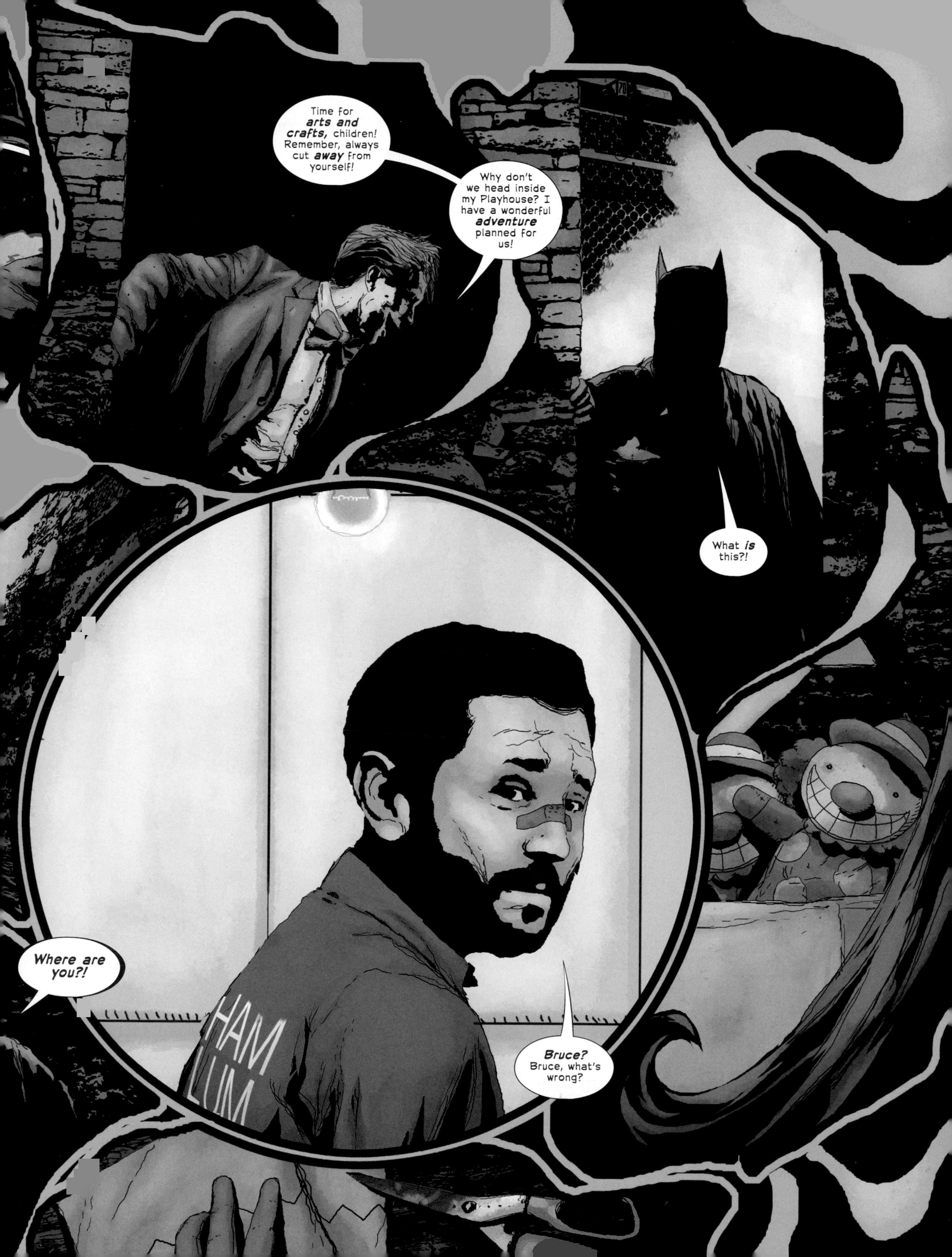
Time for *arts and crafts,* children! Remember, always cut *away* from yourself!
Why don't we head inside my Playhouse? I have a wonderful *adventure* planned for us!
What *is* this?!
Where are you?!
Bruce? Bruce, what's wrong?
HAM
UM

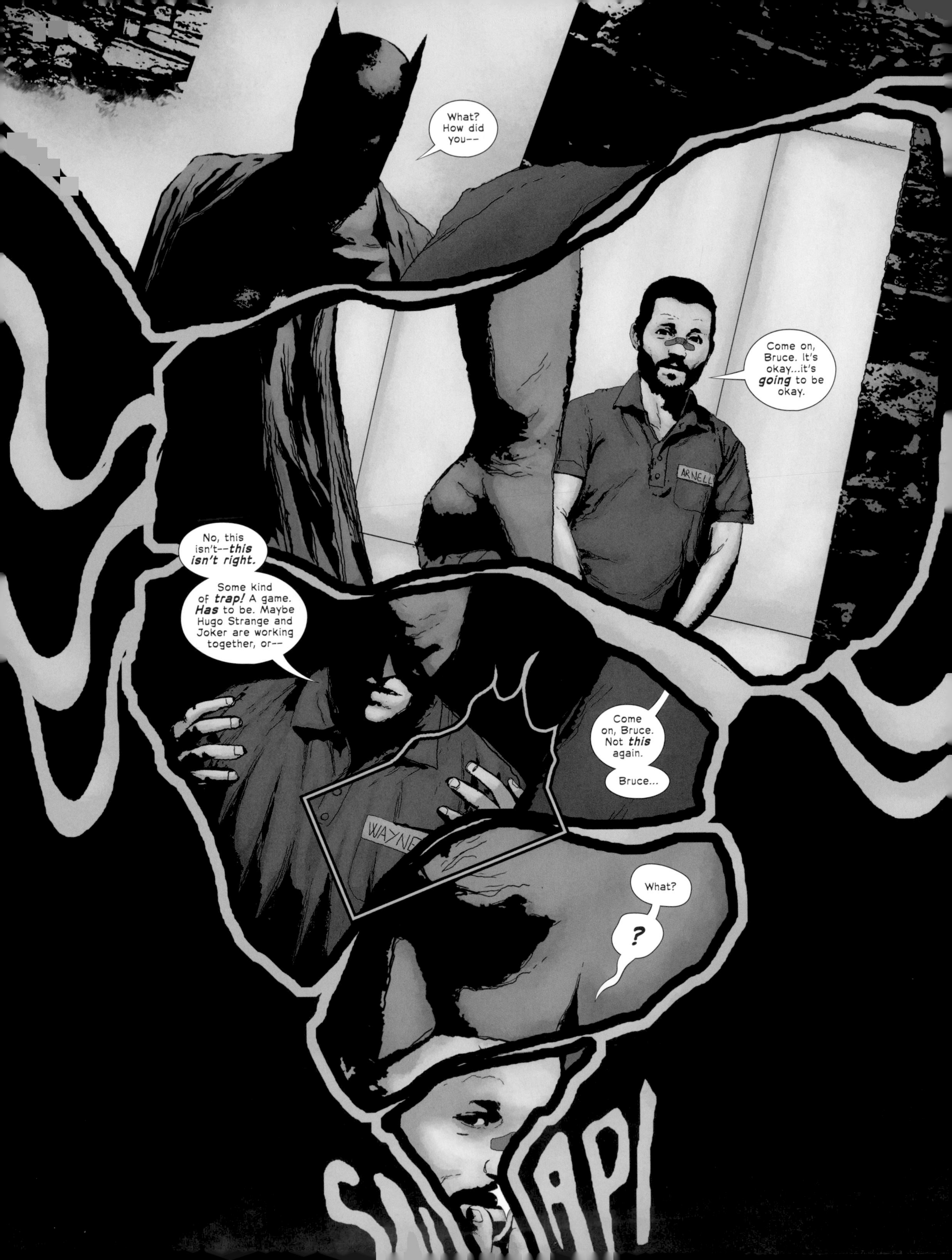
What? How did you--
Come on, Bruce. It's okay...it's going to be okay.
ARNELL
No, this isn't--this isn't right.
Some kind of trap! A game. Has to be. Maybe Hugo Strange and Joker are working together, or--
Come on, Bruce. Not this again.
Bruce...
WAYNE
What?
?

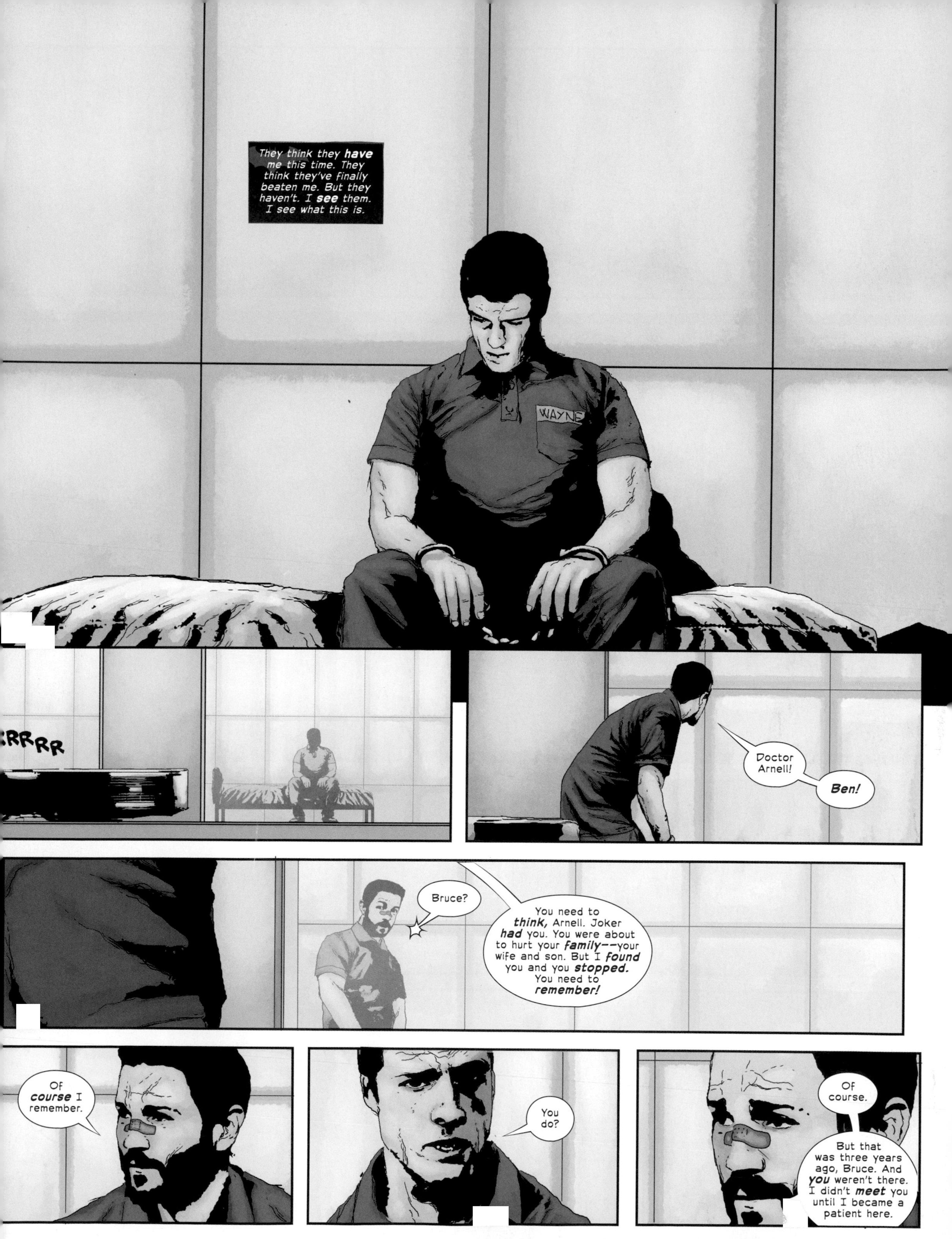

They think they **have** me this time. They think they've finally beaten me. But they haven't. I **see** them. I see what this is.
WAYNE
RRRRR
Doctor Arnell!
Ben!
Bruce?
You need to **think,** Arnell. Joker **had** you. You were about to hurt your **family**--your wife and son. But I **found** you and you **stopped.** You need to **remember!**
Of **course** I remember.
You do?
Of course.
But that was three years ago, Bruce. And **you** weren't there. I didn't **meet** you until I became a patient here.

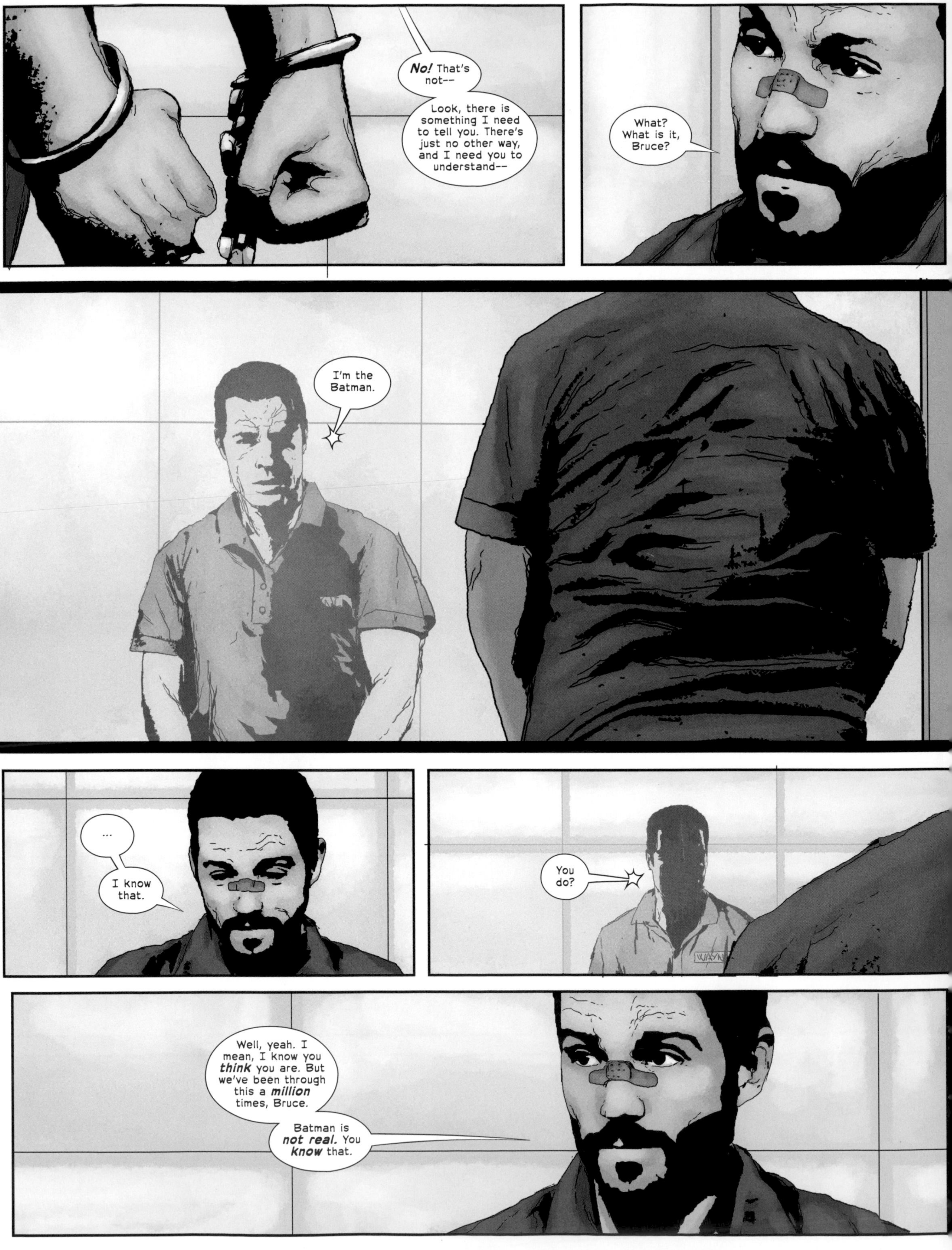

No! That's not--
Look, there is something I need to tell you. There's just no other way, and I need you to understand--
What? What is it, Bruce?
I'm the Batman.
...
I know that.
You do?
Well, yeah. I mean, I know you think you are. But we've been through this a million times, Bruce.
Batman is not real. You know that.

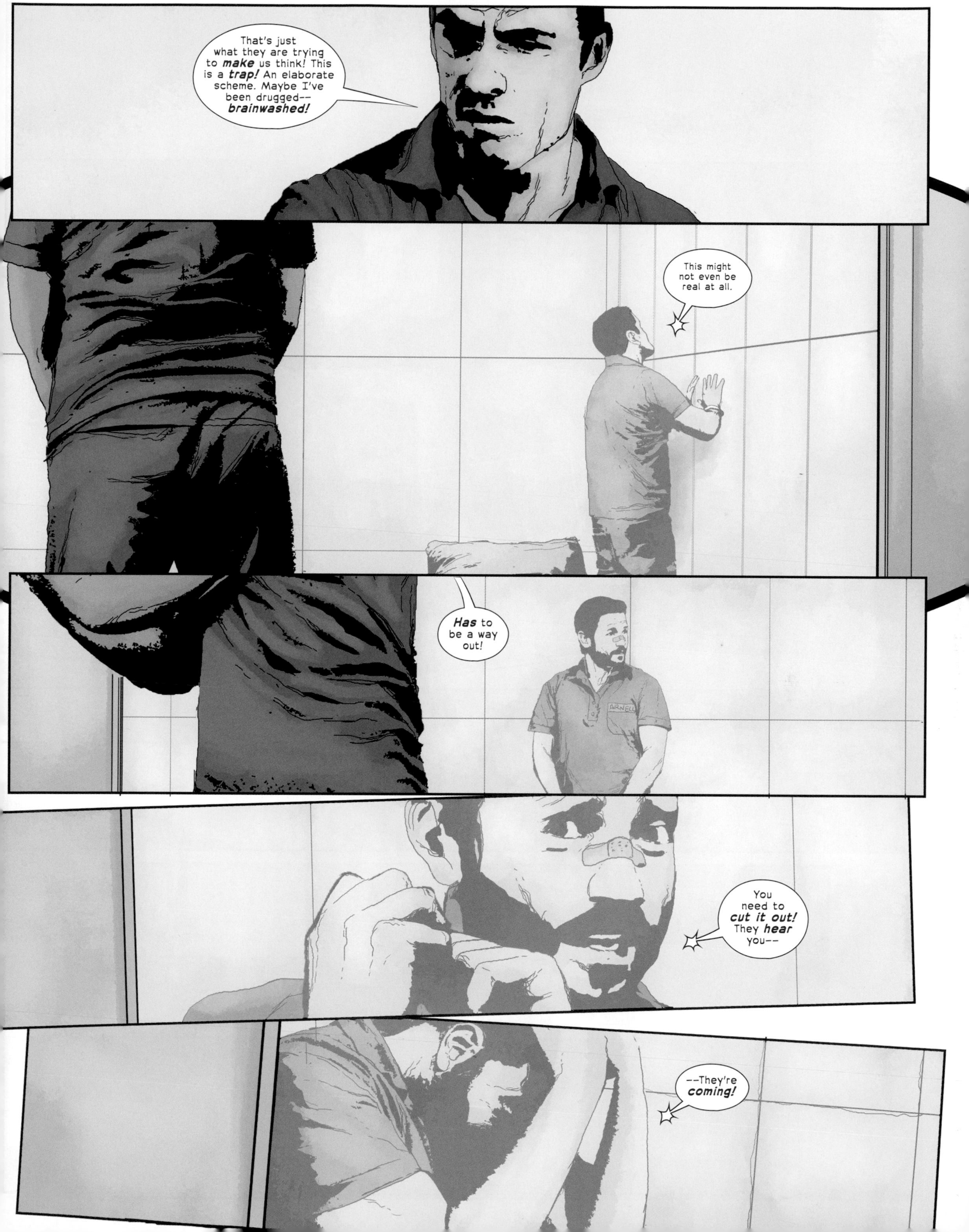
That's just what they are trying to *make* us think! This is a *trap!* An elaborate scheme. Maybe I've been drugged-- *brainwashed!*
This might not even be real at all.
Has to be a way out!
ARNELL
You need to *cut it out!* They *hear* you--
--They're *coming!*

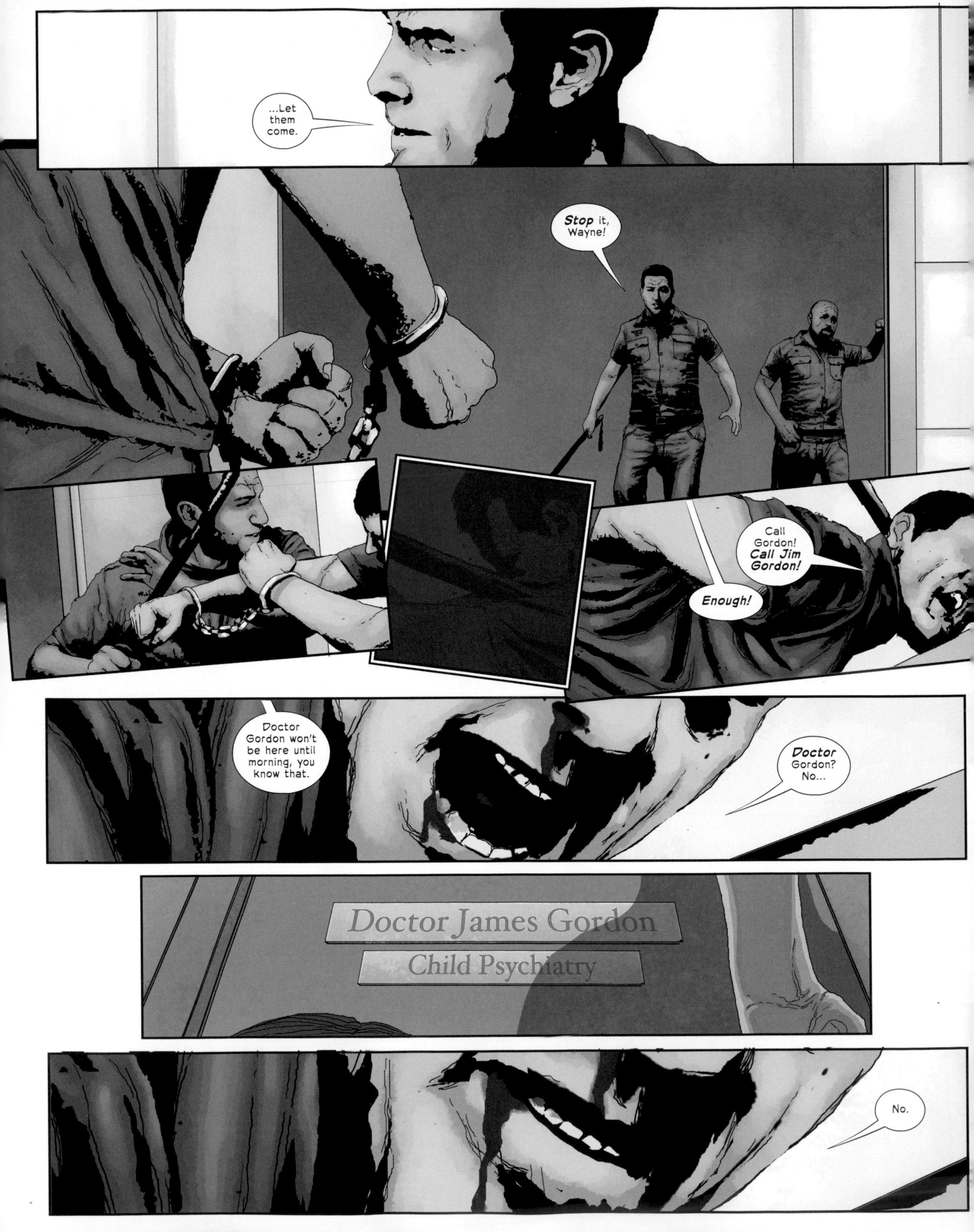
...Let them come.
Stop it, Wayne!
Call Gordon! Call Jim Gordon!
Enough!
Doctor Gordon won't be here until morning, you know that.
Doctor Gordon? No...
Doctor James Gordon
Child Psychiatry
No.

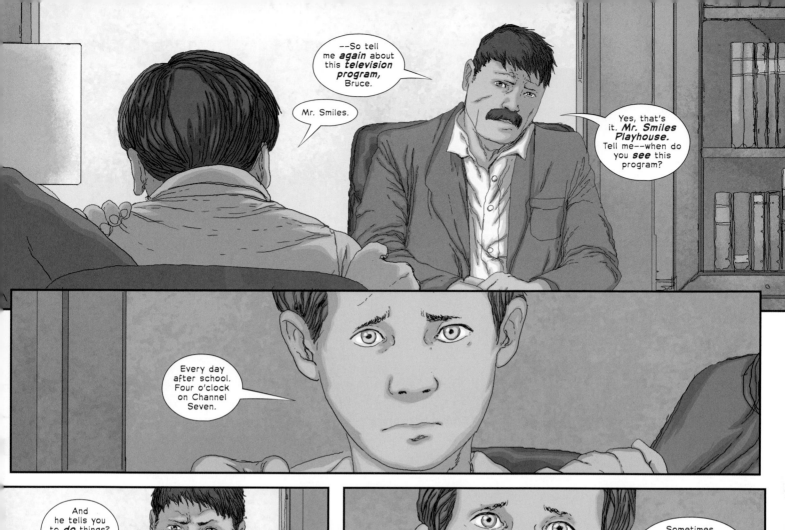

--So tell me *again* about this *television program*, Bruce.

Mr. Smiles.

Yes, that's it. *Mr. Smiles Playhouse.* Tell me--when do you *see* this program?

Every day after school. Four o'clock on Channel Seven.

And he tells you to *do* things? This--this puppet?

Sometimes. Sometimes he tells *stories.* Sometimes he shows me how to do *crafts.*

Stories? What *kind* of stories, Bruce?

...Bad ones.

What makes them bad?

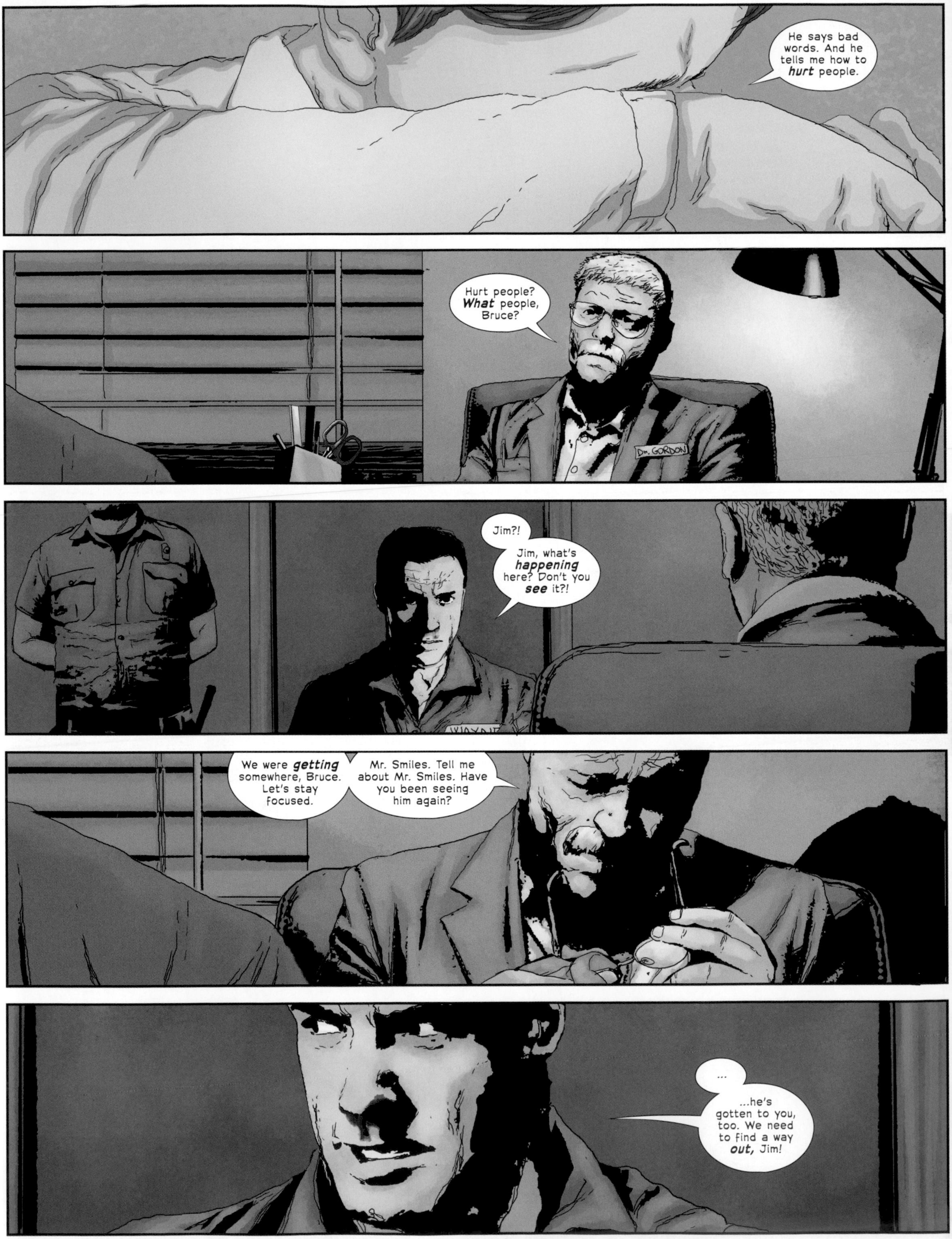
He says bad words. And he tells me how to **hurt** people.
Hurt people? **What** people, Bruce?
Dr. GORDON
Jim?!
Jim, what's **happening** here? Don't you **see** it?!
We were **getting** somewhere, Bruce. Let's stay focused.
Mr. Smiles. Tell me about Mr. Smiles. Have you been seeing him again?
...
...he's gotten to you, too. We need to find a way **out,** Jim!

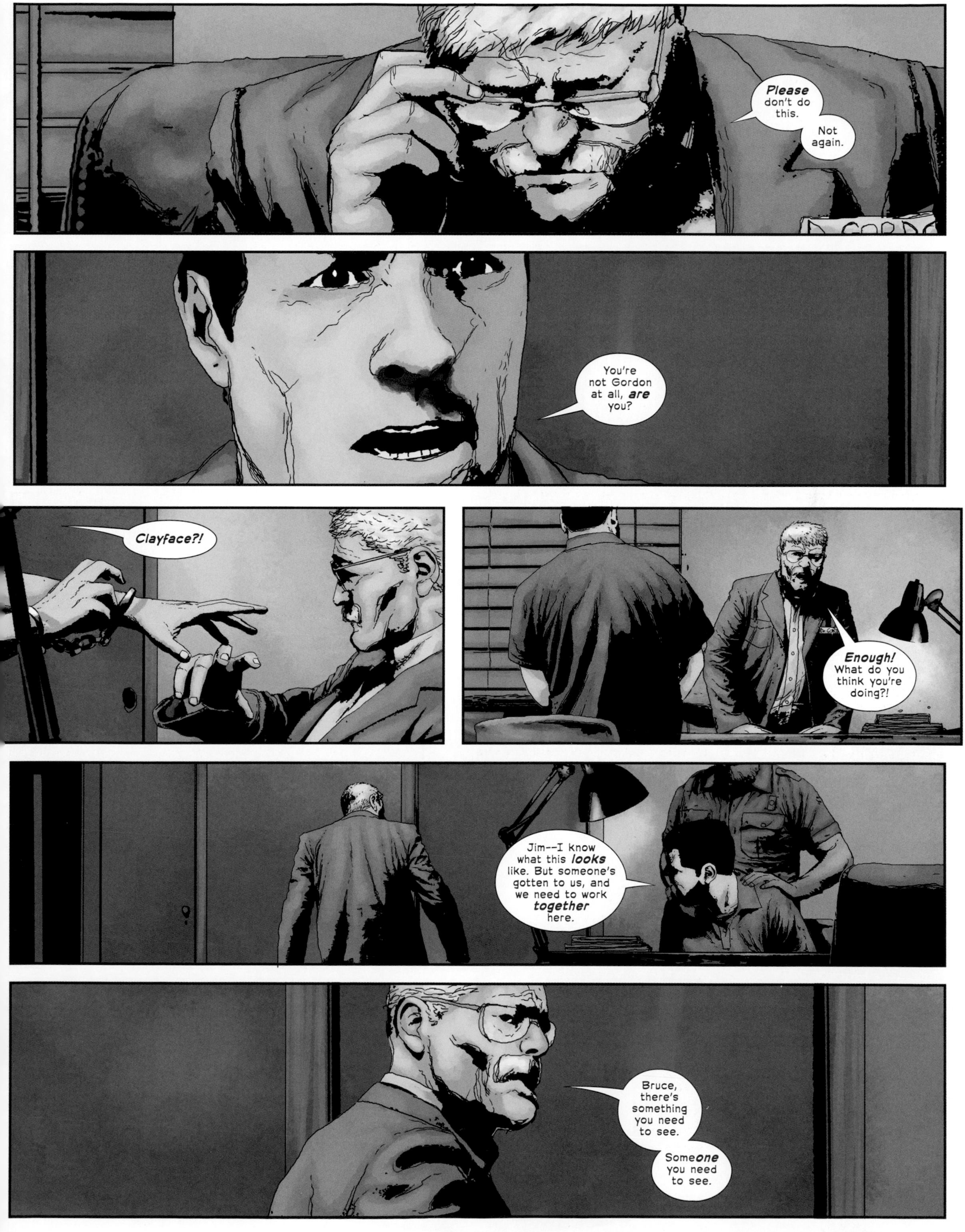
Please don't do this.
Not again.
You're not Gordon at all, are you?
Clayface?!
Enough! What do you think you're doing?!
Jim--I know what this looks like. But someone's gotten to us, and we need to work together here.
Bruce, there's something you need to see.
Someone you need to see.

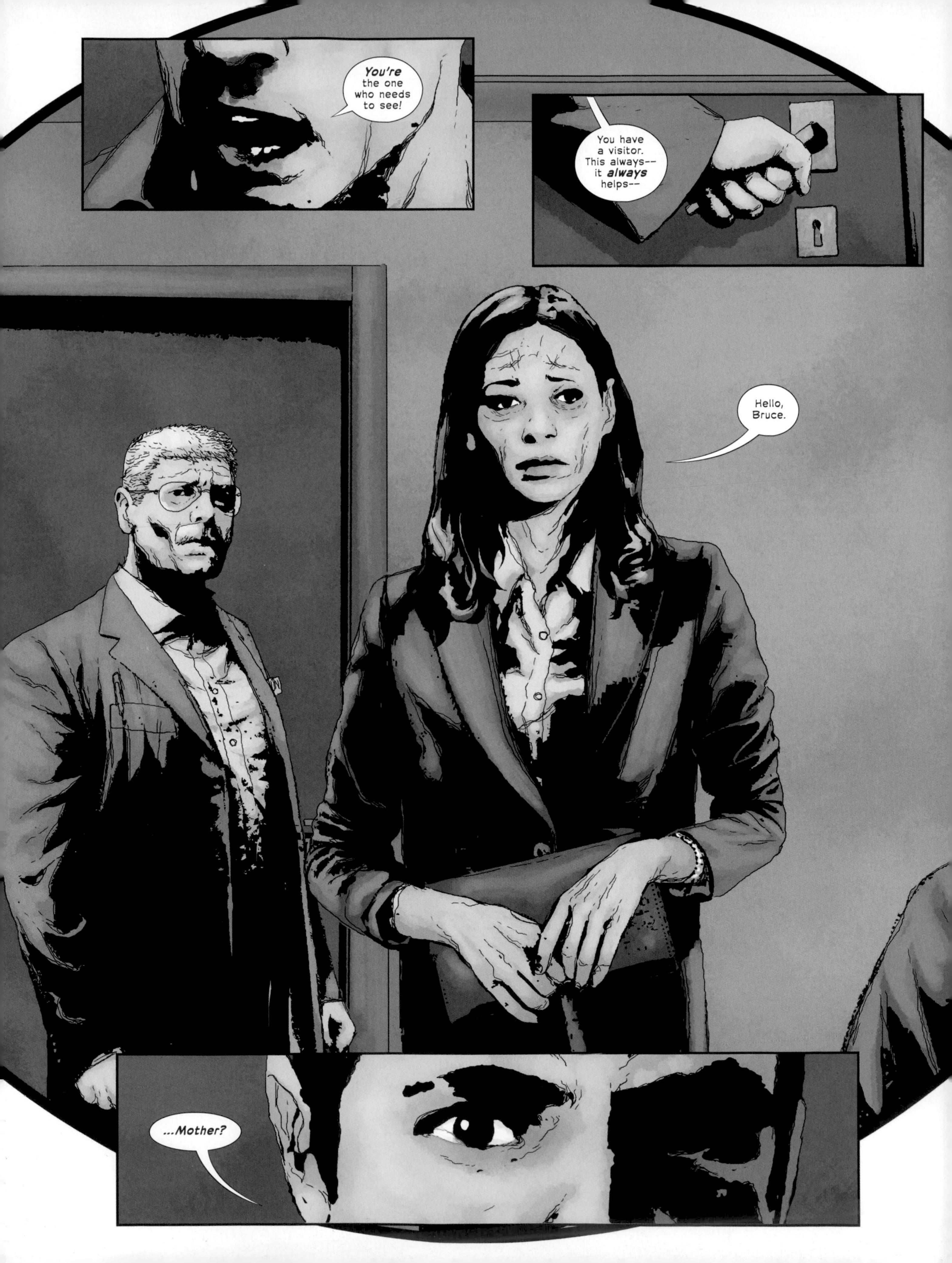
You're the one who needs to see!
You have a visitor. This always-- it ***always*** helps--
Hello, Bruce.
...*Mother?*

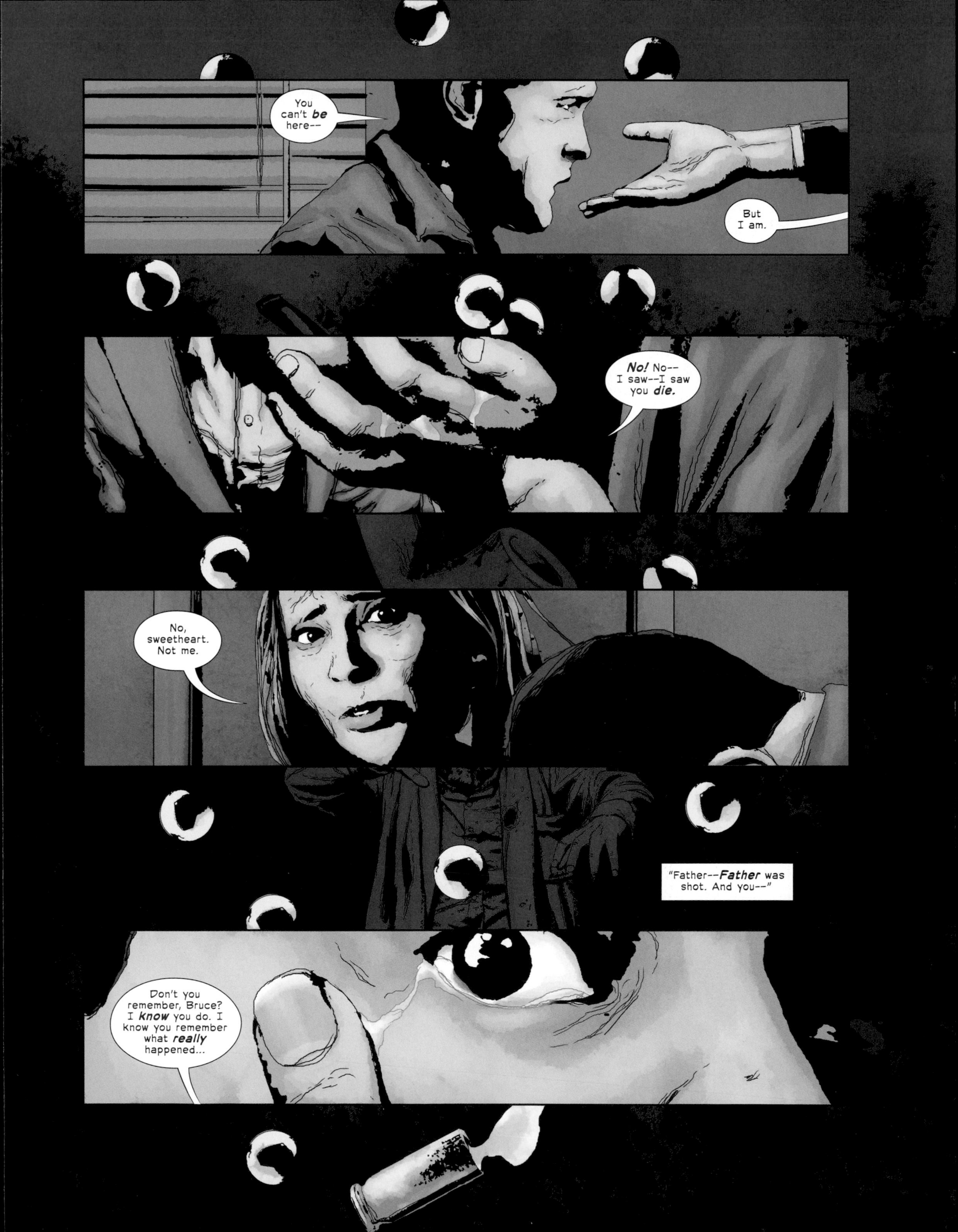
You can't **be** here--
But I am.
No! No-- I saw--I saw you **die.**
No, sweetheart. Not me.
"Father--**Father** was shot. And you--"
Don't you remember, Bruce? I **know** you do. I know you remember what **really** happened...

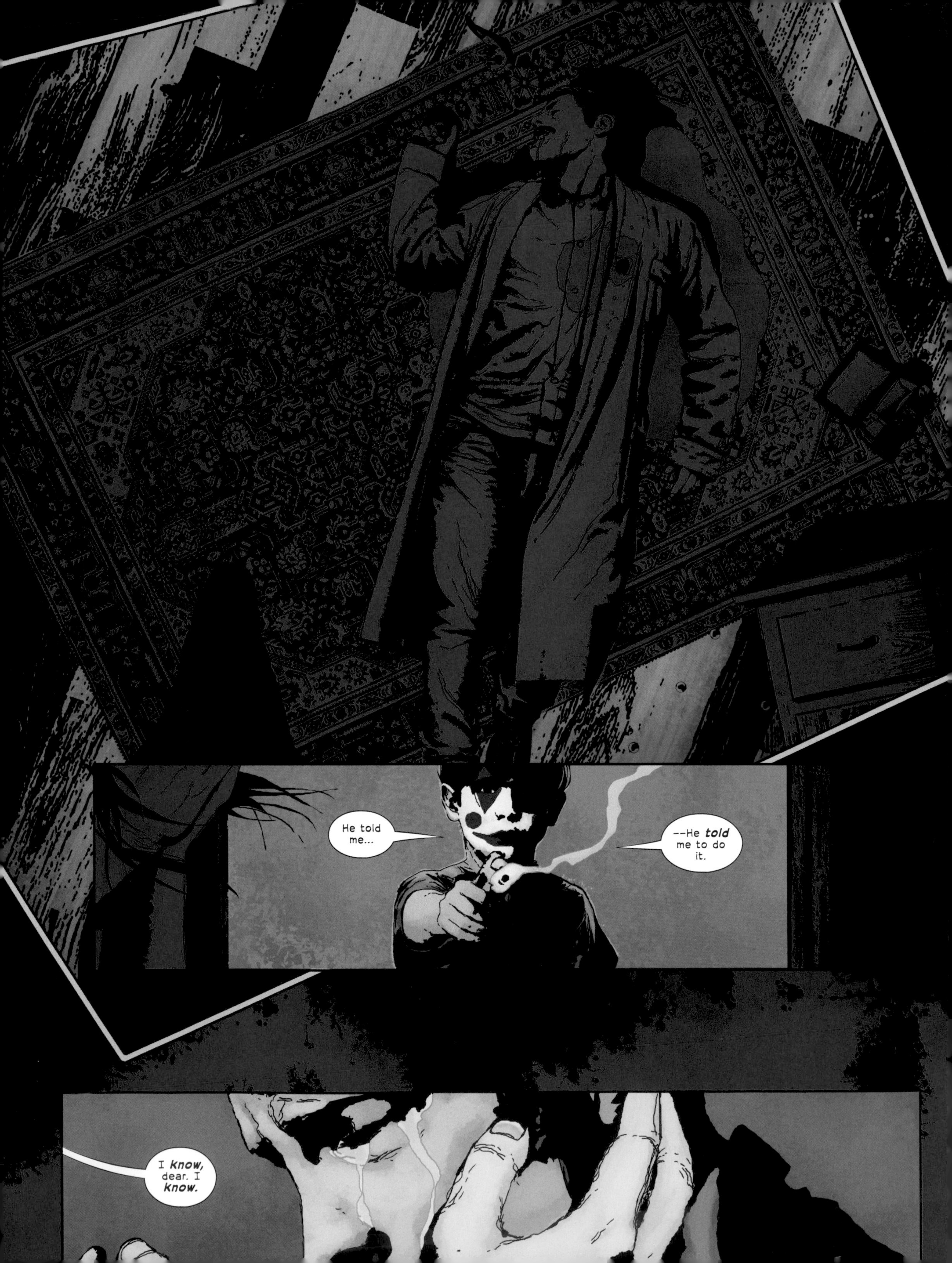
He told me...
--He *told* me to do it.
I *know,* dear. I *know.*

My mother leaves and again I am alone.

Night falls. This is my time. It--it **should** be my time.

I **know** it was real--Joker's escape. The old TV studio. I know it was real. **Wasn't it?**

But why would that old soundstage still be set up **thirty years** after the show went off the air? Unless--**no.** No, don't doubt. **Never** doubt.

I know the truth. I can never waver from my **mission.**

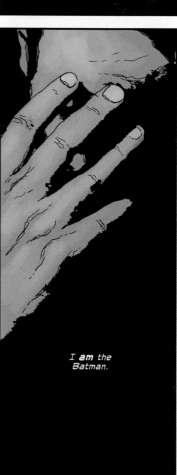

I **am** the Batman.

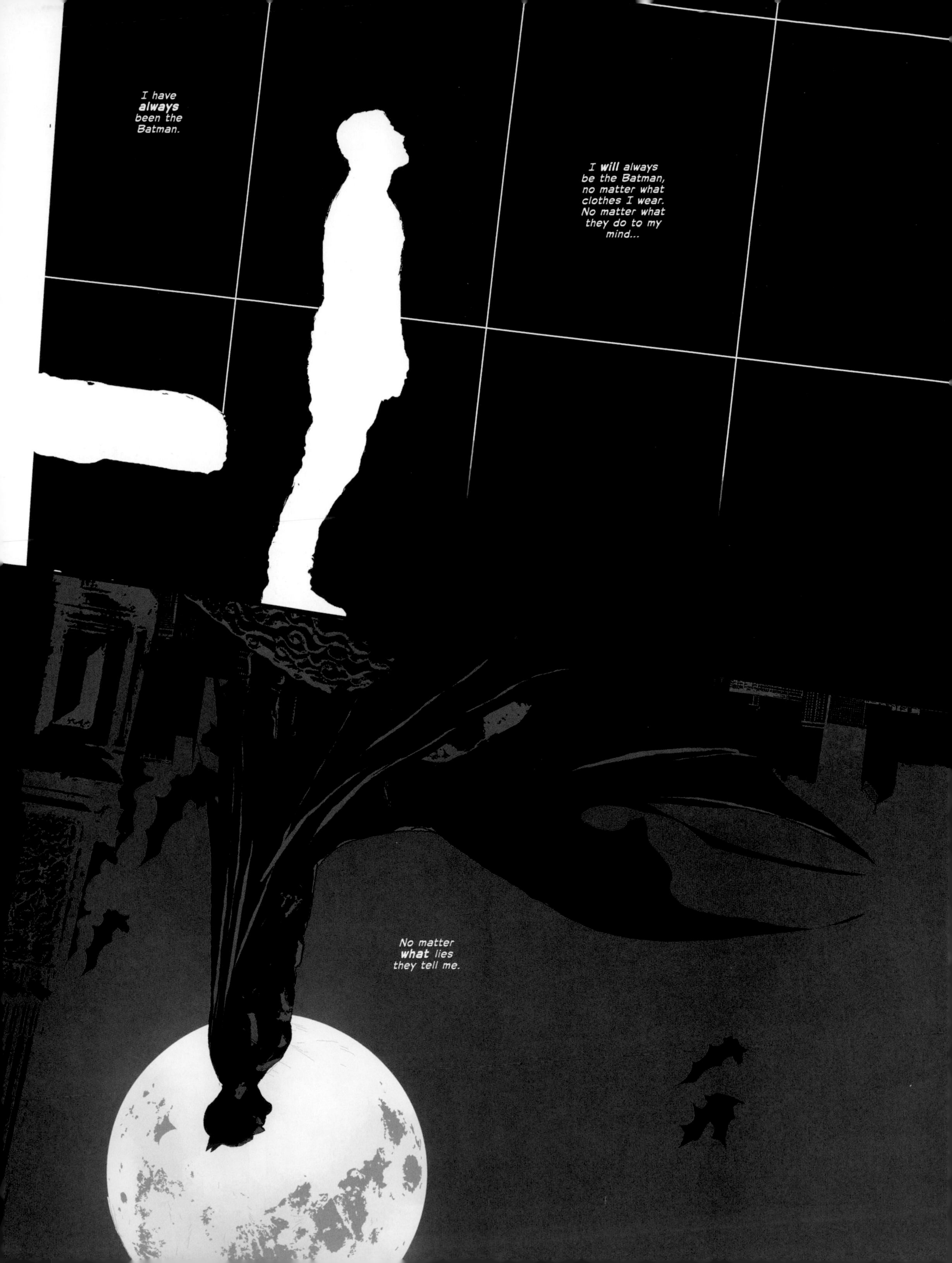
I have always been the Batman.
I will always be the Batman, no matter what clothes I wear. No matter what they do to my mind...
No matter what lies they tell me.

Arnell!

Bruce-- it's late.

I need you to listen to me. This--this whole thing. It's *very* convincing.

I--I'm not sure anymore, Ben. For the first time in my life, I'm not *sure* what to do...

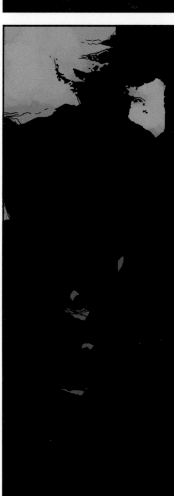

If they're threatening your family or listening-- if you *know* some-thing--if this really is a trap of some kind--

--I just need you to give me a sign--*any* sign--and I *swear* I will find a way to *get us out of here.*

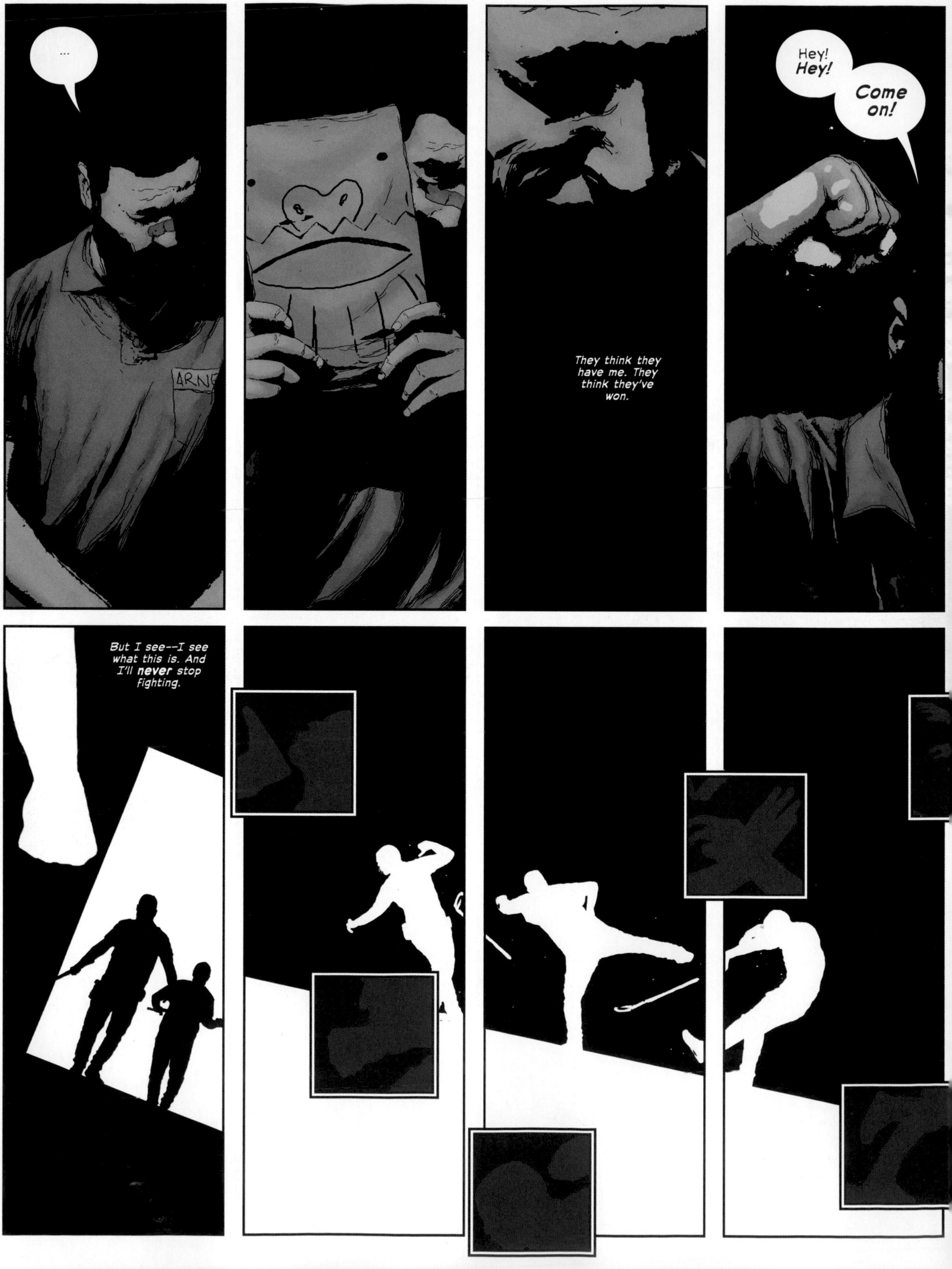
...
ARNE
They think they have me. They think they've won.
Hey! **Hey!**
Come on!
But I see--I see what this is. And I'll **never** stop fighting.

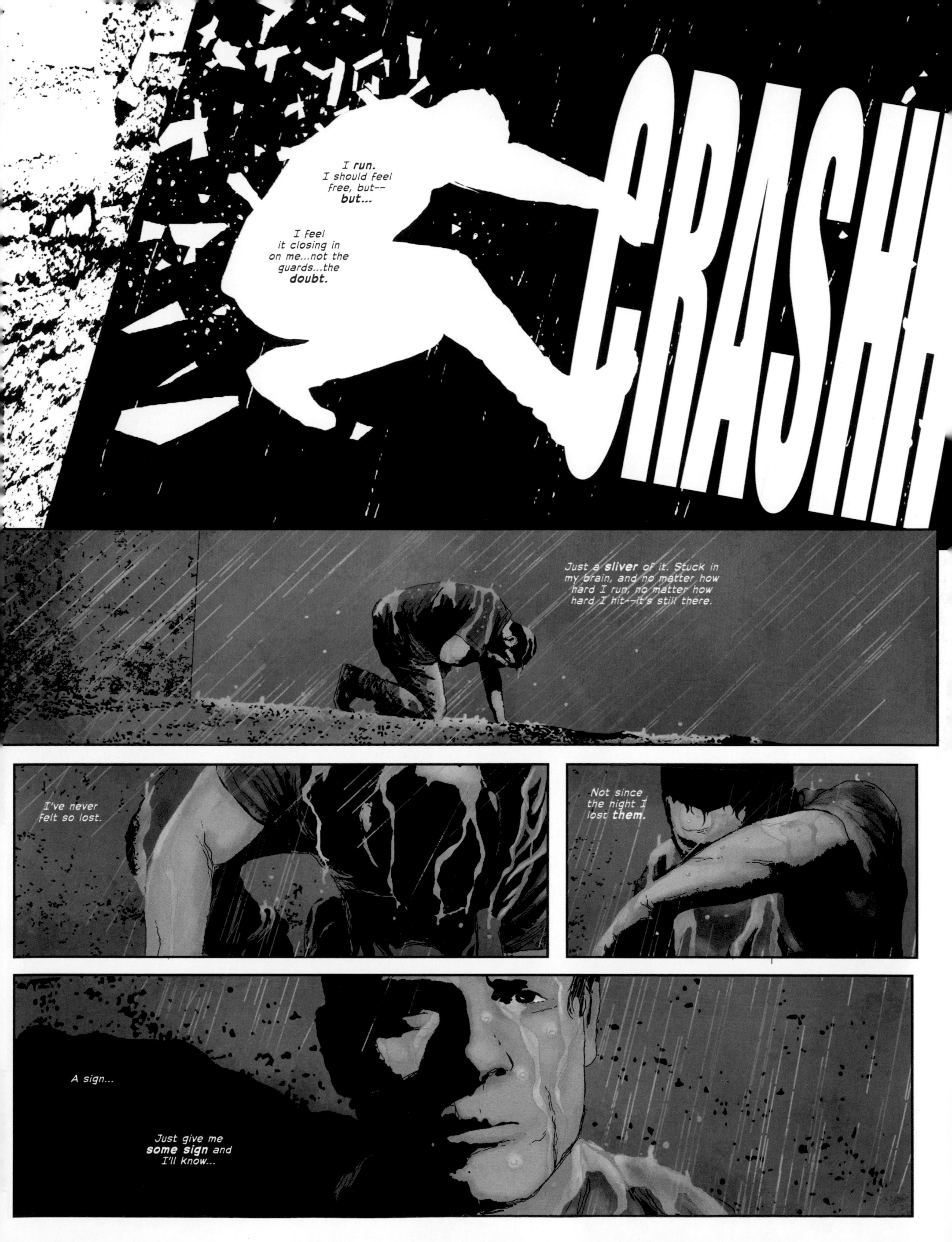

I **run.** I should feel free, but-- **but...**
I feel it closing in on me...not the guards...the **doubt.**
CRASH!
Just a **sliver** of it. Stuck in my brain, and no matter how hard I run, no matter how hard I hit--it's still there.
I've never felt so lost.
Not since the night I lost **them.**
A sign...
Just give me **some sign** and I'll know...

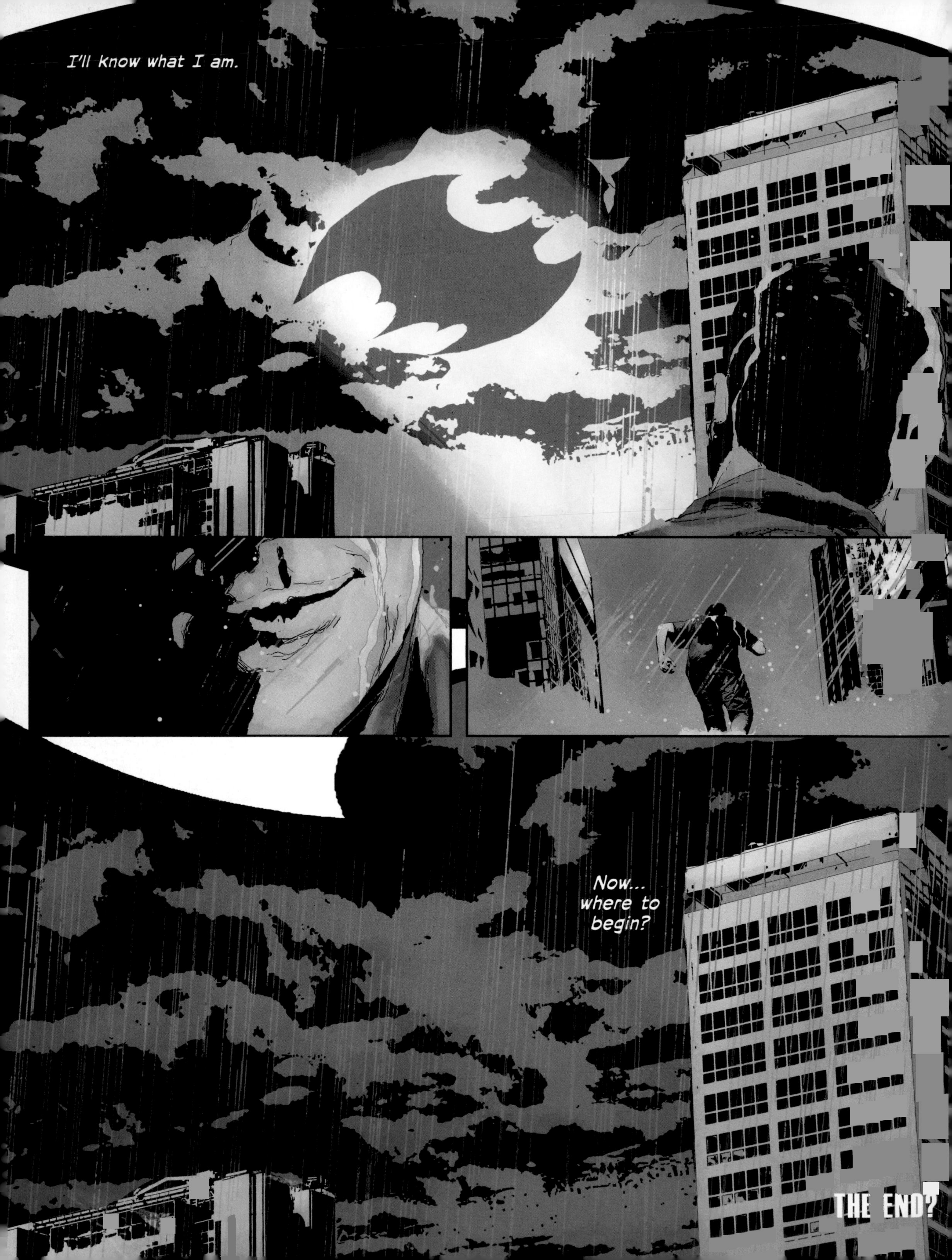
I'll know what I am.
Now... where to begin?
THE END?

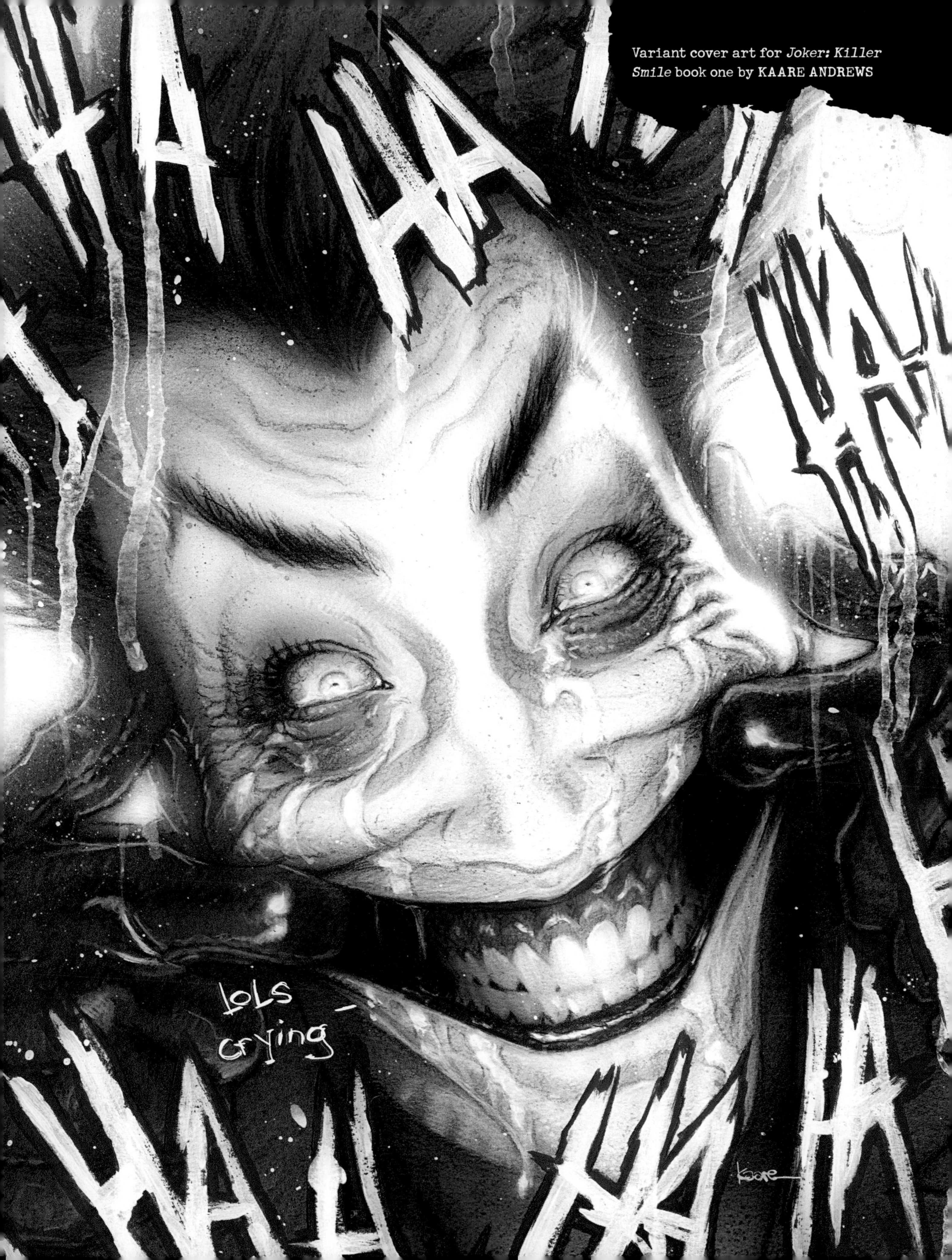
HA HA
lols
crying
kaare

Variant cover art for *Joker: Killer Smile* book one by **KAARE ANDREWS**

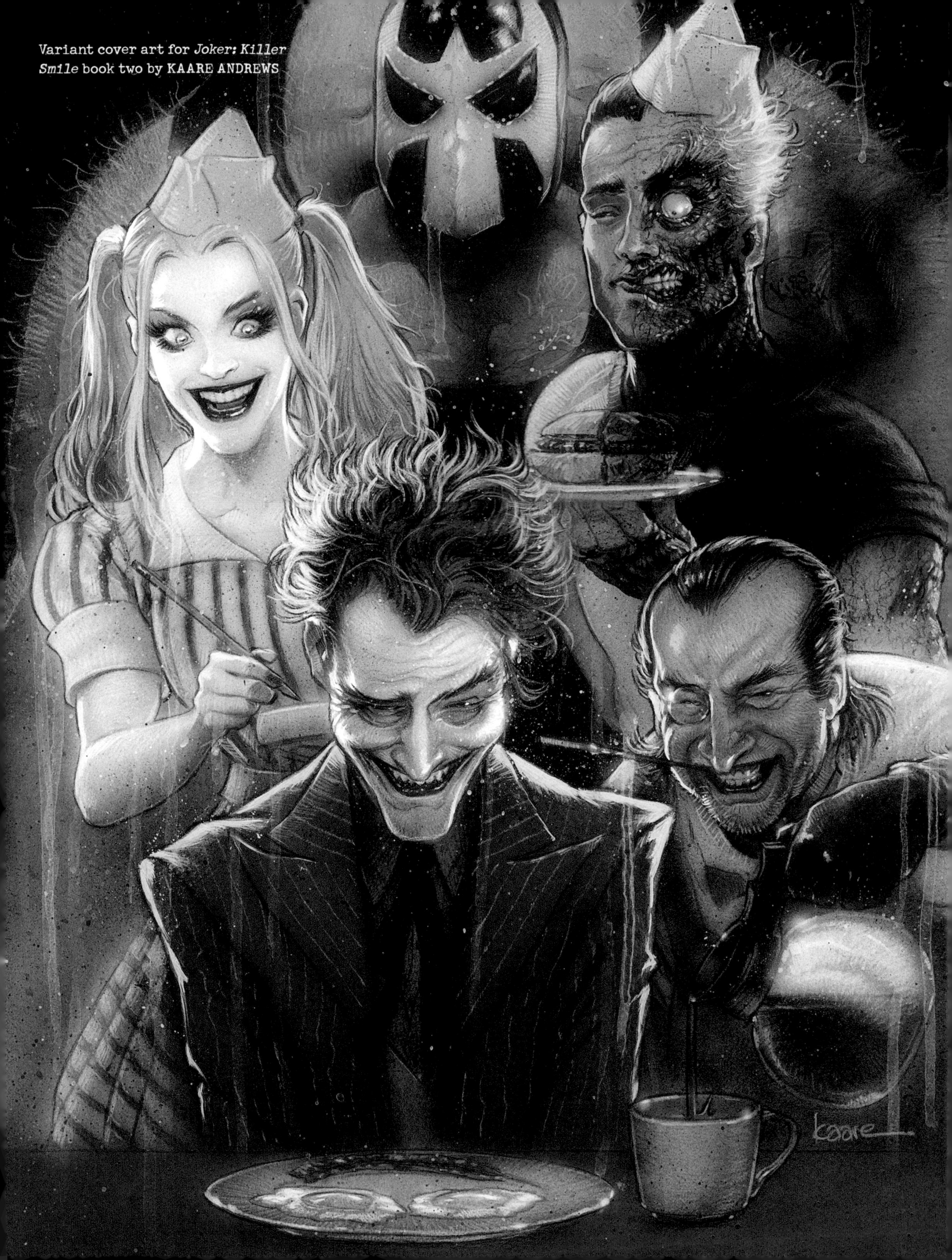
kaare

Variant cover art for *Joker: Killer Smile* book two by KAARE ANDREWS

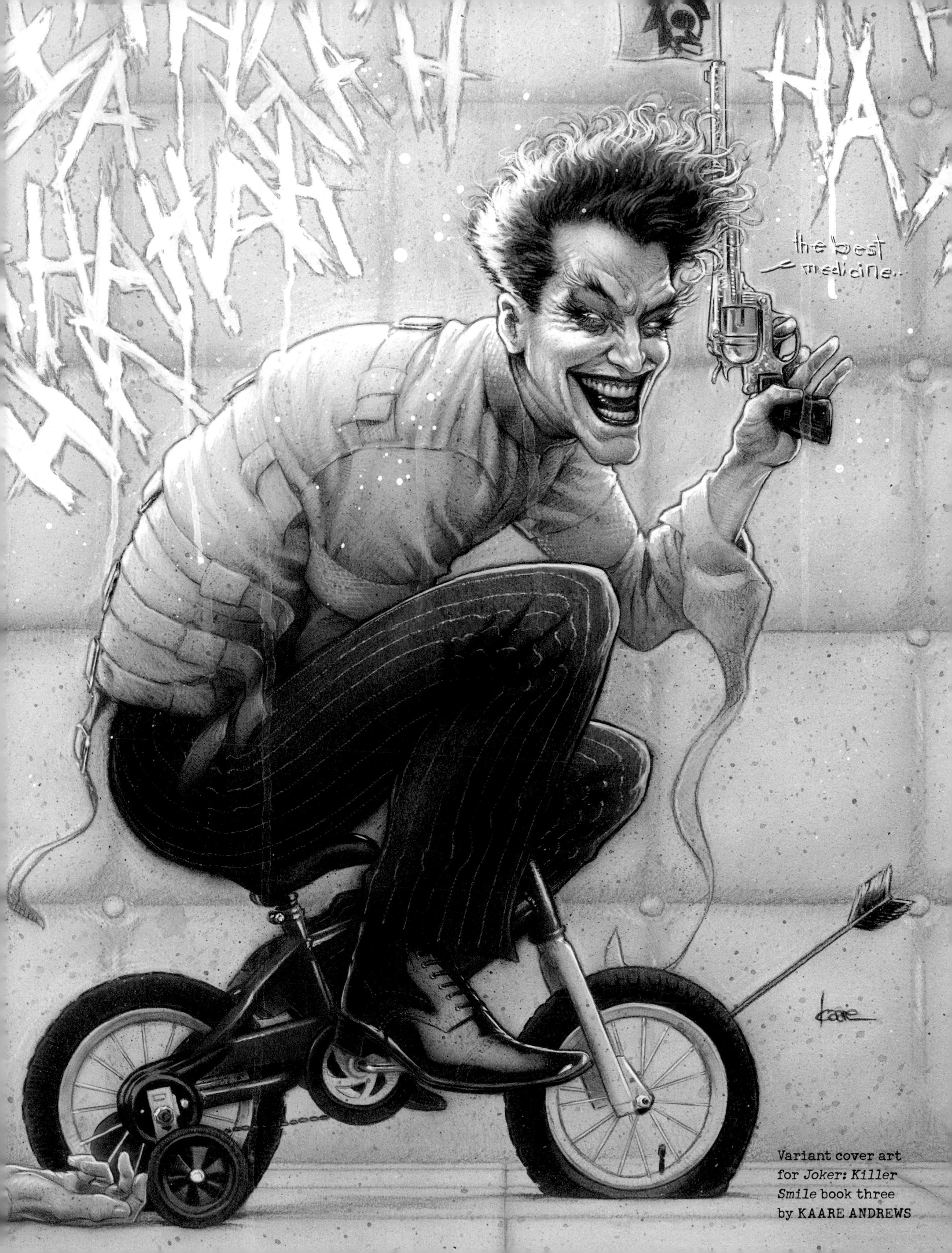
the best medicine...

Variant cover art for *Joker: Killer Smile* book three by KAARE ANDREWS

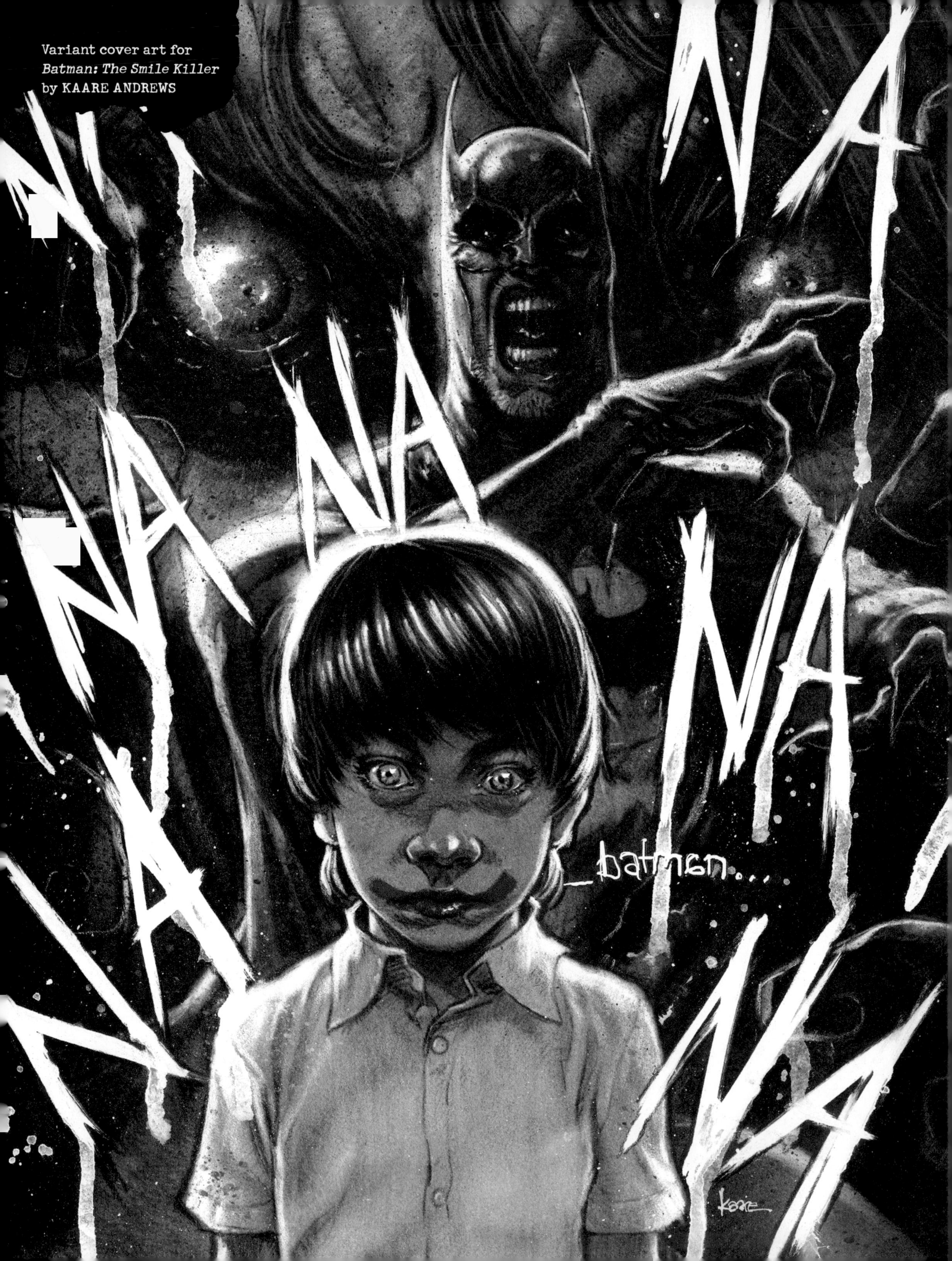
NA
NA
NA
NA
NA
NA
NA
NA
batman...
kaare

Variant cover art for
Batman: The Smile Killer
by KAARE ANDREWS

LIPSTICK TRACES
DEVELOPMENT ART BY ANDREA SORRENTINO

Promotional art for book three

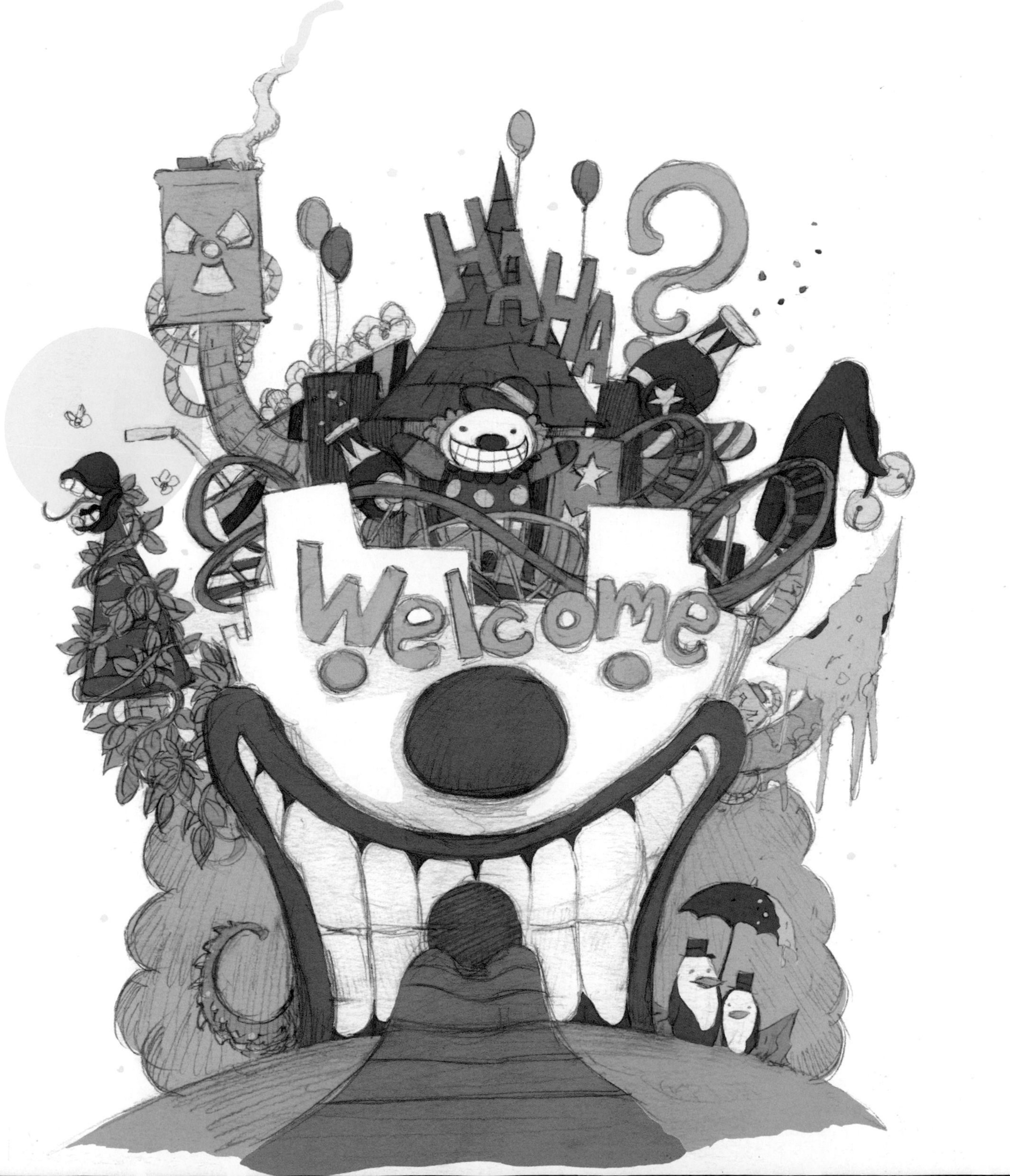

HAHA
Welcome

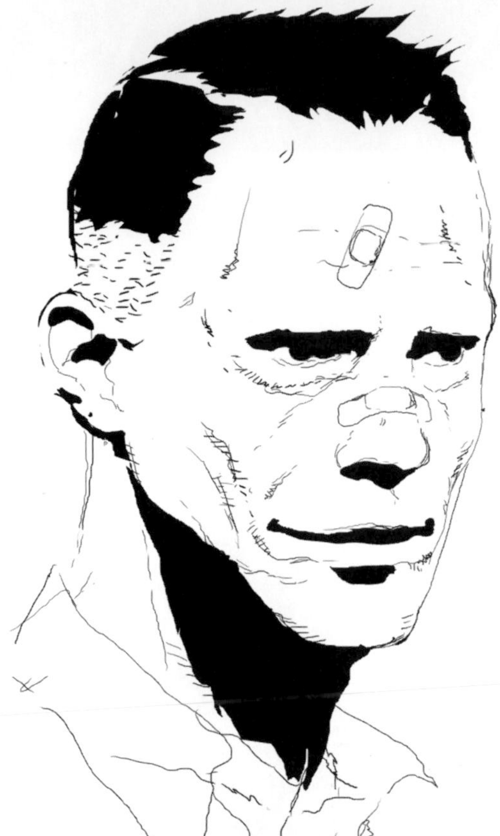

Killer Smile

JEFF LEMIRE
ANDREA SORRENTINO

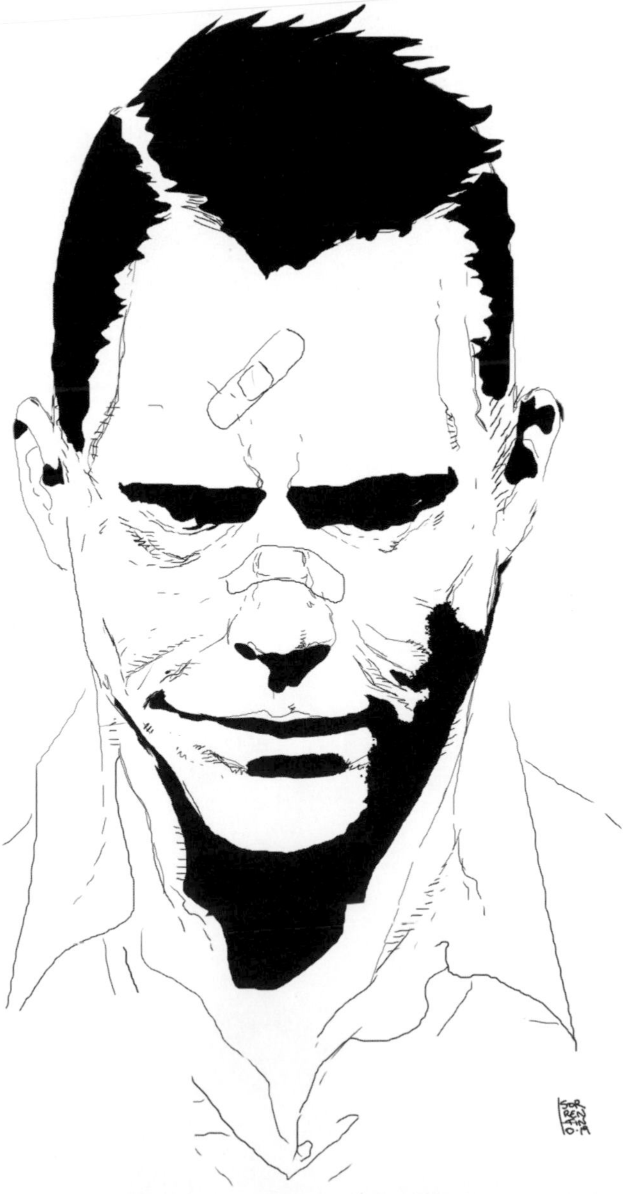

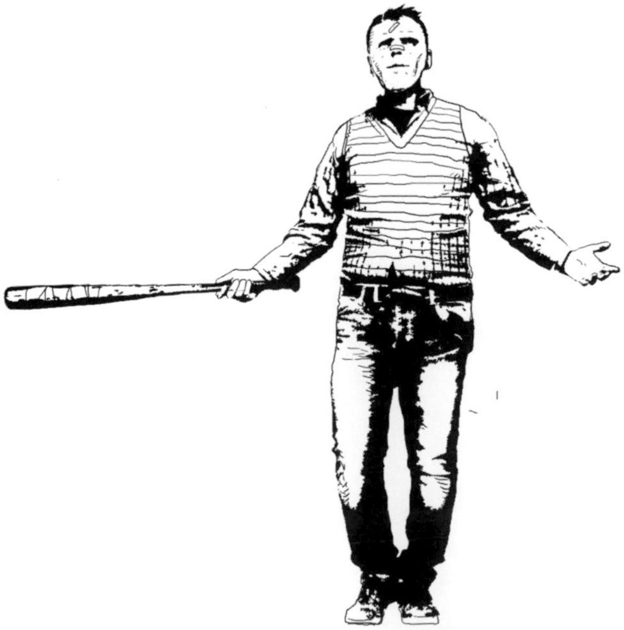

Above: Character sketches
Opposite: Unused cover art for book three

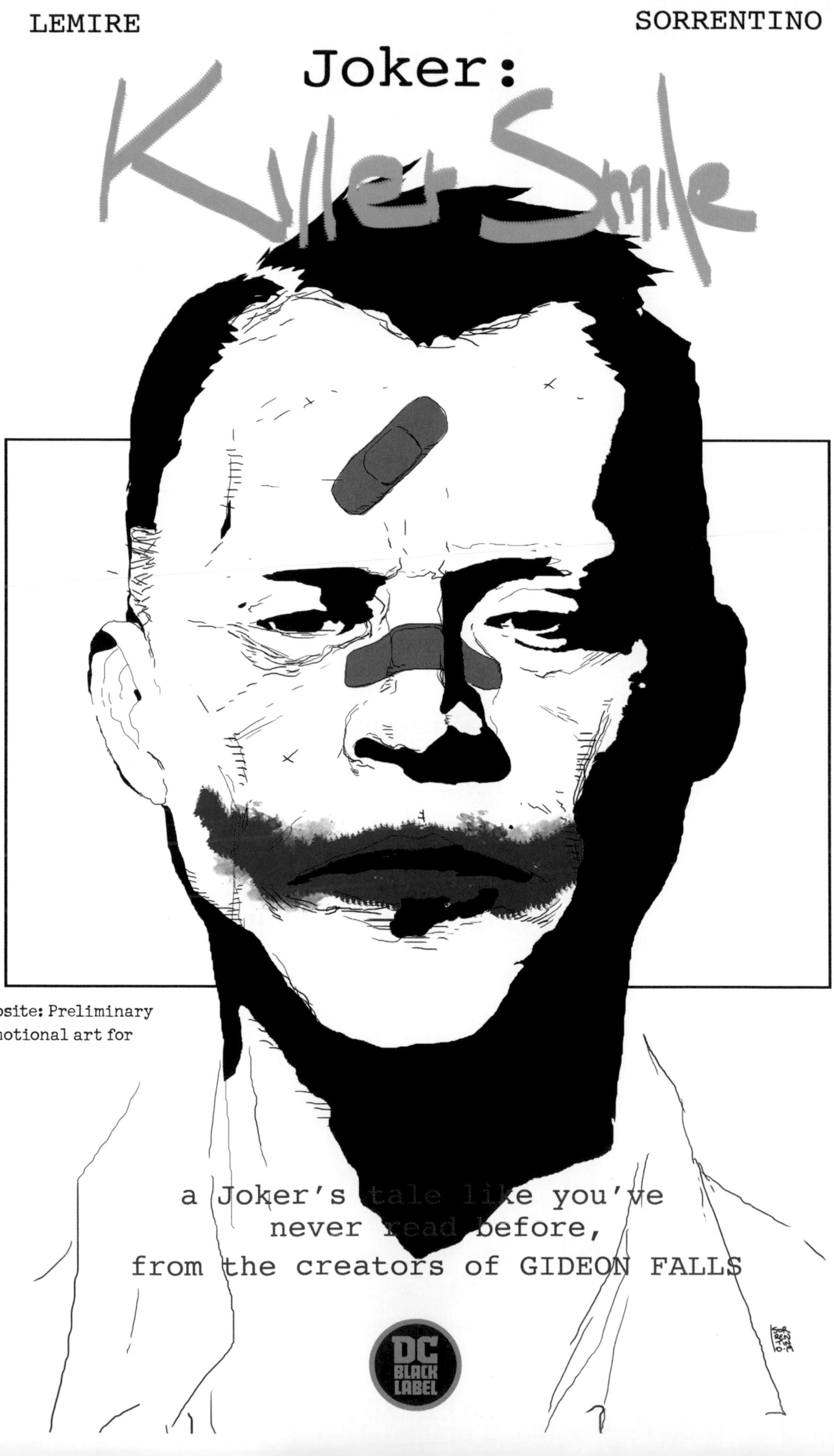
LEMIRE
SORRENTINO
Joker:
Killer Smile
a Joker's tale like you've
never read before,
from the creators of GIDEON FALLS
DC BLACK LABEL

Right and opposite: Preliminary and final promotional art for the series

ARKHAM ASYLUM DAILY REPORT

dr. Benjamin Arnell

Day:27

inmate nr.04456 'The Joker'

current mental state: <u>still totally insane</u>

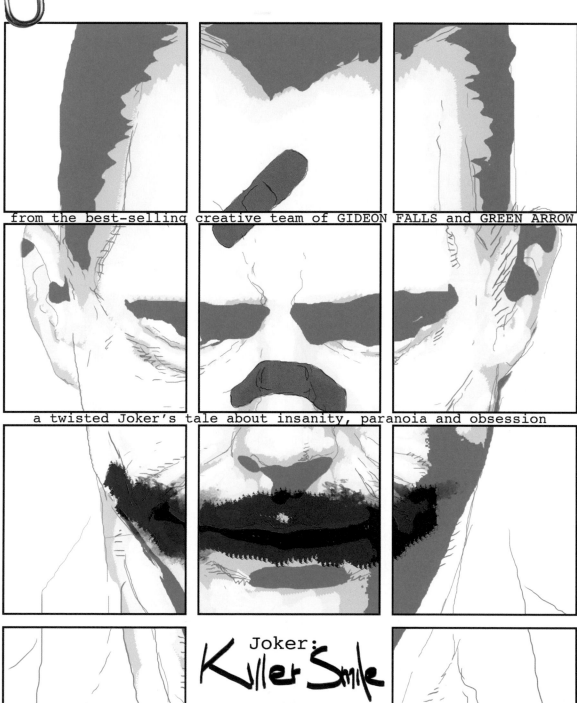

from the best-selling creative team of GIDEON FALLS and GREEN ARROW

a twisted Joker's tale about insanity, paranoia and obsession

Joker:

Killer Smile

DC BLACK LABEL

JEFF LEMIRE

ANDREA SORRENTINO

fall 2019

In two sequences for Batman: The Smile Killer, artist Andrea Sorrentino originally laid out the scenes exclusively from the point of view of the young Bruce Wayne. These early compositions are shown here next to their corresponding finished pages.

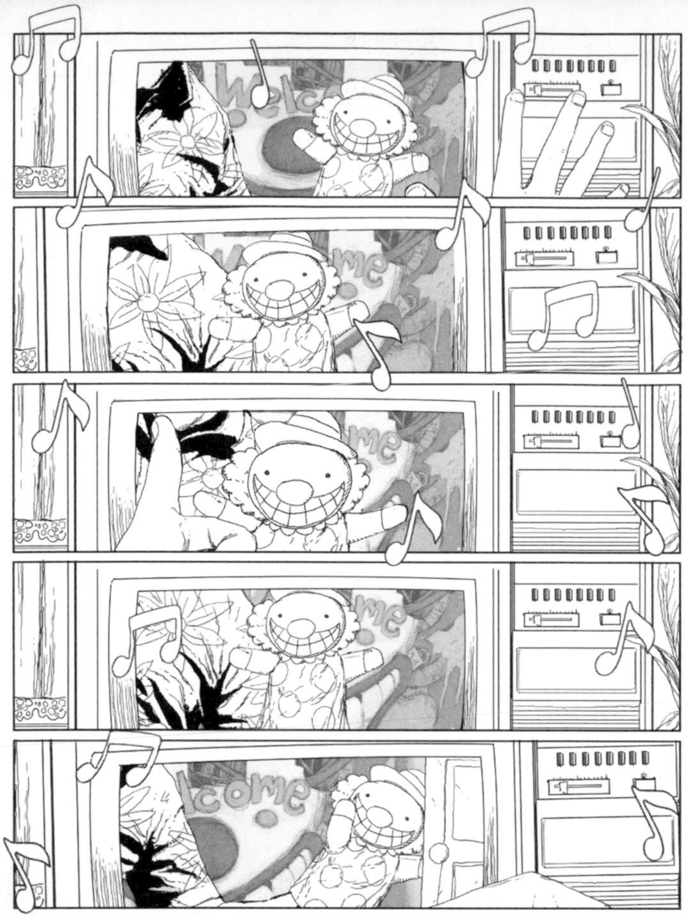

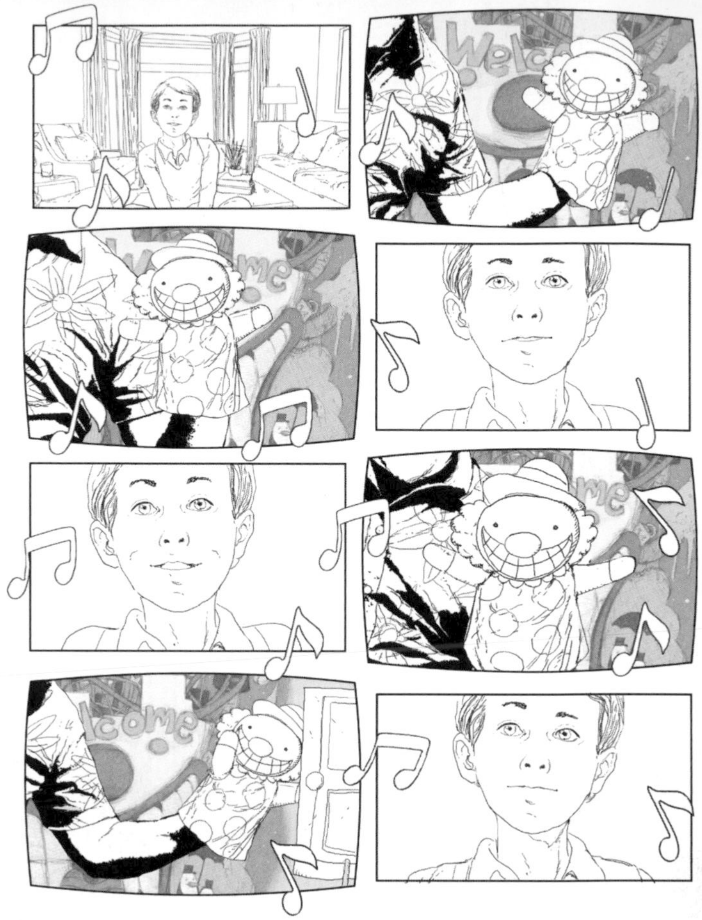

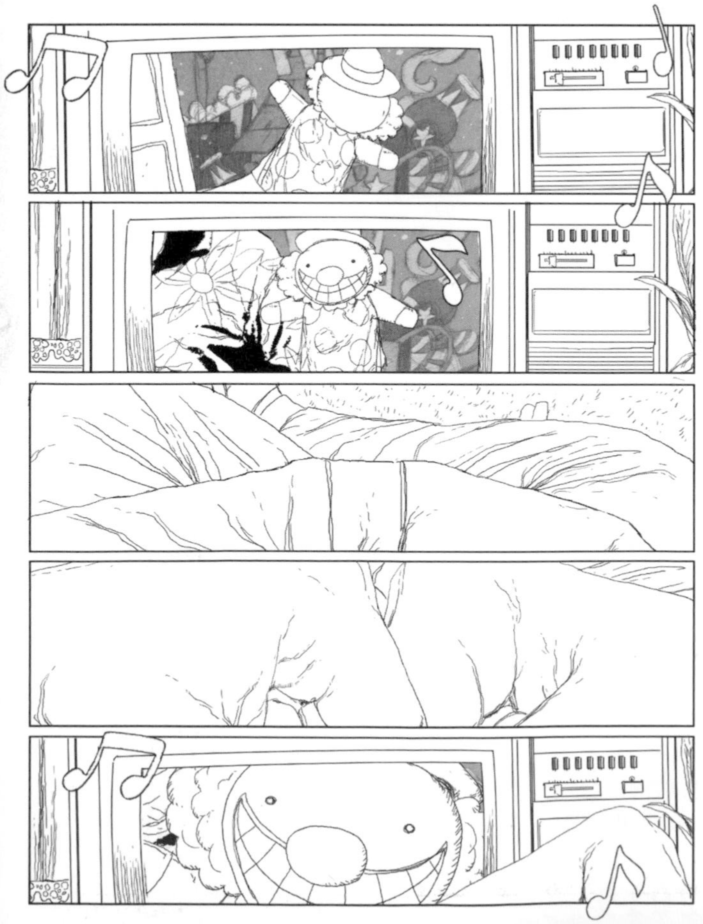

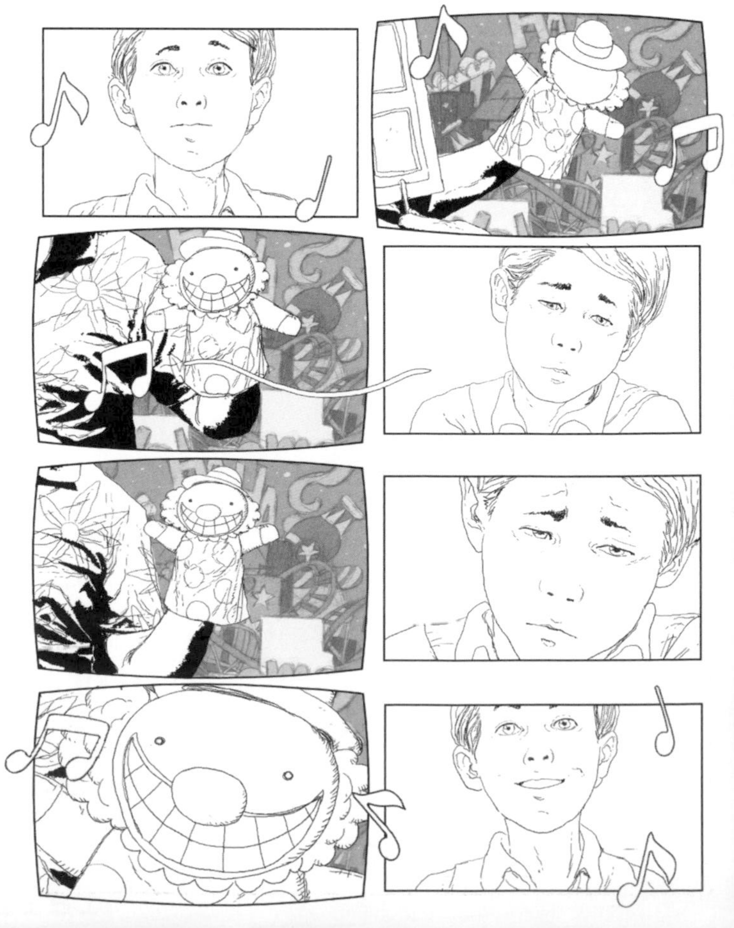

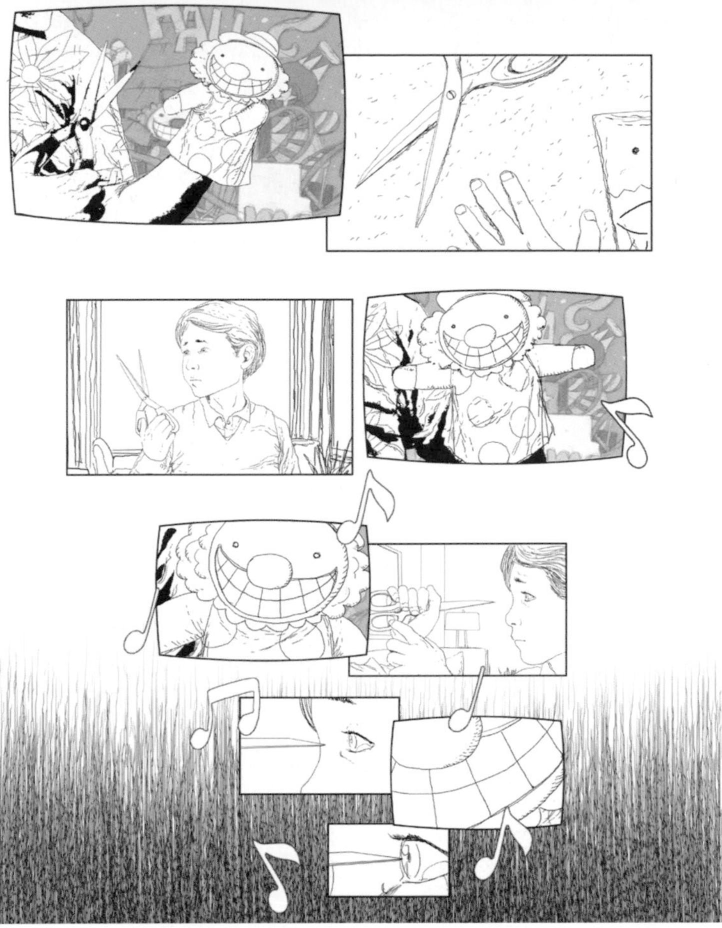

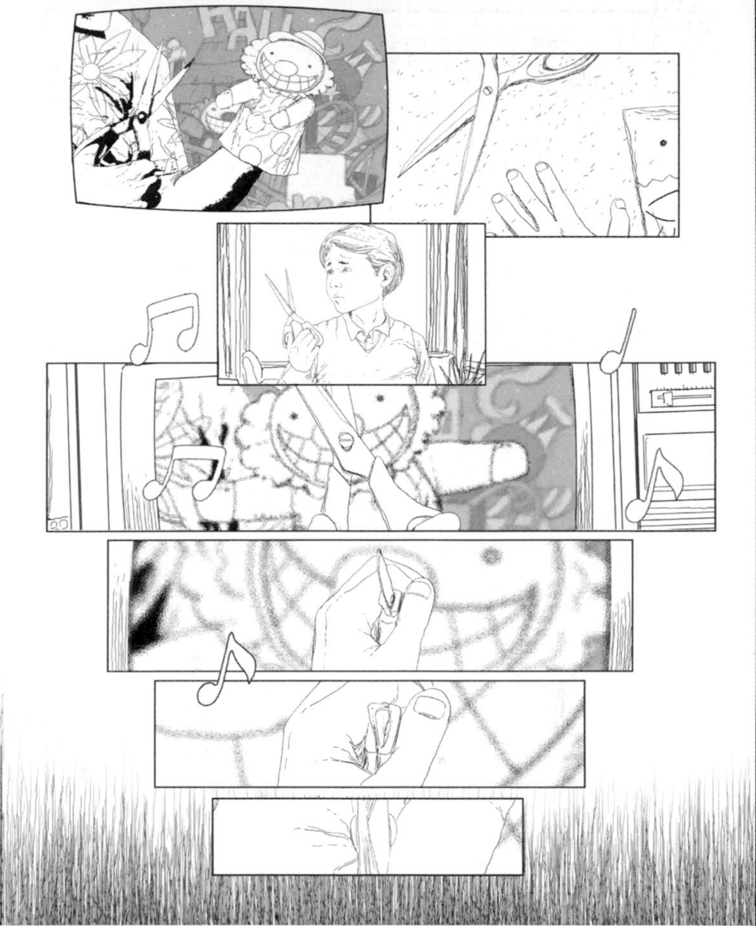

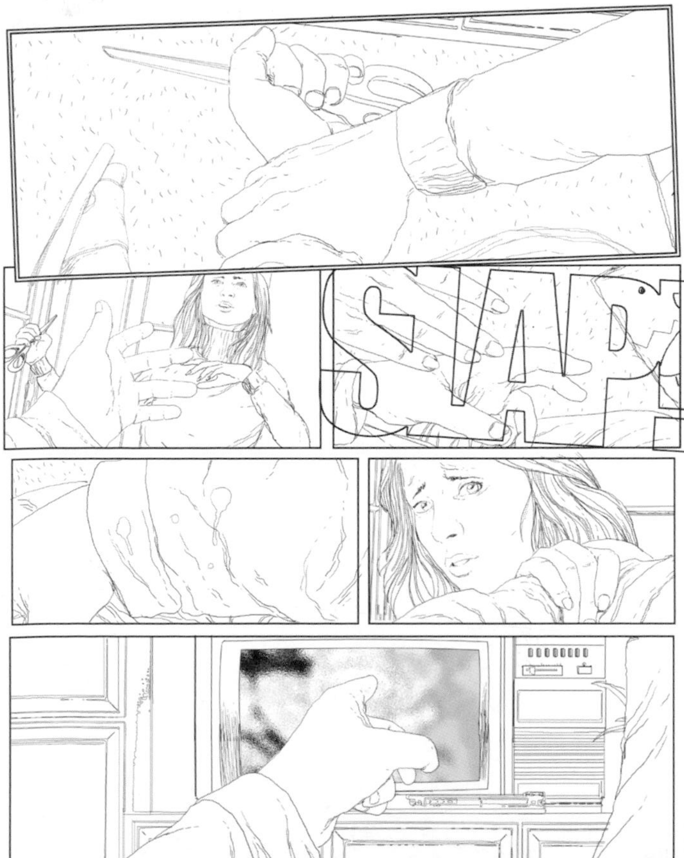
SLAP!

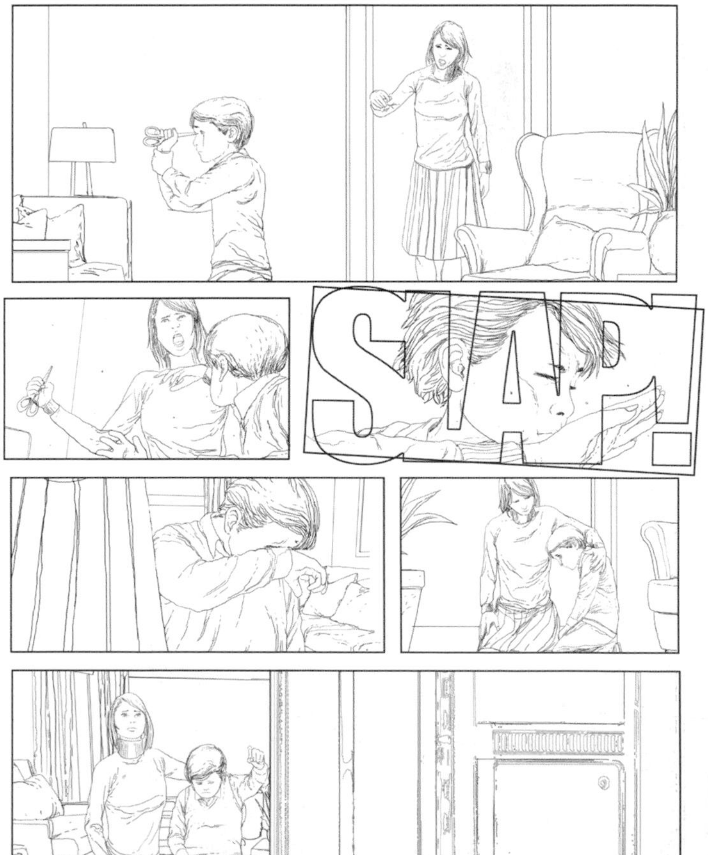
SLAP!

Mr. Smiles
and the happy village

Jeff Lemire is the *New York Times* bestselling author of such graphic novels as *Essex County*, *Sweet Tooth*, *The Underwater Welder*, and *Roughneck*, as well as the co-creator of *Descender* with Dustin Nguyen, *Black Hammer* with Dean Ormston, *Gideon Falls* with Andrea Sorrentino, and many other series. He has also written extensively for both Marvel and DC Comics, and he has collaborated with celebrated musician Gord Downie on the graphic novel and album *The Secret Path*, which was made into an animated film in 2016.

Lemire has won numerous awards for his work, including an Eisner and a Juno award in 2017. Many of his books are currently in development for film and television, including both *Descender* and *A.D.: After Death* at Sony Pictures, *Essex County* at the CBC, *The Underwater Welder* and *Plutona* at Waypoint Entertainment, *Gideon Falls* at Hivemind Media, and the Eisner Award-winning *Black Hammer* universe at Legendary Entertainment.

Lemire lives in Toronto, Canada, with his wife and son and their troublesome pug, Lola.

Andrea Sorrentino is an Italian comics artist who began his professional career working on the licensed series *God of War* for WildStorm. He followed this with acclaimed runs on *I, Vampire* and *Green Arrow* for DC and *All-New X-Men*, *Old Man Logan*, and *Secret Empire* for Marvel, and in 2018 he began a celebrated collaboration with writer Jeff Lemire on the Image title *Gideon Falls*, which won the 2019 Eisner Award for Best New Series. Sorrentino lives and works just outside of Naples, precariously close to an active volcano.

Jordie Bellaire is an Eisner Award-winning colorist best known for her work on *Batman*, *Vision*, *Pretty Deadly*, *Nowhere Men*, and her Eisner-nominated writing debut *Redlands*. You can find her in the mountains behind her house, often ill-prepared, hiking with her husband.